# CONGRESSIONAL HEARINGS ON AMERICAN DEFENSE POLICY: 1947-1971

## an annotated bibliography

# CONGRESSIONAL HEARINGS ON AMERICAN DEFENSE POLICY: 1947-1971

## an annotated bibliography

compiled by
### Richard Burt

edited by
### Richard Burt and Geoffrey Kemp

PUBLISHED FOR THE NATIONAL SECURITY EDUCATION PROGRAM
BY THE UNIVERSITY PRESS OF KANSAS
*Lawrence/Manhattan/Wichita*

Library of Congress Cataloging in Publication Data

Burt, Richard.
   Congressional hearings on American defense policy:
1947-1971.

   (National security studies series.)
   1.  United States--Military policy--Bibliography.
2.  Legislative hearings--United States--Bibliography.
I.  Title.  II.  Series.
KF7201.B86          016.35503'35'73          73-11321
ISBN 0-7006-0109-0

Printed in the United States of America

# Contents

# Foreword

During the academic year 1969-1970, the National Security Program of New York University, in cooperation with the National Strategy Information Center of New York City, sponsored a series of conferences for college and university faculty members interested in the teaching of national security, defense policy, military history, civil-military relations, defense economics, and related areas. Out of these conferences grew a number of projects designed to extend and improve academic education and scholarly research in the national security field.

Prominent among these projects is a National Security Studies Series under the general editorship of Professor Frank N. Trager of New York University. *Congressional Hearings on American Defense Policy, 1947-1971: An Annotated Bibliography* is the third publication of the series to appear. Together with *American Defense Policy since 1945: A Preliminary Bibliography* and *The Statistics of the U.S.-Soviet Military Balance, 1945-1972*, this bibliography will constitute a useful research tool for both students and advanced scholars. Other volumes in the series include:

1. *National Security and American Society: Theory, Process, and Policy*, edited by Frank N. Trager and Philip S. Kronenberg (February 1973).

2. *American Defense Policy since 1945: A Preliminary Bibliography*, compiled by John Greenwood and Robin Higham, edited by Geoffrey Kemp, Clark Murdock, and Frank L. Simonie (June 1973).

3.  *The Statistics of the U.S.-Soviet Military Balance, 1945-1972*, by Geoffrey Kemp and Clark Murdock.

4.  *Nuclear Proliferation: Phase II*, edited by Robert M. Lawrence and Joel Larus.

5.  *Modular Syllabus for Courses in National Security*, edited by T. Alden Williams and David Tarr.

Other titles may be added from time to time.

# Acknowledgments

The research for this bibliography was made possible by a grant to the Project Supervisor by the National Security Education Program of New York University. The editors would like to thank Professor Frank N. Trager, Director of the National Security Education Program, for his continued support and encouragement during the preparation of this bibliography. We would also like to thank Mr. Frank L. Simonie of the National Security Education Program for his help and guidance during the editorial process.

Finally, we would like to extend our warmest thanks to Mrs. Jill Andrews of the Fletcher School for her typing, proofreading, and editorial assistance. Her input was beyond the bounds of duty.

Richard Burt
Geoffrey Kemp

# Introduction

This annotated bibliography is intended for use by the serious scholar of postwar American defense policy. We believe that the most valuable single source of basic research material on postwar American defense policy is congressional committee hearings. Although defense budgets and other matters bearing on national security issues are discussed in newspapers and journals and in Executive branch hearings and releases, it is in committee hearings that Congress examines the administration's policies and budgetary decisions in most depth and detail.

The bibliography primarily focuses on hearings by the House and Senate Armed Services Committees and the House and Senate Defense Appropriations subcommittees. These four committees must legally authorize and appropriate funds for defense, and it is in the arena of the defense budget process that the most crucial decisions on procurement and long-term planning are made. While the relative prerogatives and activities of these committees have changed over time, all four have maintained the greatest interest in issues concerned with American defense policy.

In addition to the regularized format of the budget hearings, the Armed Services committees in both houses hold hearings to investigate security matters of special interest. These "specialized" hearings are usually conducted by a subcommittee of the larger committee. In the Senate, the Armed Services Preparedness Investigating Subcommittee conducts hearings; within the House Armed Services Committee,

special committees are formed. There is no regular
format to these special hearings. Committee staff
select knowledgeable witnesses, in and out of government, to discuss aspects of a particular issue.

Obviously, witnesses play a crucial role in congressional hearings. Up until 1970 most of the witnesses called before hearings on the defense budget
represented either the Department of Defense or particular services. This practice is slowly changing
and greater divergency of opinion is noticeable in
the special hearings conducted by the Armed Services
Committee, where there is an increasing tendency to
solicit outside opinion.

Other congressional committees also conduct hearings important to national security policy. The
House Foreign Affairs Committee and the Senate Foreign
Relations Committee are obvious examples. They must
legally authorize foreign economic assistance and thus
discuss military aid policies. The Senate Foreign
Relations Committee also exercises the Senate's con-
stitutional responsibilities in treaties and foreign
commitments. Both committees hold hearings concerning
arms control agreements, military alliances, and the
like. These two committees also discuss foreign affairs issues that have a significant military component. These hearings concern general policy areas,
and there is a greater tendency to solicit testimony
from a wider field of opinion. If the Armed Services
committees are reluctant to hold hearings on a particular security issue, for example, U.S. troop levels
in Europe, there is sometimes a tendency for the Foreign Affairs and Foreign Relations committees to
examine it.

Hearings before the House and Senate Government
Operations committees have often dealt with aspects
of security policy. Designed as investigatory committees, they do not generally consider, for example, the
structure of the National Security Council, but focus
upon government practices ranging from national security decision making, planning, program, budgeting
systems (PPBS) to military procurement practices.
As relatively new committees in Congress, their

positions are not as powerful as the Appropriations,
Armed Services, or the Foreign Affairs/Relations committees. They must, therefore, carefully choose the
areas they wish to investigate, in order not to in-
vade the territory of the stronger, more established
committees. This is more important in the House,
where normally members only sit on one committee. In
the Senate, multiple membership seems to take care of
the "boundary defining problem."

The House Science and Astronautics Committee and
the Senate Space and Aeronautics Committee also have
some input into the defense policy process, but an
increasingly small one. Formed in the wake of the
"missile gap" controversy in the late 1950s, early
hearings discussed scientific and technological aspects of the defense effort. But the Armed Services
committees' control of military research and development has effectively precluded any real participation
of the former committees. They have increasingly
turned their attention to civilian and domestic uses
of science.

Two joint Senate-House committees often conduct
hearings important to national security policy. The
Joint Atomic Energy Committee authorizes the Atomic
Energy Commission budget (including nuclear weapons
research and development) and conducts hearings that
concern the use and control of nuclear weapons --
SALT, testing, etc. The Joint Economic Committee has
recently taken an interest in defense spending,
military-industry relationships, and weapons systems
acquisition.

Basically, then, the Armed Services committees hold
the bulk of hearings directly relevant to national
security policy. But an issue of great importance
(or of perceived great importance) may be discussed
in hearings by a number of different congressional
committees. Hearings considering various aspects of
the antiballistic missile program were held by no
less than five different committees.

At the current time we are aware of no other project that has attempted to collate hearings and testimony bearing on national security policy on a

systematic basis over time.  Prior to 1970, the only
sources for complete congressional hearing listings
were the *Monthly Catalogue* published by the Government Printing Office and the United States Senate
Library's *Index to Congressional Committee Hearings*.
Both sources, however, tend to be incomplete and they
do not list witnesses or describe testimony.  A list
of witnesses appearing before congressional committees
of both houses of Congress is kept on file at the
Senate Library, but it is not readily accessible to
the public.

The *Congressional Information Service Index*, begun
in 1970, is a privately published and rather expensive
guide to congressional hearings, reports, and studies.
It consists of a monthly index containing abstracts
of hearings, reports, and studies, and is extremely
easy to use.  Like this bibliography, the various
documents are listed under appropriate committee.
But because the *Congressional Information Service
Index* was begun only in 1970, this bibliography will
complement it and will fill a major gap in congressional hearings documentation during the postwar
period.

However, it should be stressed that this bibliography is by no means an exhaustive listing of congressional committee activity.  The term "American
defense policy" includes a variety of components --
military, economic, political, and scientific -- which
at one time or another were the topic of discussion
in a variety of congressional committees.  Very early
during the compilation, the problem of defining
boundaries emerged:  What congressional hearings were
directly relevant to American defense policy?  There
was no easy solution to this problem, and the decision
to include some hearings and exclude others was taken
on a case-by-case basis.  Thus, hearings concerned
with naval petroleum stores, for instance, were included in the bibliography, while hearings concerned
with certain agricultural stockpile items were left
out.  The uppermost concern in compiling the bibliography was to produce an informative, relevant, and
usable means of researching in depth different issues

in American defense policy. *Thus, an all-inclusive bibliography was sacrificed in order to compile a shorter listing of hearings thought to bear directly on the most significant questions during the era in question.*

The same selective approach was used in annotating the specific hearings. In most cases, a complete list of witnesses and a short précis of their testimony are presented; but in cases where testimony duplicated earlier remarks or where testimony did not seem relevant to the concerns of the bibliography, it was not always included in the listings. Again, the goal of compiling a relatively short and usable research tool had priority over comprehensiveness.

In a more general sense, the selection of items for the bibliography also attempted to take into account other published accounts and descriptions of particular issues that have become available. Thus, those periods for which a great amount has already been written -- the McNamara era, for instance -- were not as exhaustively detailed as periods that have received far less attention from defense scholars -- the immediate postwar period, for instance.

In spite of these constraints, we feel that this annotated bibliography provides the scholar with both an overall impression of the kinds of issues that concerned policy makers at a given point in time and a resource index to specific hearings. A quick survey of the bibliography shows, for instance, that while manpower and fiscal concerns predominated during the early portion of the 1950s, attention gradually shifted to strategic issues in the late 1950s and 1960s. In our view, some attempt at content analysis would yield some interesting results concerning the evolution of American defense policy.

A final caveat is in order. Hearings form only a portion of the output of congressional committees. Committees also issue reports, documents, and prints (studies). These also contain a variety of useful matter. No attempt has been made to include them in the index. Like other printed material, the *Monthly*

*Catalogue* is the best and sometimes the only source of information concerning these data.

Richard Burt
Geoffrey Kemp

Medford, Mass.
March 1973

# CONGRESSIONAL HEARINGS ON AMERICAN DEFENSE POLICY: 1947-1971

## an annotated bibliography

# 1947 CONGRESSIONAL HEARINGS

## 80th Congress, First Session

HOUSE COMMITTEES

APPROPRIATIONS COMMITTEE

*Navy Department Appropriation Bill for 1948* (1947)

Sec. Forrestal, Defense Department: Unsettled problems, importance of Navy near troubled waters, strategic materials, transoceanic missiles still far off in future, need to maintain Navy strength.
Discussion of House cuts and proposed restoration, role of land-based reconnaissance planes.
Fleet Adm. Nimitz, Navy: Naval strength reduction must proceed cautiously, comparison of postwar fleet plans, discussion of House cuts.
Rear Adm. Hopwood, Navy: Budget submission, number of recruits, civilian employment, procurement, listing of House reductions and requested restoration.
Vice Adm. Mills, Navy: Bureau of Ships request, effect of House cuts on private shipyards.
Vice Adm. Hussey, Navy: Bureau of Ordnance, proposed restoration.
Vice Adm. Duncan, Navy: Naval air operations, 5,793-plane program, use of land-based planes for antisubmarine warfare.
Joseph Davitt, Navy: Naval miscellaneous expenses.

Rear Adm. Inglis, Navy: Naval intelligence,
effect of House cut.

Gen. Vandigrift, Marine Corps: Marines, House
cut, reduction in forces.

Asst. Sec. McNeil, Navy Department: Civilian
employees, Army-Navy coordination of purchases,
amount required to avoid a "shell Navy."

Rear Adm. Sprague, Navy: Navy personnel, demobilization, discussion of salaries.

*Military Establishment Appropriations for FY 48,
Subcommittee* (June, July 1947)

Sec. Patterson, War Department: Threatening
world situation, missions of occupation and defense, discussion of factors influencing size of
Army, budget cut, decentralized management, distribution of funds between ground and air forces,
budget requests from corps, officer levels.

Gen. Hall, Army: Concern over House pay cut,
size of Army officer corps, discussion of pay procedures and personnel problems, role of civilian
in Army.

Col. McAush, Army: Army career guidance plan.

A. O. Onthank, Army: Army civilian strength
decreasing, House cut would affect departmental
specialists.

Maj. Gen. Kastin, Army: Proposed cut in pay extremely serious, discussion of pay issues.

R. M. Yingling, War Department: Effect of pay
cut, budget already at minimum.

Gen. Hodes, War Department: Office of Chief of
Staff duties, effect of pay cut.

Col. Keefe, Army: Adjutant General's Office
function, FY 1948 requirement.

Col. Bean, Army: House would create finance
backlog.

Brig. Gen. Lanhan, Army: Army communications
and schooling program, cut would seriously affect
work.

Maj. Faber, Army:  Effect of cut on Army supply
operations.

Maj. Gen. Walsh, National Guard Association:
Size of National Guard, need for expansion, discussion of National Guard budgeting.

Sen. McCarran:  National Guard air units in
jeopardy.

Sen. Magnuson:  Importance of Air National Guard.

Maj. Gen. Reckord, National Rifle Association:
Association's need for more clerical help--for gun-training program.

Col. Oliver, Reserve Officers Association:
Reserve funds inadequate, loss of interest in Reserves.

Maj. Gen. Larkin, Army:  Quartermaster Corps request, increase in prices, effect of House cut, use
of scientific personnel.

Maj. Gen. Street, Army:  Military Personnel Procurement Service request, need for recruiting stations.

Maj. Gen. Akin, Army:  Signal Corps request,
need for increased media personnel.

Brig. Gen. Yount, Army:  Transportation Corps
requests, use of commercial transportation.

Maj. Gen. Bliss, Army:  Surgeon General request.

Col. Wallington, Army:  Chemical Corps requests,
use of arsenals.

Lt. Gen. Wheeler, Army:  Corps of Engineer mission, request.

Maj. Gen. Hughes, Army:  Ordnance Department requests, House cut.

Sen. Martin:  Need for scrap iron and steel.

Lt. Gen. Vandenberg, Army Air Force:  Army Air
Force request, need for 70-group Air Force, Air
Force research and development funds.

Sen. Thomas:  War Department cotton purchases.

Gen. Eisenhower, Army:  U.S. Army second strongest in the world, need for 1,070,000-man army,
House reductions serious, cuts would mean 55-group
Air Force, no modernization of ground army, delayed
research and development.

Discussion of total restoration requested by
Army, war brides.

ARMED SERVICES COMMITTEE

*Subcommittee Hearing to Authorize Sale, Loan, and Exchange of U.S. Naval Ordnance Material to Friendly Governments* (1947)

 Rear Adm. Schoeffel, Navy: Proposal to exchange naval ordnance with friendly countries with the purpose of research and development and keeping abreast of naval development.
 Discussion of political implications of trades.

*Reorganization of the Navy Department* (January 1947)

 Sec. Forrestal, Navy Department: Size of the Navy Department makes Under Secretary of the Navy necessary.

*To Authorize Construction of Experimental Submarines* (January 1947)

 Under Sec. Kenney, Navy Department: Possibilities of radical advancements in submarine construction.
 Vice Adm. Mills, Navy: Discussion of impact of Bikini tests, lessons gained from German submarine building.
 Vice Adm. Carney, Navy: Importance of antisubmarine warfare, need for high underwater speed; new Russian submarine design.

*Hearings on Supply and Procurement Setup for the Army, Navy, Marine, Air Corps* (May 1947)

 Francis Kiesling: Need for government economy, possibility of joint procurement.
 Discussion of role of Congress as "procurement

policeman." Focus on service procurement practices in San Francisco area.


*To Authorize Conversions of Naval Vessels* (May 1947)

Vice Adm. Mills, Navy: Need for new ship types and conversion, IRNV program, troop carrying submarine, a polar picket, antisubmarine warfare ships, and converted carriers.


*Hearings on UMT* (June 1947)

Dr. Compton, Commission on Universal Military Training: Low number of military enlistments, salutary effect of universal military training on Reserve readiness, need for universal military training to be civilian run.
Discussion of alternatives to universal military training, foreign examples, description of international situation, threats to security. Discussion of how atomic weapons could change suddenness of war.
Dr. Walsh: Need for integrated national security program, American world moral obligation.
Discussion of American isolationism in the 1930s and existence of Soviet revolutionary threat.
Owen Roberts, Citizens' Committee for Universal Military Training: Refutation of arguments against universal military training, need for citizens' army, consistent with U.N. Charter and weakness of the United States.
Number of witnesses from religious, peace, farm, and labor groups opposed to universal military training.


*Hearings to Operate and Expand ROTC* (June 1947)

Brig. Gen. Caffey, War Department: ROTC prime

source of officers for mobilization, importance of
ROTC for reserves.

Col. Swartz, War Department:  Need for 30,000
ROTC-trained officers annually, need for junior and
senior ROTC.

Maj. Gen. Bres, War Department:  Organization of
ROTC, need for enlargement, five-year program for
239 colleges and universities.

Discussion of inducements and need for high cal-
iber officers.

*To Repeal Profit Limitation Relating to the Construc-
tion of Vessels and Aircraft* (June 1947)

Vice Adm. Mills, Navy:  Need for flexibility in
contracting; profit-limitation provisions hamper
contract negotiations and result in increased
prices.

Discussion of naval shipyard business and contracting methods.

Rear Adm. Pride, Navy:  Changes in aircraft business, high degree of competition among 14 companies.

FOREIGN AFFAIRS COMMITTEE

*Assistance to Greece and Turkey* (March, April 1947)

Sec. Acheson, State Department:  Withdrawal of
British, existence of armed insurgent groups sup-
plied by Communists in Greece, economic strategy
in Turkey.  Importance of both countries, effect on
Middle East.

Discussion of Yalta, Tehran, Potsdam conferences,
nature of the aid, Chinese civil war, role of U.S.
intervention in postwar world.

William Clayton, State Department:  Economic

crisis in Greece and Turkey, extent of problem, role of U.N.

Testimony by various State Department officials on current crisis.

Rear Adm. Wooldridge, Navy: Strategic importance of Greece and Turkey, discussion of lend-lease ships transferred to Soviets during war.

Rep. Crawford: Opposition to involvement.

Rep. Fisk: Truman Doctrine means global imperialism.

Testimony by religious and peace groups opposed to Truman Doctrine and anticommunism.

*Inter-American Military Cooperation Act* (June, July 1947)

Sec. Marshall, State Department: Act of Chapultepec, coordinated training programs and standardization of equipment and procedures.

Discussion of protecting U.S. interests in Latin America, need for western hemisphere unity, number of military missions in Latin America.

Sec. Patterson, War Department: Collective security, importance of United States to Latin American security, need for modernization.

Discussion of surplus sales, advantages of Latin American countries using U.S. arms.

Gen. Eisenhower, Army: Need for unity, training Latin American officers in U.S. schools, rules surrounding arms transfers.

Discussion of continent "defense," need to foster democracy.

Fleet Adm. Nimitz, Navy: Transferral of naval vessels to Latin America, cost of transfer, list of larger combatant ships possessed by Latin American countries.

Sec. Forrestal, Navy Department: Collective security in Latin America, strategic interests, importance of coordination.

Lt. Gen. Vandenberg, Army Air Force: Air power could be applied throughout the continent, technical advances, need for extended defenses, an added impetus to aircraft industry.

Lt. Gen. Ridgway, Inter-American Defense Board: Need for military cooperation; political and military cooperation inseparable.

Discussion of possible Latin American arms race and capture of weapons by revolutionaries.

Maj. Gen. Henry, Inter-American Defense Board: Northern hemispheric defense, U.S.-Canadian agreements.

Norman Thomas: Proposal will strengthen power of dictators in Latin America and will be used against popular uprisings.

Testimony by other groups opposed to agreement.


## JOINT COMMITTEES OF HOUSE AND SENATE


JOINT ATOMIC ENERGY COMMITTEE


*Confirmation of Atomic Energy Commission and General Manager, Senate Subcommittee* (January, February, March 1947)

David Lilienthal, Atomic Energy Commission appointee: TVA experience, Atomic Energy Commission organization, role of Military Applications head, work of the Manhattan project.

Testimony of other appointees to commission--experience and background.

Bernard Baruch: Acheson-Lilienthal report, discussion of U.N. plan.

Discussion of Lilienthal's ties to the Communist party.

SENATE COMMITTEES

ARMED SERVICES COMMITTEE

*National Defense Establishment (Unification), Part 1*
(March, April 1947)

Sec. Forrestal, Navy Department:  Need for service integration, experiences of World War II,
integration of civilian economy with military requirements of three service branches.

Discussion of autonomy of the services, need for
some measure of service independence, authority of
the Secretary of Defense.  Formulation of the defense budget, authority of the service secretaries
and chiefs of staff.

Sec. Patterson, War Department:  Role of the
Joint Chiefs of Staff, preparation of the National
Security Agency of 1947, problems of World War II
Army-Navy committee system.

Discussion of need for balanced defense program,
effect of act on national economy, Eberstadt plan
of defense organization.

Asst. Sec. Symington, War Department:  Unhealthy
interservice competition, Air Force support for
measure.

Gen. Eisenhower, Army:  Unified command vital
for military victory, no such thing as separate
sea, land, and air war.  Need for defense flexibility.

Discussion of determining basic functions of the
services, role of Naval Air and Marine Corps.  Line
of command of 1947 National Security Agency.

Gen. Spaatz, Army Air Force:  Need for equal Air
Force status, role of air power.

Discussion of Navy responsibilities, Air Force
research and development, advisability of equal
status for Air Force.

Fleet Adm. Nimitz, Navy:  Act incorporates lessons of World War II, organizational history of

Allied command, need for a Joint Chiefs of Staff.

Discussion of Secretary's authority, role of Assistant Secretary, possibilities of over-centralization.

Adm. Sherman, Navy: Discussion of whether Army or Navy actually agreed to Act, chronology of Act's drafting, role of Central Intelligence Agency, outline of the defense budget process, ability of the services to appeal Secretary's budget decision.

Maj. Gen. Norstad, Army Air Force: Strategic Bombing Survey results, need for separate Air Force, role of Naval aviation.

*--Part 2* (April 1947)

Asst. Sec. Kenney, Navy Department: Need for efficient defense organization, supply organization must remain with the services, role of Munitions Board.

Discussion of potential service rivalry, dangers of over-centralization.

Vice Adm. Carney, Navy: Navy logistics under proposed Act, Joint Chiefs decision making, National Defense Establishment logistics support plan.

Under Sec. Royall, Army Department: Act is a compromise, different approaches to unification, savings resulting from Act, 1947 National Security Agency organization chart.

Sen. Hart: Navy fears, need to preserve Air Force and Marine capabilities.

Gen. Vandegrift, Marine Corps: Discussion of the Marine representative on Joint Chiefs, need to protect Marine functions.

Melvin Maas, Marine Reserve Officer Association: Opposition to Act, need for separate Marines, over-centralization of Secretary of Defense.

*--Part 3* (April, May 1947)

Lt. Gen. Vandenberg, Central Intelligence Agency:

Need for effective intelligence apparatus, history of Office of Strategic Services, roles and duties of the Central Intelligence Agency. Will not duplicate service intelligence.

Sen. Lodge: Tendency of services to cling to outmoded weapons and tactics, need for strong Secretary of Defense, deleterious effects of interservice rivalry.

John Bracker, Naval Reserves: Opposed to unification.

James Webb, Bureau of the Budget: Role of Bureau of the Budget, defense budget process.

Col. Oliver, Reserve Officers Association: Need for independent service intelligence agencies.

Fleet Adm. King, Navy: Proposes plan for defense reorganization, need to integrate national security policy with other government considerations.

Charles Wilson: Need to preserve service identity, organizational flexibility.

Fleet Adm. Halsey (Ret.), Navy: Need to define more carefully missions of the services.

Rep. Andrews: Report from House Armed Services Committee.

Ferdinand Eberstadt: Need to relate for political and military policy, and for Joint Chiefs and some service autonomy, dangers of over-centralization.

Functions of National Defense Establishment's boards and committees.

Maj. Gen. Reckord, National Guard: National Guard overlooked in legislation.


*--Part 4*

Stuart Cramer, Munitions Board: Operations of Munitions Board, plant maintenance and operation.


*Disposition of Government Surplus Airports and Facilities* (June 1947)

*Procurement of Supplies and Services by War and Navy Departments* (June 1947)

Asst. Sec. Kenney, Navy Department:  Need to eliminate duplication in procurement, need to coordinate procurement.  Outline of proposal, including areas of negotiated contracts and competitive bidding.

*Armed Services Procurement Act of 1947* (July 1947)

Asst. Sec. Kenney, Navy Department:  Discussion of service procurement practices, differences in Army-Navy practices.
Under Sec. Royall, Army Department:  Army procurement techniques, contracting.
Lt. Gen. Vandenberg, Army Air Force:  Procurement by negotiation essential for Air Force, B-29 experience.

*Expansion of the ROTC* (July 1947)

Col. Swartz, War Department:  Increasing ROTC payments, flying instruction.
Maj. Gen. Bres, Army:  Five-year program of college expansion.

*Making Certain Changes in the Organization of the Navy Department* (July 1947)

Asst. Sec. Kenney, Navy Department:  Need for better supply management in the Navy, Navy logistical management.
Discussion of Navy cutbacks since war.
Fleet Adm. Nimitz, Navy:  Need to increase powers of Chief of Naval Operations, discussion of role of Chief of Naval Operations.

FOREIGN RELATIONS COMMITTEE

*Assistance to Greece and Turkey* (March 1947)

Sec. Acheson, State Department:  Situation in
Greece and Turkey, Truman Doctrine, British withdrawal; situation in Greece and Turkey not necessar-
ily precedent for future aid program.

Discussion of U.N. responsibilities, situation
in the Middle East, Korean situation.

Sec. Patterson, War Department:  Military aspects
of Greece and Turkey situation, British withdrawal,
Communist rebel threat.

Sec. Forrestal, Navy Department:  Turkish and
Greek navies, discussion of requests for sales from
other states.

Under Sec. Clayton, State Department:  The sever-
ity of Greece's and Turkey's monetary situations.

Charles Bolte, American Veterans Committee:
Need for strengthened U.N., peace between United
States and Soviet Union.

Rev. Muste, Fellowship of Reconciliation:
United States should refuse to take over British
imperial commitment.

Testimony from other groups pro and con the
issue.

# 1948 CONGRESSIONAL HEARINGS

## 80th Congress, Second Session

APPROPRIATIONS COMMITTEE

*Military Functions Appropriation for 1949, Subcommittee* (June 1948)

Sec. <u>Royall</u>, <u>Army</u>:  Restoration of House cut, draft bill, Army budget by office function, 18-division (6 Reserve) FY 1949 Army objective, adding additional division year by year.

Discussion of Reserve forces, cost of universal military training.

Gen. <u>Bradley</u>, <u>Army</u>:  Increasing need for ground forces, ordnance and equipment rehabilitation. Corps (service) requirements.

Maj. Gen. <u>Richards</u>, <u>Army</u>:  Amounts requested restored, problems created by cut.

Brig. Gen. <u>Westover</u>, <u>Army</u>:  Reserve and ROTC spending, 18-division plan, importance of Reserve and ROTC.

Brig. Gen. <u>White</u>, <u>Air</u> Force:  House cut would seriously control Air Force Reserve activities.

Lt. Col. <u>Dey</u>, <u>Army</u>:  Inter-American Army and Air Force missions to Latin America.

Maj. Gen. <u>Kasten</u>, <u>Army</u>:  Army pay and personnel.

Col. <u>Sewell</u>, <u>Army</u>:  Army education branch activities.

Maj. Gen. Larkin, Army:  Quartermaster Corps, effect of rising costs.

Brig. Gen. Fitch, Army:  Army procurement, recruiting.

Maj. Gen. Heileman, Army:  Military transportation.

Maj. Gen. Akin, Army:  Signal service, procurement.

Maj. Gen. Crawford, Army:  Army Engineer request, joint Army-Air Force construction program.

Maj. Gen. Hughes, Army:  Ordnance, effects of House cuts.

Maj. Gen. Cramer, Army:  Increase in personnel, size of National Guard.

Maj. Gen. Arnold, Army:  Restoration of funds.

Col. Boyer, Reserve Officers Association:  Reserve program in trouble, no support from either services or Congress.

Maj. Gen. Walsh, National Guard Association:  Growing strength of the Guard, discussion of tripling prewar strength to 682,000.

Lt. Gen. Rawlings, Air Force:  Summary of FY 1949 fiscal program, 70-group Air Force (expansion of 55 to 65), programs deferred by cut.

*Navy Department Appropriation Bill for 1949, Subcommittee* (June 1948)

Sec. Sullivan, Navy:  Need to maintain naval strength, importance of flush-deck carrier.

Discussion of Joint Chiefs' vote on carrier, Joint Chiefs' unanimity, role of carriers, vulnerability to land-based aviation, new program for guided missile ships, manpower requirements.

Adm. Denfield, Navy:  Navy manpower needs, need for 14,500-man naval aviation program and major missions of Navy.

Discussion of antisubmarine warfare.

Under Sec. Kenney, Navy:  Petroleum reserve, Office of Secretary request, personnel requirements, summary of appropriation categories, budget summary.

    J. S. Davitt, Navy:  Miscellaneous expenses, use of scientists.

    Rear Adm. Lil, Navy:  Naval research, need for larger staff.

    Gen. Cates, Marine Corps:  Marine strength, House cut, Marine Corps Reserve.

    Vice Adm. Mills, Navy:  Bureau of Ships, need for restoration, shipbuilding and conversion program; risks taken if fleet not modernized.

    Rear Adm. Noble, Navy:  Bureau of Ordnance, procurement.


## ARMED SERVICES COMMITTEE


*To Establish the Women's Army Corps in the Regular Army and to Authorize the Appointment of Women in Navy and Marine Corps* (February 1948)

    Gen. Eisenhower, Army:  Need for women for particular jobs in the military establishment.

    Discussion of promotion problems.

    Sec. Forrestal, Defense Department:  Need for competent women, discussion of WAC, WAVE, and WAF programs, competence of women.

    Adm. Denfield, Navy:  Womanpower part of preparedness, success of women in the Navy.

    Gen. Bradley, Army:  Work of women in the Army, inability of Reserves to fill in for work done by women in World War II.

    Gen. Vandenberg, Air Force:  Indispensable use of women in World War II, British use of women in the military, the aircraft "ferrying" program.

    Other witnesses include representatives from services on roles and duties of women in the military.


*To Provide for Administration of the CIA* (March 1948)

Rear Adm. Hillenkoeller, Central Intelligence
Agency:  Mission of the Central Intelligence Agency,
need to regard employment with Central Intelligence
as carrier service.  Importance of confidential
authorization and appropriations.


*To Establish Civil Air Patrol of Civilian Auxiliary
of the USAF* (April 1948)

Maj. Gen. Beau, Air Force:  Services of the
Civil Air Patrol--antisubmarine warfare, anti-
sabotage, courier service; history of the Civil Air
Patrol.  Proposed cadet training program.
Discussion of Air Force-Civil Air Patrol rela-
tionship.


*Selective Service* (April, May 1948)

Sec. Forrestal, Defense Department:  Nonencroach-
ment of universal military training night force,
maintenance of regular forces only through selective
service.  Need for strong Air Force and Navy.
Discussion of the balanced force concept, increasing the strength of the military establishment.
History of American isolationism, need for strong
forces and vigilance.  Discussion of 70-group Air
Force and universal military training.
Sec. Symington, Air Force:  70-group Air Force,
Air Force manpower needs.
Gen. Spaatz, Air Force:  Air Force strength,
strategic bombing with atomic weapons, concept of
continental air defense, trend in Air Force manpower build-up.
Sec. Sullivan, Navy:  Need for increased naval
personnel, doctor shortages.
Adm. Denfield, Navy:  Changes in international
situation.  Need for naval conversion, protecting
sea lanes for strategic materials, size and deployment of Navy active and reserve fleets.  Importance

of Navy and Marine capabilities if strategic forces
are to be successful.

Gen. Bradley, Army:  Army has become an administrative force, need for larger land forces.  Inadequacy of strategic bombing alone; Army must take
bases in an air war; request for 18-division Army.

Discussion of poor state of Army equipment and
effect of universal military training.

Charles Thomas, American Chemical Society:
Scientific talent more useful in private sector for
national defense.

Witnesses from peace groups, religious orders,
farm groups, and labor groups opposed to supporting
selective service and universal military training
programs.

*To Authorize President to Permit Stoppage of Work on
Combatant Vessels* (May 1948)

Sec. Sullivan, Navy:  Necessary for Navy to move
on to higher priority projects instead of completing
vessels begun during World War II.

Discussion of guided missile and submarine developments, need for new type carriers, history and
exploits of Naval aviation record.

Adm. Denfield, Navy:  Discussion of Air Force 70-
group proposal, Navy IRNV program, obsolescence of
ships to be cancelled, and new submarine development program.

*To Provide for the Development of Civil Transport
Aircraft Adaptable for Auxiliary Military Service*
(May 1948)

Robert Gross, Lockheed Aircraft:  Performance of
civil airliner in World War II, postwar aviation
contraction and costs of new aircraft production.
Potential of new aircraft development and discussion of civil aircraft in war line.

Arthur Raymond, Douglas Aircraft:  Use of Air

Force procurement and need to develop new aircraft
which could not be financed under existing high
costs.

Witnesses include other executives from aircraft
companies on need for government contract to
finance development of military transport.

Maj. Gen. Kuter, Air Force:  Size of Military
Air Transport Service, only one-tenth that of World
War II; need for new military transport.

*Hearings to Establish Composition of the Air Force*
(June 1948)

Under Sec. Barrows, Air Force:  Need for 70-
group Air Force, flexibility of authorizations.

Gen. Vandenberg, Air Force:  Congress has been
attentive to Air Force problems, strains of current
world situations.  Necessity of 70-group Air Force
and strength of American Air Establishment.

Discussion of Air Force long-range procurement
plans and Navy's claims of superiority of aircraft
carrier.  Discussion of an academy of the air.

SENATE COMMITTEES

ARMED SERVICES COMMITTEE

*R&D by the War and Navy Departments* (March 1948)

Dr. Bush, R&D Board:  Military contracting for
research and development, role of R&D Board.

Maj. Gen. McAulifee, Army:  Coordination with
Research and Development Board, importance of
science in World War II.

Rear Adm. Lee, Navy:  Provisions of act, role of
service department, Research Advisory Committee.

Maj. Gen. Craigie, Air Force:  Air Force projects noncommercial in nature; need for government
support for private research.

*UMT* (March, April 1948)

Sec. Marshall, State Department:  Soviet menace
in Europe, need to strengthen active forces, Reserves, and ROTC.
Discussion of present military force as "a hol-
low shell," need for readiness, large mobilization
capability.  Discussion of uses of air power, need
for strong Army and Navy.
Sec. Forrestal, Defense Department:  Universal
military training commission, need for large number
of specialists; universal military training would
create trained reserve of over three million.
Discussion of military weakness, authorization
ceilings, weakness of Reserves.
Dr. Compton, Committee on Universal Military
Training:  Operation of universal military training, refutation of arguments against universal military training, cost of universal military
training--$3 billion.
Testimony of interested groups--farm, veteran,
labor, temperance--on universal military training.
Testimony of service secretaries and chiefs in
favor of universal military training.
Testimony of presidential candidate Henry Wal-
lace on size of U.S. military establishment and
plans to reduce it.

FOREIGN RELATIONS COMMITTEE

*European Recovery Program, Part 1* (January 1948)

Sec. Forrestal, Defense Department:  Importance
of Europe to national security, Europe a vacuum,

meaning of real security, a strong Europe will prevent war.

Statements and testimony of a variety of outside
witnesses, primarily concerned with economic aspects
of recovery program.

# 1949 CONGRESSIONAL HEARINGS

## 81st Congress, First Session

HOUSE COMMITTEES

APPROPRIATIONS COMMITTEE

*National Military Establishment Bill for FY 50* (1949)

Sec. Johnson, Defense Department: Need for unified establishment, "reasonable" degree of preparedness, 48-group Air Force, 677,000-man Army,
costs of Berlin airlift, management problems of Office of the Secretary of Defense, single budgeting
procedure, implementation of NATO.
Discussion of Greece and Turkey, question of
Secretary's authority.
Franz Schneider, Defense Department: New budgeting procedure, savings, inflated budget estimates,
summary of Military Establishment appropriations.
Asst. Sec. McNeil, Defense Department: Office
of the Secretary of Defense staff necessary for
unification.
Sec. Gray, Army: Improved Army management,
standardization, procurement.
Gen. Bradley, Joint Chiefs of Staff: Need for
military preparedness, need for restoration of
House cut, Army support for 58-group Air Force.
Discussion of "balanced" forces, Air Force's
tactical air support capability.
Sec. Mathews, Navy: Responsibilities of Navy

secretary, reduction in forces, ships, aircraft.

Adm. Denfield, Navy:  Need for preparedness; no single plan for defense adequate; need for prompt offensive beyond territory.

Discussion of lack of adequate naval supplies, Soviet submarine development, future of battleship, history of carrier cancellation, Navy need for carrier.

Gen. Cates, Marine Corps:  Marine Corps strength, mission, Reserves.

Rear Adm. Hopwood, Navy:  General breakdown of Navy budget, operations and maintenance procurement, civilian components, personnel and pay, Reserve forces, House reductions.

Statements of Naval bureau spokesmen.

Statements of Army service spokesmen.

Sen. Flanders:  Need for strong economy to back up military forces; military spending should be reduced in the face of anticipated deficit.

Discussion of areas amenable to budget cuts, importance of research and development, proposed $3 billion reduction.

C. B. Lister, National Reserve Association: Rifle courses program.

Maj. Gen. Walsh, National Guard Association: National Guard support for rifle program.

Col. Boyer, Reserve Officers Association:  Need for better Reserve training.

Sec. Symington, Air Force:  Air Force appropriations, need for air defense, 58-group program, organization of bomber groups, active and reserve, breakdown of 58-group Air Force, costs of B-50, B-54.  Breakdown of budget request--operations and maintenance, procurement, personnel, air installations.

Discussion of jet transitions, radar research.

Statements from Munitions Board concerning stockpiling program.

ARMED SERVICES COMMITTEE


*Hearings to Authorize Composition of the Army and the Air Force* (January 1949)

Sec. Royall, Army: War not imminent, need for flexibility in planning. Separation of Air Force from Army.

Discussion of congressional ceiling limitations of Army, Air Force, and Navy strengths, need for Ready Reserves. Authorized strengths higher than actual required levels. Discussion of fiscal considerations.

Gen. Bradley, Army: Need to combine into single act congressional authority of Army and Air Force strength. Occupation duties, need for Strategic Reserves.

Discussion of need for 70 air group and proposals for universal military training.

Sec. Symington, Air Force: Need for air power and a congressionally-determined personnel limit.

Discussion of 70 air group and impact of fiscal considerations. Discussion of B-70 program.

Maj. Gen. Walsh, National Guard Association: Danger of federalizing National Guard.

Discussion of Air National Guard status.

Statements by state commanders of National Guard and Reserve units describing lack of funds and organization.


*Hearings to Authorize Air Force Land-Based Air Warning and Control Installations* (February 1949)

Gen. Fairchild, Air Force: Importance of air defense, the time to deploy such a system is great.

Maj. Gen. Saville, Air Force: System would consist of radars, control centers, communication and interceptor aircraft. Description of fighter defense principles, interception and organization.

Col. McCaul, Marine Corps:  Need for land-based systems so that naval air defense can operate effectively.

Lt. Col. Ekman, Army:  Army agreement with Air Force program.

Gen. Saville, Air Force:  Installation of radar sites in Alaska, discussion of air defense effectiveness.

*Hearings to Provide for Under Secretary of Defense* (February 1949)

Sec. Forrestal, Defense Department:  Responsibilities of Secretary too great, need for Under Secretary, discussion of delegation of authority.

*Subcommittee Hearings to Authorize Establishment of Joint Long-Range Guided Missile Proving Grounds* (February 1949)

Gen. Fairchild, Air Force:  Air Force overall responsibility, program jointly administered.  German V-1 and V-2 displayed importance of missiles in the future.

Maj. Gen. Sayler, Army:  Army support for project.

Rear Adm. Gallerey, Navy:  Navy concurrence.

Dr. Compton, R&D Board:  Types of missiles, missile ranges, description of operation, and desciption of testing range.

Discussion of safety and missile accuracy.

*Hearings to Authorize a Unitary Plan for the Establishment of an Air Engineering Development Center, Subcommittee #3* (April 1949)

Dr. Perchelderfer, National Advisory Committee for Aeronautics:  Need for supersonic research, revolutionary changes in aeronautics.

Sec. Symington, Air Force:  German breakthroughs
in research during World War II, need for air supremacy and technological superiority.

Dr. Cornell, R&D Board:  Need for propulsion and
wind tunnel research for both high speed aircraft
and missiles.

Capt. Diehl, Navy:  Need for technological superiority.

Lt. Col. Vaughn, Army:  Army guided-missile program, need for unified testing center.

H. L. Dryden, National Advisory Committee for
Aeronautics:  Technical measurement of speed, uncer-
tainties in supersonic flight, behavior of shock
waves on aircraft performances.

Discussion of X-1 and X-2 research aircraft, XB-
47 bomber program.  Discussion of need for trained
personnel.


*Committee Hearings on B-36 Test* (May 1949)

Rep. Vinson:  Need for impartial tests of the
vulnerability of the B-36 bomber, congressional
resolution to simulate U.S. Navy fighter attack on
B-36.

Discussion of congressional lack of expertise in
aviation affairs.


*Subcommittee Hearings to Amend Act to Authorize the
Construction of Experimental Submarines, Subcommittee #1* (May 1949)

Rear Adm. Clark, Navy:  Need to raise authorized
ceiling of submarines, postwar price rise.


*Subcommittee Hearings to Establish Decoration Medal
for Berlin Airlift, Subcommittee #3* (May 1949)

Testimony includes characteristics of airlift,

number of aircraft, costs, maps, airlift capabilities and requirements.
     Col. Duncan, Air Force:  Discussion of Berlin
Operation, vital statistics of Berlin airlift.


*Subcommittee Hearings to Promote National Defense by
Sending NACA Personnel to Graduate School, Subcommittee #1* (May 1949)

     Robert Lacklen, National Advisory Committee for
Aeronautics:  Importance of air supremacy in future
wars, complexity of supersonic flight, discussion
of Communist party members in National Advisory
Committee for Aeronautics.


*Hearings to Convert National Military Establishments
into an Executive Department of Defense and to Provide the Secretary of Defense with Appropriate Responsibility and Authority* (June 1949)

     Sec. Johnson, Defense Department:  Need for
maintenance of strong postwar defense posture,
Secretary Forrestal's plea for clarification of the
Secretary's duties, need for Secretary to direct
and control military departments, need for additional Secretarial staff, need for Chairman of
Joint Chiefs of Staff, reconstitution of Munitions
and R&D boards.
     Discussion of creation of Assistant Secretary of
Defense, role of Congress, need for civilian control, role of Chairman of Joint Chiefs of Staff,
and accountability to Secretary.
     Herbert Hoover, Hoover Commission:  Report of
Hoover Commission, failure of National Security
Agency of 1947 to establish unity of command, need
for military unity in strategy and command, problems of military waste.
     Discussion of inefficiencies, check on Secretary
of Defense, role of civilian boards in Department
of Defense.

Ferdinand Eberstadt, Hoover Commission: Organizational problems in National Military Establishment, need to (1) strengthen, (2) add civilian as-
sistants, and (3) improve budgeting procedures.

Discussion of possibility of more harmonious
military establishment, membership on National Security Council and prerogatives of Secretary of Defense in proposed Department of Defense.

Frank Hecht, Navy League: View that Secretary
of Defense is too powerful, arguments of fiscal efficiency bogus, warnings of over-centralization.

Gen. Bradley, Army: Need for Chairman for Joint
Chiefs of Staff; fears of overpowerful Chairman exaggerated.

Discussion of need to clarify Chairman's responsibilities and authority.

Adm. Denfield, Navy: Need for objective Chairman; discussion of seniority in the Navy.

Gen. Vandenberg, Air Force: Seniority important
in Joint Chiefs.

Gen. Cates, Marine Corps: Discussion of provision that if a Chief of Staff were made Chairman
he could not return to Chief position.

*Full Committee Hearings to Reorganize Fiscal Manage-
ment in the National Security Establishment* (July
1949)

Asst. Sec. McNeil, Defense Department: Bill to
establish Office of Comptroller in Department of
Defense, discussion of duties and procedures. Need
to centralize budget requests of three services.

Discussion of need to base defense budget on military requirements and not division of defense dol-
lars, need to eliminate budget competition.

*Investigation of the B-36 Bomber Program* (August,
October 1949)

Rep. Van Zandt: Background and chronology of
the B-36 controversy.

Sec. Lovett, Air Force:  Long-range plans for developing B-36, B-36 range and bomber lead, engine development.

Discussion of testing program, contracting and development problems.

Gen. Smith, Air Force:  Genesis of B-36 bomber development process during the war; need to bridge B-29 to B-52 gap with B-36.  Importance of strategic bombing with atomic weapons; B-36 only aircraft to enable United States to launch an attack from the continental United States.

Discussion of development program and testing results, Air Force strategic requirements, B-47 and B-45 development.

Rep. Patterson:  B-36 program during World War II.

Gen. Vandenberg, Air Force:  Mission of the B-36, vulnerability; discussion of role of Navy carrier aviation.

Gen. LeMay, Air Force:  Importance of strategic bombing, role of Air Force Aircraft and Weapons Board, discussion of night bombing tactics and follow-on to B-36.

Gen. Vandenberg, Air Force:  Need for strategic bombing, first priority of the Air Force, doctrine of civilian-industrial bombing, capabilities of the B-36.

Discussion of B-36 selection process.  Discussion of 70-group Air Force aircraft goal.

Sec. Symington, Air Force:  Capabilities of B-36, mobilization requirements of the Air Force, low projected loss rate.

Discussion of Secretary Symington's reconsideration of the B-36 during 1948.  Role of strategic bombing in World War II.

Jack Northrop, Northrop Aircraft:  Discussion of B-35 and B-49 bombers, role of reconnaissance aircraft.

Discussion of B-49 cancellation.

William Allen, Boeing:  Discussion of the B-54, potential of the B-52, and effect on B-36 obsolescence.

Donald Douglas, Douglas Aircraft:  Discussion of
Air Force contracting practices.

James Kindeberger, North American:  B-45 and F-
93 cancellations, need for maintaining healthy aircraft industry.

Gen. Arnold, Air Force:  B-36 most outstanding
bomber in the Air Force, bomber follow-on practices,
importance of strategic bombing, doubts validity of
interception tests.

Gen. Spatz, Air Force:  Concept of strategic
bombing, nuclear deterrence, performance of the B-
36, difficulty of interception over the Soviet Union, danger in cutting Air Force to 48 air group.

Lt. Gen. Twining, Air Force:  Air Force recommendations for B-36.

Lt. Gen. Norstad, Air Force:  Implementation of
Air Force recommendations, B-50 cancellation.

Marx Leva, Office of the Secretary of Defense:
Participation of Office of the Secretary of Defense
in B-36 program, R&D Board, role of Secretary Forrestal's decisions, B-54 cancellation.

Sec. Johnson, Defense Department:  Attempt to
clear innuendoes of political intrigue in approving
B-36 requests.  Traces own participation in decision.


*Hearings on the National Defense Program:  Unifica-
tion and Strategy* (October 1949)

Sec. Mathews, Navy:  Problem of certain Navy personnel secretly releasing information, role of modern aircraft carriers and the need to develop Navy
tactical air capability.

Discussion of decision to cancel supercarrier,
reiteration of naval roles and missions.  Discussion of interservice rivalry and functioning of the
Joint Chiefs.

Adm. Radford, Navy:  Need for a strong Navy, particularly naval aviation.  Atomic warfare not mili-
tarily sound--"a cheap and easy victory."  The
vulnerability of the B-36, inaccuracies in bomber.

Myth of strategic bombing in World War II.

Discussion of nature of future wars, need for limited air capability in foreign waters, and over-estimation of atomic war effects.  Immorality of mass bombing.

Adm. Hopwood, Navy:  Effect of budget cuts on naval procurement.

Asst. Sec. McNeil, Defense Department:  Navy's budget cut greater than other services, discussion of need for naval airpower.

Capt. Trapnell, Navy:  Jet fighter development, vulnerability of B-36, ability of Banshee fighter to down B-36, ability of radar to detect and track B-36.

Discussion of Air Force withholding information from Navy on B-36.

Lt. Comm. Harrison, Navy:  Ability of modern air defense system to defeat strategic bombers, Soviet air defense capability.

Comm. Leonard, Navy:  Ability of high-altitude Navy fighters to down B-36.

Comm. Martin, Navy:  Ability of radar to detect high-flying B-36.

Comm. Metsger, Navy:  Advantages of fighter-interceptors, particularly those equipped with rockets.

Asst. Sec. Hyatt, Navy:  Vulnerability of modern bombers, B-36 would suffer same losses as B-17 over Germany.

Brig. Gen. McGee, Marine Corps:  Insufficient emphasis on tactical missions, need for small, light tactical aircraft.  Use of air support in World War II, Soviet tactical air capabilities.

Adm. Blandy, Navy:  Navy threatened; strategic bombing not as effective as believed in World War II; atomic weapons overestimated.  Importance of traditional naval missions.

Discussion of impact of service unification on Navy.

Adm. Halsey, Navy:  Need for new supercarrier, role of carrier in World War II.

Adm. Burke, Navy:  Need for modern carriers,

tactical air capability, U.S. forces in need of more flexibility than merely bombing.

Fleet Adm. Nimitz, Navy: Need for tactical capability in global war, ability to control the seas, A-bomb not an efficient weapon of war.

Sec. Symington, Air Force: Atomic war not immoral, concept of deterrence. Air Force does possess tactical air ability, realities of modern warfare.

Gen. Vandenberg, Air Force: Air Force capabilities; strategic bombing gets results; ability to knock out enemy capability.

Gen. Bradley, Joint Chiefs of Staff: Joint Chiefs' planning objectives, Soviet aggression, need for balanced forces, importance of strategic bombing and worthiness of B-36 in bomber mission. History of B-36 decision and discussion of Joint Chiefs' understanding of Navy mission.

Sec. Johnson, Defense Department: Military unification, but acceptance of service diversity. Navy mission an important one.

FOREIGN AFFAIRS COMMITTEE

*Mutual Defense Assistance Act of 1949* (July, August 1949)

Sec. Acheson, State Department: Act necessary to achieve peace and security, consistent with collective security, size of Soviet peacetime force, threat of Communist infiltration. $1.4 billion for NATO, Korea, Iran, the Philippines, Latin America, and Canada. Communist groups in these countries the reason for aid, need to prevent future piecemeal conquests.

Discussion of size of aid package, line extent of American commitment, nature of military advice, nature of military assistance and sales since V-J Day.

Sec. Johnson, Defense Department:  Military aid
essential for Marshall Plan and NATO success; European military production a long-term prospect;
United States cannot afford to wait.  U.S. commitment in manpower only advisory in nature.

Discussion of U.S. rearmament, situation in
China, importance of Korea.

John Marshall, former Secretary, Defense Department:  Support for program; United States cannot
let down momentum.

Discussion of China, the projected length of the
Cold War.

Ambassador Harriman, State Department:  European
recovery, Military Assistance Program essential for
economic program.

Ambassador Grady, Greece:  U.S. military assistance in Greece.

Edgar Mourer, columnist:  Need for European military independence.

Testimony by concerned veterans' groups, religious and political groups pro and con the proposed
legislation.


JOINT COMMITTEES OF HOUSE AND SENATE


JOINT ATOMIC ENERGY COMMITTEE


*Investigation into the U.S. Atomic Energy Project*
(May 1949)

David Lilienthal, Atomic Energy Commission:
Charges that U.S. atomic energy program has been a
failure and incredibly mismanaged untrue; scope of
U.S. atomic energy program.

Discussion of personnel problems, management,
charges of Communist infiltration.

Extensive testimony on Atomic Energy Commission
management.

SENATE COMMITTEES

ARMED SERVICES COMMITTEE

*National Defense Facilities Act of 1949* (March 1949)

Sec. Royall, Army: Construction and expansion of training facilities for active forces, Reserves, and National Guard.

*Army-Air Force Composition Authorization: Composition of the Air Force* (March, April 1949)

Sec. Royall, Army: Need for realistic, long-term authorization for Army-Air Force strength; war not imminent; legislation essential to Army-Air Force separation.

Gen. Bradley, Army: Need for Army-Air Force authorization like that of the Navy. History of congressional authorization for the Army; discussion of Army troop ceiling of 837,000. Air Force's 70-group program, strategy of strategic bombing, role of group forces.

Discussion of budget formation of three services.

Asst. Sec. Zuckert and Gen. Vandenberg, Air Force: Need for authorizational flexibility; discussion of meaning of 70-group program, size of Air Force.

Maj. Gen. Walsh, National Guard Association: Support for measure.

*National Security Act Amendment of 1949* (March, April, May 1949)

Sec. Forrestal, Defense Department: Conversion of National Military Establishment into Department of Defense. Appropriate responsibility and authority of the Secretary of Defense. Failure to endow

authorization in Secretary will create risks to national security; fears of defense centralization
unfounded.

Discussion of Hoover Commission recommendations,
authorization of the Secretary of Defense, problems
of lack of Chairman for Joint Chiefs and insufficient staff for service secretaries.

Discussion of inefficient service duplication.

Ferdinand Eberstadt, Hoover Commission: Fear
that Office of the Secretary of Defense will become
a corporate empire; centralization does not automatically mean efficiency.

Discussion of lines of authority in the Defense
Department, problems with the establishment of a
Chairman of the Joint Chiefs of Staff.

Frank Pace, Bureau of the Budget: Proposed act
would aid President; need for increased Secretary
of Defense authorization to help President.

Discussion of setting budget ceiling, role of
Secretary of Defense in determining budget.

Sec. Symington, Air Force: Air Force favors centralization, need for strong Defense Department
leadership, fear of Chairman of Joint Chiefs of
Staff becoming dictator unfounded.

Adm. Denfield, Navy, Gen. Bradley, Army, Gen.
Vandenberg, Air Force: Support for Chairman of the
Joint Chiefs of Staff, meaning of the "principal
military advisor" clause, duties of the Joint Chiefs.

Discussion of service roles in budgeting; discussion of mission assignments and power of the Secretary of Defense.

Herbert Hoover, Hoover Commission: Lack of clear-
cut secretarial authority in National Security
Agency of 1947; need for stronger Secretary and
functional budgeting system; disapproves of Chairman
for Joint Chiefs.

Discussion of defense management, need for stan-
dardized procedures.

Sec. Patterson, War Department: Urges adoption
of bill, centralization necessary for mobilization.

*Malmedy Massacre Investigations: Massacre of Soldiers
at the Battle of the Bulge* (April, June 1949)

Extensive hearings on murder of U.S. troops and
administration of military justice.

*Construction at Military and Naval Installations*
(July 1949)

Sec. Johnson, Defense Department:  Importance of
separately defined roles and missions of services.
Results of Key West and Newport conferences.

FOREIGN RELATIONS COMMITTEE

*North Atlantic Treaty, Part 1* (April, May 1949)

Sec. Acheson, State Department:  Traditional
U.S. policy, impact of World War II, U.N., viola-
tions by Soviet Union.
Explanation of Ure treaty, Military Assistance
Program, discussion of relationship with U.N., nature of Soviet threat, future of U.S. commitments.
Warren Austin, State Departmentt:  Increasing
unity of non-Soviet world, the U.N. Charter, Article 51 of Charter.
Sec. Johnson, Defense Department:  Treaty, not
military alliance, role of military assistance, discussion of surplus program, Military Assistance Program, and future of commitments.
Ambassador Harriman, Economic Cooperation Administration:  Growing confidence in Europe, changing
attitude toward Germany, morale in Europe.
Robert Lovett, Defense Department:  European insecurity, Communist threat, must emphasize self-help;
United States must encourage federation of Europe.
Gen. Bradley, Army:  Military significance of
treaty, need to establish defense frontier in

Europe, nature of Military Assistance Program, deterrent effect of treaty.

*--Part 2* (May 1949)

Number of witnesses representing political groups in favor of and opposed to treaty.

*Military Assistance Program* (August 1949)

Sec. Acheson, State Department: North Atlantic Treaty, interdependence of economic recovery and national security, community of interests in North Atlantic area. Plan--$1.1 billion of military aid to Europe, need for flexibility.

Discussion of costs, North Atlantic Council.

Sec. Johnson, Defense Department: Isolationism no longer viable, objectives of program, screening requests, procurement and forward contracting authorization.

Discussion of the Far East situation.

Gen. Bradley, Joint Chiefs of Staff: U.S. leadership, integrated defense plans.

Ambassador Harriman, Economic Cooperation Administration: Support for united, rearmed Europe; need to bolster European morale.

Norman Thomas: Need to stall military assistance until collective security built up, appeal for disarmament.

Witnesses from veterans', women's, and religious groups in favor of and opposed to the proposal.

# 1950 CONGRESSIONAL HEARINGS

## 81st Congress, Second Session

APPROPRIATIONS COMMITTEE

*DOD Appropriations for FY 51* (1950)

Sec. Johnson, Defense Department, and Gen. Bradley, Joint Chiefs of Staff: Defense budget process, role of Joint Chiefs, need for more powerful forces, Army strength, aircraft procurement, Navy size.

Discussion of size of Air Force, research and development support, status of Army preparedness, unification of services.

Asst. Sec. McNeil, Defense Department: Evaluation of budget requirements, FY 1951 budget, summary detailed by cost category, how contract authority works in procurement, military personnel costs.

Gen. Bradley and Gen. Collins, Army: Status of military strength not sufficient to fight a major war, situation in Pacific, Communist forces in Asia, Japanese situation.

Sec. Voorhees, Army: Occupied areas.

Gen. Collins, Army: Assistance to Greece and Turkey, major procurement and research and development, Military Defense Assistance Program, mission of Reserves and National Guard, Army role in nuclear era, Army research and development, development of a tank program.

Sec. Mathews, Navy: Naval role, cargo transport, Navy budget, research and development.

Adm. Sherman, Navy: Changes in Navy budget since 1945, maintenance of Reserve Fleet; discussion of effect of NATO on defense budgets, Navy and Marine ship and aircraft strength, antisubmarine warfare program, breakdown of Navy personnel.

Sec. Symington, Air Force: 70-group Air Force, responsibilities of Air Force, Air Force procurement, need for modernization and vigorous research and development--interceptors, guided missiles, and air defense.

Gen. Vandenberg, Air Force: Role of atomic warfare, 70-group Air Force, discussion of Air Force strength and 70-group debate.

Lt. Gen. Rawlings, Air Force: Air Force FY 1950 request, fiscal category requests, use of unobligated funds, cost of Air Force and 11-group Air National Guard.

John Ohly, Mutual Defense Assistance: Military Assistance Program B-29 transfer to United Kingdom, agreement conditions.

Dep. Asst. Sec. Merchant, State Department: Military aircraft seized by Chinese Communists.

Maj. Gen. Arnold, Army: Military personnel costs, operations and maintenance, major procurement.

Statements by Army Ordnance, Chemical, Engineers, Quartermaster, Transportation.

Rear Adm. Hopwood, Navy: Policy approach of "performance" budgeting, development of an appropriation structure, operations and maintenance, personnel procurement.

Gen. Cates, Marine Corps: Fleet Marine forces, security forces, training activities.

Rear Adm. Moebus, Navy: Naval air budget, antisubmarine warfare, aircraft procurement and modernization.

Statements from Navy Bureau of Ships, Ordnance, Supply, Petroleum Reserves.

Maj. Gen. Nugent, Air Force: Aircraft procurement, personnel, discussion of guided missiles.

Statements from Air Force Armaments, Air Materiel.

Gen. Eisenhower, Army:  Opposed to unilateral disarmament, need for strong economy, 70-group Air Force not sacrosanct, need for antisubmarine warfare capability.

Discussion of adequacy of FY 1951 budget.

Asst. Sec. Butterworth, Defense Department:  Military Defense Assistance Program, discussion of congressional access to information.

Asst. Sec. McNeil, Defense Department:  National Security Agency, personnel.

Frank Weil, Presidential Committee on Relations and Welfare of Armed Services:  Military morale, importance of USO.

William Webster, R&D Board:  Role of R&D Board.

Maj. Gen. Timberlake, Air Force:  Munitions Board, Reserve plant program.

James Lay, National Security Council:  Function of National Security Council.

Maj. Gen. Walsh, National Guard Association: Budget barely large enough to operate on.

Brig. Gen. Evans, Reserve Officers Association: Need for more training, greater support.

Sec. Johnson, Defense Department:  Defense Department supplemental increases requested, money requested by the services was granted by Executive.

Discussion of NATO Hague meetings, H-bomb construction, increase in aircraft procurement.

Asst. Sec. McNeil, Defense Department:  Statistics of budget supplemental.


*Supplemental Appropriations* (July 1950)

Sen. Thye:  Discussion of appropriation to National Guard.

Maj. Gen. Walsh, National Guard Association: National Guard-Bureau of the Budget disagreements; National Guard training levels continually lowered; need for restoration of House cut.

Lyle Garlock, Defense Department:  Defense

Department gives consideration of National Guard
strength.

Maj. Gen. Decker, Army:  Difficulty of calling
up National Guard, discussion of regular Army ignor-
ing National Guard.

Sec. Johnson, Defense Department:  Korean invasion, amount requested, combat potential, breakdown
of supplemental request, full mobilization not requested.

Short statements by Navy and Air Force on amounts
requested.

Lt. Gen. Ridgway, Army:  $3-billion Army request,
purpose of request, repelling Korean invaders,
strength of Army 590,000 at time of attack, support
for Military Defense Assistance Program, U.N. effort.

Maj. Gen. Decker, Army:  Breakdown of supplemental request, summary by Army services.

Sec. Finletter, Air Force:  Air Force request,
aircraft production.

Sec. Mathews, Navy:  Korean situation, Navy request, discussion of adequacy of defense funds.

ARMED SERVICES COMMITTEE

*Hearings to Authorize Construction of Modern Naval
Vessels* (1950)

Adm. Sherman, Navy:  Need for balanced Navy,
particular need for increased submarines and carrier conversion.

Discussion of nuclear submarine development and
defense budget review by Joint Chiefs; need to emphasize military strength over fiscal considerations.

*Selective Service Act Extension* (January 1950)

Gen. Bradley, Joint Chiefs of Staff:  No

intentions of exercising provisions of draft, but
need to convince Russians of determinations and
NATO allies of willingness to contribute to collective defense.

Sec. Acheson, State Department: Background of
North Atlantic Treaty, need to convince allies to
increase their troop strengths.

Discussion of universal military training.

Gen. Collins, Army: U.S. commitments, effects
of demobilization on the Army; Reserves and National Guard incapable of supporting mobilization.

Maj. Gen. Hershey, Selective Service: Size of
draft pool, numbers of potential mobilization, discussion of how state Selective Service boards operate.

Rep. Javits: Existence of racially segregated
units in the Army.

Maj. Gen. Walsh, National Guard Association:
Need to maintain Selective Service as an emergency
measure, Guard not benefiting from Selective Service.

Witnesses from religious, temperance, and peace
groups opposed to Selective Service.


*Subcommittee Hearings to Provide for Additional Offi-
cers for the National Guard* (February 1950)

Maj. Gen. Fleming, National Guard Association:
Officers already exist, need for permanent authority.

Maj. Gen. Walsh, National Guard Association:
Need for better National Guard housing and equipment.


*Army Organization Bill* (March 1950)

Sec. Gray, Army: Need to maintain 1941 organization of the Army as established by the War Powers
Act; discussion of internal organization; no effect
on strength of the Army, need for organizational

flexibility as recommended by the Hoover Commission. Explanation of each section of the bill.

Gen. Collins, Army: Discussion of role of Reserves and National Guard in the Army, powers and duties of the Secretary of the Army, historical evolution of the Army.

*Hearings to Extend Selective Service Act of 1948* (May 1950)

Gen. Bradley, Joint Chiefs of Staff: Soviet pressure, Berlin, Formosa, Indochina, and Hungary. Importance of the North Atlantic Treaty and ability to mobilize in between four to six months.

Discussion of collective defense alliances, necessity of draft, and areas of Communist pressure.

## JOINT COMMITTEES OF HOUSE AND SENATE

## JOINT ATOMIC ENERGY COMMITTEE

*Civil Defense against Atomic Attack* (March 1950)

Paul Larsen, Office of Civilian Mobilization: Definition of civil defense, need to stimulate local programs.

William Gill, National Security Resources Board: Studies necessary for planning, current programs in existence.

Dr. Kiefer, National Security Resources Board: Housing and community planning program, experience in Japan and Germany, need for readiness procedures and emergency facilities.

Gordon Dean, Atomic Energy Commission: Atomic Energy Commission's civil defense responsibilities.

Dr. Warren, Atomic Energy Commission: Atomic

Energy Commission sponsored courses in medical
hazards of atomic attacks, experience of Hiroshima.
   Mayor Bowrob, Los Angeles:  Need for federal action to integrate state and local action.
   Testimony of mayors, American Legion representatives, and others urging stronger federal civil
defense programs.


## JOINT DEFENSE PRODUCTION COMMITTEE


*Defense Production Act:  Hoarding and Strategic Ma-
terials* (December 1950)

   William Harrison, National Production Authority:
Act to prevent accumulation and hoarding of scarce
and strategic materials over and above reasonable
personal and business demands.
   Discussion of steel and aluminum hoarding, price
of scrap metal.


## SENATE COMMITTEES


## APPROPRIATIONS COMMITTEE


*Third Supplemental Appropriation:  FY 51* (1950)

   Charles Wilson, Defense Production Administration:  Need for increase in borrowing authority,
inflation during Korean War.
   Statements by other government agencies and departments on need for increased authority.
   Adm. McCormick, Navy:  Increased appropriations
for Navy; Chinese invasions, increase in personnel
and guided missile program.
   Gen. Cates, Marine Corps:  Four-division and

four-air-wing Marine Corps; need for increased appropriations.

Gen. Twining, Air Force: Increased aircraft procurement.

Lt. Gen. Hull, Army: Increased size of Army.


## ARMED SERVICES COMMITTEE


*Army Organization Act of 1950* (May 1950)

Sec. Pace, Army: Act only deals with internal organization of standing army. Legislation necessary before 1941 authority runs out.

Asst. Sec. Gray, Army: Army Chief of Staff made responsible to Secretary of the Army. Discussion of Secretary's prerogatives and responsibilities.

Gen. Collins, Army: Chief of Staff's responsibilities, discussion of general scope of authority.


*Mutual Defense Assistance Program, 1950, Held with Committee on Foreign Relations* (June 1950)

Sec. Acheson, State Department: U.S. obligations under NATO, conception of integrated defense, increased confidence in Europe, situation in Greece, Turkey, Iran, and Far East.

Discussion of European morale, efforts of allies.

Sec. Johnson, Defense Department: Defense planning accomplished, shipments so far, and appraisal of Soviet intentions.

Discussion of regional areas and problems of Hague meeting of NATO allies.

Discussion of length of commitment, expression of hope that billion-dollar-a-year commitment will not go on indefinitely.

Ambassador Harriman, Economic Cooperation

Administration: Economic recovery in Europe, increasing military production. Discussion of Communist propaganda, role in labor movements.

Paul Hoffman, Economic Cooperation Administration: Economic Cooperation Administration's currency fund; cautions against excessive military
investment; need for economic recovery.


*Selective Service Extension Act* (June 1950)

Sec. Johnson, Defense Department: Proposal for
three-year extension of draft, need to protect commitment to NATO, cost of act, effect of act on pro-
moting voluntary enlistments.

Discussion of international situation--Soviet
A-bomb test, fall of China, expansion of Soviet
navy.

Discussion of racial segregation in the Armed
Forces, status of the reservists and National
Guard.

Gen. Bradley, Joint Chiefs of Staff: Selective
Service a vital part of the Administration's $13-
billion budget.

Gen. Collins, Army: Selective Service part of
integrated free-world defense plan.

Maj. Gen. Hershey, Selective Service: Operation
of Selective Service system, effect on voluntary
enlistments, size of draft pool.

Testimony of racial, religious, and peace groups
on extension of the draft.


*The Korean Situation* (August 1950)

Ambassador Pauly: Soviet Union behind Korean
aggression, Soviet occupation of North Korea, discussion of Soviet propaganda techniques, decision
for American troops to leave Korea.

*UMT* (August 1950)

   Sec. Johnson, Defense Department:  Korean events
emphasize need for universal military training,
need for increased manpower and readiness; discussion of Soviet intentions, failure of the U.N.
   Gen. Bradley, Joint Chiefs of Staff:  Universal
military training only answer to U.S. long-run
manpower needs, educational and moral benefit of
universal military training.  Universal military
training would strengthen Reserves and National
Guard.
   George Craig, American Legion:  Universal military training an answer to juvenile delinquency,
need to convince Soviet Union of American determination.
   Testimony of mothers' groups, religious, farm,
and peace groups on universal military training
legislation.


*Federal Civil Defense Act* (December 1950)

   Mayor Hynes, Boston:  Boston prime target, need
for federal government to establish communication
centers for attack warning, federal requirements
for shelters, and federal plan for manpower assistance if attacked.
   Testimony of other mayors supporting federal
program.
   James J. Wadsworth, Civil Defense Association:
Civil defense a state, not a federal, responsibility.  Discussion of cost of nationwide program.
   Federal responsibilities include coordination
and Red Cross mobilization.  Federal-state civil
defense cost-sharing plan.
   Discussion of other federal civil defense admin-
istrations on details of program.
   Dr. Warren, Atomic Energy Commission:  Biological research on radiation effects.

FOREIGN RELATIONS COMMITTEE

*Mutual Defense Assistance Program*

See Senate Armed Services Committee (June 1950)

# 1951 CONGRESSIONAL HEARINGS

## 82nd Congress, First Session

HOUSE COMMITTEES

ARMED SERVICES COMMITTEE

*Hearings to Authorize the Use of Incompleted Submarine for Explosive Tests* (1951)

Adm. Witten, Navy:  Use of incompleted submarine to determine hull shock resistance for atomic submarine under development.

*Committee Hearings on Organization of the Department of the Air Force* (January 1951)

Discussion of civilian control over Air Force, General Vandenberg's plea for an "air staff."
Sec. Finletter and Gen. Vandenberg, Air Force: Discussion of National Security Act, legal status of Air Force, need for higher number of officers.
Gen. Vandenberg, Air Force:  Need for clear command and control, need for Chief of Staff to command strategic forces in combat situations.
Discussion of Air Force's five commands.

*Hearings on Universal Military Training* (January, February, March 1951)

Asst. Sec. Rosenberg, Defense Department:  Elements of national strength, reasons for choosing 18- to 19-year-old age bracket, four-month training provision; possibility that veterans could be called up if universal military training not adopted.

Discussion of size of draft pool, effect of universal military training on Reserves, and civilian authority over military.

Sec. Marshall, Defense Department:  Need for universal military training, desired force of 3.4 million, large force in being.  Need for specialists in armed forces; changing character of full-scale war.

Discussion of Korean War, tactics of Gen. MacArthur, difficulty of mobilizing Reserves.

Maj. Gen. Hershey, Selective Service:  Possibility of all-out general war, danger of current situation, history of draft conscription, need for extending Selective Service Act of 1948, lowering age of inductees, extending service and delaying discharges.

Discussion of need for technical skills for military service, Compton Commission suggestion of a National Security Training Commission, fairness of proposed system.

Rep. Bailey:  Need to provide veterans' hospitals with adequate staffs.

Erle Cocke, Jr., American Legion:  Need for universal military training, raising strength of military.  Support for induction of 18-year-olds and 26 months active service.  Advocates National Security Training Corps and permanent universal military training program.

Rep. Steed:  Possibility that proposed legislation would destroy National Guard by making guardsmen liable for draft.

Rep. Javits:  Need for "race, creed, color" insert in universal military training legislation.

Discussion of Communist propaganda calling the United States "racist."

Omar Ketchum, Veterans of Foreign Wars:  Need

for universal military training, changing draft age requirements of 19-26 to 18-35. Argues that measure contains too many exemptions.

Discussion of time necessary for reservists to prepare for combat after active duty call-up.

Rep. Denny: Proposes scheme that would mix basic training with college education.

Discussion of need for civilian control of military establishment.

Brig. Gen. Evans, Reserve Officers Association: Support of universal military training, but concern over a standing force of 3.5 million, need for fiscal responsibility and larger Reserve forces to enable a smaller standing force. Danger of depleting Reserve forces.

Discussion of difficulty of building effective Reserve forces.

Frank Sparks, Wabash College: ROTC programs, need to defer college students.

Discussion of unfairness of program in drafting students from non-ROTC colleges.

Maj. Gen. Hershey, Selective Service: Tests for student deferments.

Discussion of grading system.

Rep. Hinshaw: Social impact of universal military training; supports allowing students to finish college before facing military service.

Maj. Gen. Byers, Army: ROTC deferments, need for ROTC officers, discussion of ROTC cost per student and numbers and names of colleges offering Army ROTC.

Rear Adm. Watkins, Navy: Cost of Navy ROTC, description of program.

Brig. Gen. Parks, Air Force: Air Force ROTC, costs, summary of program.

E. Raymond Wilson, Friends Committee: Opposition to universal military training, fear of militarism, financial bankruptcy. Failure of Baruch proposal, need for disarmament, role of U.N. Anomaly of rearming Germany and Japan five years after their defeat.

Discussion of immorality of conscription

systems, psychological harm of draft.  Discussion
of need for U.N. peace-keeping system and limited
world government.

Frederick Libby, National Council for the Prevention of War:  European allies, short terms of
conscription, alleged power of Joint Chiefs, revolutionary potential of Asia, need for economic development.

Miss Elizabeth Smart, Women's Christian Temperance Union:  Opposition to peace-time conscription,
18-year-olds too young for armed forces, problem of
alcoholism in armed forces.

John Swomley, National Council against Conscription:  Need for termination date in bill to control
size of military.  Fear that military is draining
nation's resources.  Eighteen-year-olds too young
for armed forces, unlikelihood of future war in
Europe.

J. T. Sanders, National Grange:  Large standing
army injurious to farm manpower; need for farm
deferments.

Donald McQuade, Catholic War Veterans:  Need for
universal military training, seriousness of world
situation.  Opposition to drafting 18-year-olds.

Mrs. William Slagle, mother:  Need to coordinate
military training with education.  Opposition to
conscription of 18-year-olds.  "Are we in such dire
straits that we need to conscript our babies for a
global crusade?"

Jack Kyle, National Defense League:  Immediate
defense threat, need for universal military training and strong Reserves.

Discussion of inevitability of war.

Rep. Barden:  Opposed to defeatist Cold War
mood; universal military training should be viewed
as an emergency program, not continuous.

Clinton Howard, International Reform Federation:
Religious messages bearing on universal military
training, drinking in armed forces--"may they put
their trust in the God of battles and not in the
devil of booze."

Joseph Buchiet, Labor Youth League:  Opposition

to universal military training, possibility of
other "Koreas." No danger from Soviet Union.

Discussion of Youth League's credentials and
ties with Communist party.

Mrs. C. D. Wright, General Federation of Women's
Clubs: Support for universal military training,
adequate training for young soldiers.

Witnesses include a number of religious pastors,
ministers, and spokesmen from religious orders
opposed to universal military training.

S. M. Brownwell, National Education Association:
Using 18-year-olds will not increase number of
draft pool, 18-year-olds already in college. Proposed law a waste of manpower.

Stanley Ruttenberg, Congress of Industrial Organization: Need to defer married men, to end dis-
crimination in armed forces, and to provide certain
occupational deferments.

Dr. James Conant, Universal Military Training
Commission: Support for universal military training, size of draft pool, need for adequate forces
to avoid global war.

Clarence Mitchell, NAACP: Condemnation of Army
segregation, progress in Navy and Air Force.


*Reserve Components* (January, April, July, August
1951)

Gen. Evans, Reserve Officers Association: Drastic problems facing the Reserves, the relevance of
the Korean War, uncertainty of present Reserve program, injustices. Need to increase size of
Reserves, need to induct presently deferred individuals for Reserve service, and need to remove
officer ceilings on Reserves.

Discussion of partial mobilization effects,
problems dealing with Department of Defense.

Omar Ketchum, Veterans of Foreign Wars: Injus-
tice of reservists carrying brunt of Korean episode, disruption of reservists' careers.

Discussion of plan to make call-up more predict-
able.

Col. McMullen, Air Reserve Association:  Problem
in maintaining pilot and technician reserve; need
for more funds, better equipment.

Clarence Adamy, American Veterans:  Major com-
plaint--lack of comprehensive, equitable procedure
for recall to active duty.  Advocates point system
procedure.

Statements by state and regional National Guard
and Reserve Adjunct General on specific problems
facing units in various states.

Asst. Sec. Rosenberg, Defense Department:  Need
to convert Guard and Reserve to ready status.  Korean crisis necessitated the calling of veterans;
plan to return reservists home as quickly as possible.  Need for universal military training.

General discussion of universal military training proposal.

*Hearings to Fix Personnel Strengths of the Marine
Corps and Establish Relationship to JCS* (May 1951)

Adm. Sherman, Navy:  Opposition to independent
status of Marine Corps, integral part of Navy.
Size of Marine Corps should be geared to the Navy.
Danger of allowing Marine Corps to grow dispropor-
tionately and absorb Navy's resources.  Legal right
of Secretary of the Navy and the Chief of Naval
Operations to exercise authority over the Marine
Corps.

Discussion of need to protect size of Marine
Corps.

Rep. Mansfield:  Need for Marine Corps representation on the Joint Chiefs of Staff, inability of
Navy to represent the views of the Marine Corps.

Discussion of Marine readiness prior to Korea,
legal status of the Marine Corps.

Gen. Devereux, Marine Corps:  Need for strengthened Marine Corps and representative on Joint
Chiefs.

Discussion of Navy's ability to understand Marine problems.

Gen. Collins, Army:  Marine Corps should be pro-
portionate to the Navy, no need for Joint Chiefs
representation.
Discussion of whether Marine Corps is separate
military service, of Navy's authority over Marines.
Gen. Vandenberg, Air Force:  Marine Corps a specialized component of the Navy, like Strategic Air
Command in the Air Force, mission dependent upon
naval campaign.  Enlarging Marine Corps would create "second Army."
Discussion of Marine mission.
Gen. Cates, Marine Corps:  Need for four Marine
divisions and air wings, support of Joint Chiefs
membership.
Discussion of effect of Marine growth on Marine
efficiency, necessity to draft.

## Hearings to Make Revisions to Officer Personnel Act of 1947 (May 1951)

Rear Adm. McMahon, Navy:  Need for emergency revisions due to Korean situation.  Navy practice of
separating officers while calling up Reserves in-
consistent and unsatisfactory.  Hope of returning
to stable force levels when world situation permits.
Discussion of Navy separation procedures.

## Hearing to Amend Act to Authorize Experimental Submarine (June 1951)

Rear Adm. Walton, Navy:  Cost overrun in the
construction of advanced submarines.
Remainder of hearing in executive session.

## Hearings to Establish Advisory Committee to Facilitate R&D Work by the Services (June 1951)

Col. Triplet, Army:  Need for military research
and development to overcome Soviet manpower

superiority.  Explanation of research and development advisory committee and provision for long-term
research contracts.

Discussion of limited ability of services to
contract for research, interdepartment relationship
of services to National Advisory Committee for Aeronautics, other government agencies.

Col. Boushey, Air Force:  Description of Air
Force Air Research and Development Command, contracting procedures.

Dr. Piore, Navy:  Research and Development Review Board, discussion of duplication of research.


## Military and Naval Construction (June, July 1951)

Gen. Doolittle (Ret.), Army Air Corps:  Construction of Air Force Research and Development
Command.

Sec. Finletter, Air Force:  Rebuilding Strategic
Air Command base structure, importance of strategic
bombing.

Dep. Sec. Lovett, Defense Department:  Review of
defense program, need for base modernization.


## Hearing to Suspend Authorized Personnel Strength of the Armed Forces (July 1951)

Brig. Gen. Schuyler, Air Force:  Differences of
authorized and appropriated service strengths, need
to go beyond these strengths, particularly for the
Air Force.


## Subcommittee Hearings to Amend Civil Defense Act of 1950 Relating to Alaska (August 1951)

E. L. Bartlett, Alaskan Congressional Delegate:
Strategic importance of Alaska, inability of Alaska
to pay 50-50 on civil defense program.

James J. Wadsworth, Civil Defense Association:

Difficulty of shelter program for Alaska.

*Hearing on Reserve Components Bill* (September 1951)

Gen. Evans, Reserve Officers Association: Plan providing for three categories of Reserves--ready, stand-by, and retired.

Discussion of the limitation of the President in the call of the Ready Reserve, congressional prerogatives in setting Reserve ceilings.

Gen. Beckford, National Guard: Support for three-tiered Reserve system, need for National Guard role in declared national emergency, how universal military training could damage the National Guard.

## JOINT COMMITTEES OF HOUSE AND SENATE

### JOINT ATOMIC ENERGY COMMITTEE

*Progress Report--Atomic Energy Committee* (November 1951)

Rear Adm. Collier (Ret.), Navy: H-bomb program, excellent organization and construction effort.

Discussion of Taft-Hartley regulations flaunted at H-bomb site.

### JOINT DEFENSE PRODUCTION COMMITTEE

*Progress Report--Defense Production Administration* (April 1951)

William Harrison, National Production Authority:

Emergency tax amortization, need for short-run emergency controls, long-run tax breaks to increase mobilization.

Discussion of effect of government policies on small businesses.

## *Progress Report--Office of Defense Mobilization* (April 1951)

Charles Wilson, Office of Defense Mobilization: Korean invasion, NATO; new tank, aircraft, and jet engine production goals, costs in comparison with World War II--$23 billion in defense obligation nine months after Korean outbreak.

Discussion of government contracting methods of the Reconstruction Finance Corporation, inflationary effect.

## SENATE COMMITTEES

## APPROPRIATIONS COMMITTEE

## *DOD Appropriations for FY 1952* (1951)

Dep. Sec. Lovett, Defense Department: Total budget estimate, activities provided by budget request, massive procurement, budget for Korean War, impact on economy.

Asst. Sec. McNeil, Defense Department: Procurement, inventory control.

John Small, Munitions Board: Small business procurement, contracting procedures.

Sec. Pace, Army: Army budget request, management, cost-reduction procedures.

Sec. Mathews, Navy: Navy budget, planning, inflation increases.

Asst. Sec. McCone, Air Force: Air Force budget

request, programming and control, wing organization, performance and cost comparison of B-17E vs.
B-47B, price changes.

Dep. Sec. Lovett, Defense Department: Office of
the Secretary of Defense role in budget formulation, new obligational authority by cost category,
size of armed forces.

Discussion of adequacy of current military effort

Asst. Sec. Rosenberg, Defense Department: Defense Department manpower situation, effect of Korea.

Adm. Sherman, Navy: Navy mission Soviet
expansion, breakdown into budget categories.

Discussion of carrier strength, adequacy of budget.

Gen. Cates, Marine Corps: Marine program, personnel strength.

Sen. Lodge: Air Force strength should be expanded from 95 to 150 groups, need for tactical air
power improvements.

Sen. Wherry: Need to establish ring of air
bases around the Soviet Union.

Sec. Finletter, Air Force: 95-wing program, Air
Force major mission--"prevention of disaster."

Gen. Vandenberg, Air Force: Discussion of 95-
vs. 150-wing force.

Gen. Collins, Army: Strength of Army, role of
land army in nuclear age.

Asst. Sec. McNeil, Defense Department: Aircraft
procurement.

Statements by Reserve and National Guard spokesmen.


ARMED SERVICES COMMITTEE


*To Facilitate R&D Work by and/or on Behalf of the
Army, Navy, and Air Force* (1951)

Col. Triplet, Army, and others:  Need to secure
talents of scientists and engineers for service research and development programs.
Discussion of contracting procedures.


*UMT and Service Act of 1951* (January, February 1951)

Sec. Marshall, Defense Department:  Universal
military training best means of enlarging military
strength at low cost.  Need for preparedness--
adequate standing force and vitalized Reserves and
National Guard.  Need to draft 18-year-olds.
Discussion of increased manpower needs, necessity of supporting worldwide commitments.
Asst. Sec. Rosenberg, Defense Department:  Needs
of military establishment must be met without disrupting civilian life, importance of proper manpower utilization in the Defense Department, problem
of building forces by 700,000 in short time period.
Discussion of 18-year-old draft, four-year enlistment, 27-month draft.  Discussion of ROTC programs, manpower pools, cost of universal military
training.
Asst. Sec. Johnson, Army:  Comparative international military service, manpower pools, Army
needs.
Vice Adm. Roper, Navy:  Effect of Korean build-
up on Navy.
Sec. Tobin, Labor Department:  U.S. manpower resources, World War II manpower experience, changes
in population patterns.
Dr. Compton, M.I.T.:  Report of Universal Military Training Commission, 18-year-old draft, effect
on education and morals.
Dr. Dodds, Princeton University:  Moral capacity
of an 18-year-old, discussion of universal military
training disrupting college careers, opposition to
college deferment.
Witnesses include other educators discussing effect of universal military training on universities.

Maj. Gen. Hershey, Selective Service: Problems
of draft unacceptability, need to maintain large
manpower pool.

Discussion of program's effect on Reserves and
National Guard.

Edward Overly, Department of Agriculture: Plan
will allow agricultural deferments if necessary.

Adm. Sherman, Navy: Support for universal military training and partial mobilization. Need for
longer than 27-month service, importance of training.

Gen. Collins, Army: Eighteen-year-old soldiers
are excellent; discussion of combat-support ratio.

Gen. Vandenberg, Air Force: Air Force increases, discussion of 27-month draft.

Gen. Bradley, Army: Duties of the Joint Chiefs,
need for partial mobilization, necessity of drafting 18-year-olds, discussion of costs of universal
military training.

Erle Cocke, American Legion: Need to protect
strength of Reserves and National Guard, support
for 18-year-old draft.

Omar Ketchum, Veterans of Foreign Wars: Support
for universal military training, support for 18-
year-old draft, amendment to place conscientious
objectors in detention camps.

Maj. Gen. Walsh, National Guard Association:
Support for universal military training, need to
channel inductees into National Guard and Reserve
forces.

Brig. Gen. Evans, Reserve Officers Association:
Need for universal military training to build up
Reserve components.

Testimony includes statements from religious,
farm, political, and labor organizations on proposed system.


*Assignment of Ground Forces of the United States to
Duty in the European Area*

See Senate Foreign Relations Committee (February
1951)

*Air Force Organization Act of 1951* (April 1951)

Sec. Finletter, Air Force:  Offers advice to
change act to create more authority for Air Force
Chief of Staff, discussion of line of authority in
act, relation of Air National Guard and Reserves.
Thomas King, Reserve Officers Association:  Ap-
peal for greater Air Force Reserve autonomy.
Paul Robbins, National Society of Professional
Engineers:  Amendment to insert engineers in Air
Force Act.

*Amendments to Federal Civil Defense Act of 1950*
(April 1951)

Samuel Sabin, Civil Defense Administration:
Need for larger part federal funds in Alaska state
sharing program.
Hubert Gallager, Civil Defense:  Crucial importance of Alaska, vulnerability, need for protection.
Testimony of Alaskan officials in support of
measure.

*Marine Corps Strength and Joint Chiefs Representation*
(April 1951)

Sen. Douglas:  Marine Corps ceiling, need for
strong Marine Corps, Army influence on Joint Chiefs
preventing it.
Discussion of top-heavy Army, support missions,
strength of a single Marine division, Marine Corps
not elite but mission important.
Gen. Holcombe (Ret.), Marine Corps:  Contribution of Marines, possible role in Joint Chiefs, Marine Corps interest not served by Navy, Marine
Corps threatened.
Brig. Gen. Day, Marine Reserve:  Marine operations in Korea, combat effectiveness.
Adm. Sherman, Navy:  Marine Corps not being

neglected, Marine strength rising faster than other
services, Chief of Naval Operations can represent
Marines, Marines an arm of the Navy.

Discussion of Marine combat operations, role of
Marine Commandant in Navy decision making.

Sec. Mathews, Navy: Opposed to Marine position
on Joint Chiefs of Staff, discussion of Navy need
for Marine capability.

Dep. Sec. Lovett, Defense Department: Complexity of Marine Corps's legal status, existence of
other specialized mission groups in the services,
problems of representing Marines in Joint Chiefs
without creating an additional military department.

*Military Situation in the Far East, Held with Foreign
Relations Committee: On Relief of General MacArthur*
(May 1951)

Gen. MacArthur, Army: Integration of U.N.
forces, quality of Republic of (South) Korea, Soviet intentions in the Far East, Joint Chiefs recommendation of China blockade, limitations on
bombing, right of the President to recall.

Discussion of appeasement or victory, importance
of Formosa, need to pressure China. General discussion of global Communist tactics, use of atomic
weapons, U.S. preparedness.

Sec. Marshall, Defense Department: Restriction
of operations on Gen. MacArthur, origins of restrictions, Soviet power, American troop morale,
hazards of MacArthur's recommendations.

Discussion of Communist foreign policy, Chinese
Communist threat, possibilities of a Korean armi-
stice, Soviet psychological warfare.

*--Part 2*

Gen. Bradley, Joint Chiefs of Staff: Risk of
global war, concept of limited war, role in Mac-
Arthur removal, limitations on MacArthur.

Discussion of General Bradley's right to claim
immunity in answering questions concerned with private conversations.

Gen. Bradley, Joint Chiefs of Staff: Strategic
values in the Far East, discussion of Joint Chiefs
decision making and role of State Department.

Gen. Collins, Army: Current battle situations,
Chinese equipment, concurrence with MacArthur dismissal, role of Joint Chiefs in dismissal, point of
difference with MacArthur.

Discussion of prerogatives of field commander.

Gen. Vandenberg, Air Force: Soviet jet capability, comparisons of total strategic capability,
Joint Chiefs role in MacArthur dismissal.

Discussion of need to expand Air Force.

Adm. Sherman, Navy: Navy minesweeping operations, effect of a naval blockade, discussion of
whether present Korean strategy will be successful,
and characteristics of current U.S. naval strength.

Adrian Fisher, State Department: Discussion of
State Department document anticipating fall of Formosa, discussion of Voice of America.

## --Part 3 (June 1951)

Sec. Acheson, State Department: U.S. policy
toward Formosa, U.S. policy prior to North Korean
invasion, State Department document on Formosa,
discussion of classification regulations, how Korean problem could be solved, U.S. objectives in
Korea, nature of Chinese threat, extent of presidential power, diplomatic reasons for opposing naval blockade and bombing of Manchuria.

Discussion of Soviet intentions, U.S. interests
in Far East, effect of Japanese peace treaty and
recognition of Red China.

Lt. Gen. Wedemeyer, Army: State Department's
pessimistic views toward Korea, firsthand knowledge
of Chinese Communist leaders, discussion of Chinese
"puppet" troops, discussion of history of the Wedemeyer mission, and why National Chinese government
fell.

Discussion of U.N. and possible role of U.N. and right of field commander to disagree publicly with policy.


--*Part 4* (June 1951)

Louis Johnson, former Secretary, Defense Department: Decision to intervene in Korea, withdrawal of troops in 1949, decision to defend Korea.

Discussion of strategic value of Korea, President's action on FY 1950 defense budget and manner of MacArthur dismissal. Discussion of wisdom of FY 1951 $13-billion budget, global Soviet threat.

Vice Adm. Badger, Navy: Communist pressure in Asia--Southeast Asia, Indonesia, Burma. Importance of Formosa, American postwar China policy, military aid programs to China.

Discussion of importance of Korea, effect of Yalta Conference on Chinese leaders, and reason for U.S. failures in China.

Maj. Gen. Hurley, Army: Mistakes of U.S. policy in China, U.S. foreign policy after Yalta Conference. Principles of the Atlantic Charter, effect of Yalta.

Discussion of Iranian experience, U.N.'s ability to practice collective security, experiences with Chiang Kai-shek in China--differences with Stilwell.

General description of U.S. policy toward Chinese Communists during World War II.

Gen. Barr, Army: Chinese Communist military tactics, discussion of fighting along the Yalu, the Indian landing, and experiences during Chinese civil war, reasons for Chiang's defeat.

Maj. Gen. O'Donnell, Army: Bombing operations in Korea, difficulty of bombing Yalu bridge, losses of aircraft in Korea.

Discussion of need for 70-group Air Force.

*--Part 5*

Appendix and index.


*Military and Naval Construction* (August 1951)

Sec. <u>Finletter</u>, <u>Air</u> <u>Force</u>:  "Three Pillars" of
the Air Force, tremendous construction necessary
for 95-wing program.  Major construction programs--
all but six overseas.


*Civil Defense Program:  Civil Defense Task Force of
the Preparedness Subcommittee* (September 1951)

Gov. <u>Caldwell</u>:  Public not convinced of necessity of civil defense, congressional foot-dragging,
need to organize public.
Dep. Sec. <u>Lovett</u>, <u>Defense</u> <u>Department</u>:  Defense
Department's contribution to civil defense, mili-
tary recognition of importance.
Sec. <u>Finletter</u>, <u>Air</u> <u>Force</u>:  Likelihood of Soviet
nuclear attack increasing, possibility of sneak at-
tack, relationship of civil defense to air defense.
Discussion of need to convince public of seriousness of situation.



FOREIGN RELATIONS COMMITTEE


*Mutual Security Act of 1951*

Sec. <u>Acheson</u>, <u>State</u> <u>Department</u>:  Military Assistance Program cannot be relaxed, situation in
regional areas, amounts requested.
Admission of Greece, Turkey, and Spain into
NATO.
Discussion of total foreign aid amount, aid management and occupation costs.

Sec. Marshall, Defense Department:  Soviet
threat, situation in regional areas, Korean war,
effect of inflation.

William Foster, Economic Cooperation Administration:  Progress to date, problems in Southeast
Asia, European production.

Gen. Collins, Army:  Strategic material for European readiness.

Gen. Gruenther, NATO:  Problem in Europe, importance of air power, division make-up, need for
airlift capability.

Maj. Gen. Scott, Defense Department:  Breakdown
of categories and types of material to be furnished
by Military Assistance Program, cost categories and
eligible countries that have asked for aid.

George McGhee, State Department:  Military Assistance Program in Near East, South Asia, and
Africa.

Maj. Gen. Arnold, Army:  Military aid to Greece
and Turkey.

Asst. Sec. Miller, State Department:  Latin
American Military Assistance Program.

Thomas Cabot, Defense Department:  The relation
of military and economic aid, discussion of pros
and cons of reorganization.

Asst. Sec. Rusk, State Department:  Military Assistance Program in Far East, Communist aggression.

Gen. Bradley, Joint Chiefs of Staff:  Military
equipment furnished to Europe.


*Assignment of Ground Forces of the United States to
Duty in the European Area* [Foreign Relations and
Armed Services Committees] (February 1951)

Gen. Eisenhower, Army:  Mission in NATO, Communist threat, need for flexibility, organization of
NATO, adequacy of separate NATO contributions, European awareness of danger.

Sec. Marshall, Defense Department:  U.S. forces
necessary to defend North Atlantic community, six

U.S. divisions--will be keystone of European defenses.

Discussion of six division adequacy, need for
air and naval bases in Europe.

Sec. Acheson, State Department:  Importance of
ground forces, sufficiency of allies' contribution,
presidential power to send troops.

Gen. Bradley, Joint Chiefs of Staff:  No vast
ground army to be sent, possibility of dispatching
U.S. troops after an attack.

Discussion of size of six divisions, Wherry Resolution.

Adm. Sherman, Navy:  Naval forces should also
participate in NATO defense, Air Force could not
win war alone, procedure of NATO to determine force
requirements.

Gen. Vandenberg, Air Force:  All services need
defense, importance of ground support for Air Force
activities, U.S. ability to destroy Russian war
potential.

Testimony of political, religious, and veterans'
groups on resolution.


*Military Situation in the Far East:  On Relief of
General MacArthur*

See Senate Armed Services Committee (May 1951)


*United States Foreign Aid Programs in Europe, Subcom-
mittee* (July 1951)

Statements by Generals Eisenhower and Gruenther
and Military Assistance Advisory Group advisor for
NATO countries, primarily concerned with the organization of NATO, Economic Cooperation Administration, and Military Assistance programs.

# 1952 CONGRESSIONAL HEARINGS

## 82nd Congress, Second Session

HOUSE COMMITTEES

ARMED SERVICES COMMITTEE

*Universal Military Training* (January 1952)

Sen. Wadsworth, National Security Training Commission:  Commission's tasks, how universal military training best established and administered, creation of training corps with six-months military training for 18-year-olds.  Need for prompt enactment of universal military training.

Discussion of installations to be built, college deferments, impact on Reserves.

Adm. Kinkaid, National Security Training Commission:  Need for large Reserves, character building, morale of trainees.

Discussion of drinking alcoholic beverages, logistical problems of training 800,000 men a year.

Dr. Compton, National Security Training Commission:  18-year-old best age bracket, continuous six-months training, need for USO recreational services, other fringe benefits.

Lt. Gen. McLain, National Security Training Commission:  Inequities of present system, cost saving through National Security Training Commission, propaganda and indoctrination value of system.

Sec. Lovett, Defense Department:  Danger in

present international situation, unfairness of
calling veterans back to service, military training
only alternative.

Discussion of universal military training relationship with Reserves.

Asst. Sec. Rosenberg, Defense Department: ROTC
exemption from universal military training, need
for gradual implementation of universal military
training.

Discussion of possible immorality in universal
military training camps.

Gen. Collins, Army: Long-range manpower problem, need for backlog of trained soldiers, need for
greater readiness than that provided by Reserves or
National Guard.

Discussion of draft levels and proposed training
methods.

Adm. DuBose, Navy: Unique naval problems with
Naval Reserves, discussion of training program.

Gen. Shepherd, Marine Corps: Design of Marine
universal military training program, program for
inductees below induction requirements.

Gen. Vandenberg, Air Force: Air Force universal
military training program, welfare and morals of
trainees, technical training plans.

J. T. Sanders, Grange: No need for vast government universal military training bureaucracy, de-
traction from national security, immorality with
universal military training, need for U.N. peace-
keeping. Discussion of group's opposition.

Frederick Libby, National Council for the Prevention of War: Opposition to large program in
peacetime.

James Patton, National Farmers' Union: Need for
agricultural deferment, opposed to indoctrination
in war psychology.

John Lynn, American Farm Bureau: Universal military training not effective use of manpower, expansion of services possible without universal
military training.

Number of witnesses from church groups, academic

institutions, and labor groups in opposition to
universal military training proposal.

*Waste in Defense Department Procurement: Special
Subcommittee on Procurement* (February, March 1952)

Hearings to consider standardization of cataloguing. Congressional proposal to establish single cataloguing system.

Asst. Sec. Foster, Defense Department: Immensi-
ty of Defense Department supply program, need for
federal cataloguing system.

Discussion of Pentagon waste, cataloguing procedures. Witnesses include service and General Services Administration spokesmen concerning defense
cataloguing procedures.

*Subcommittee Hearings to Retain National Guard in Ac-
tive Status in National Emergency* (May 1952)

Gen. Collins, Army: Unprecedented peacetime
demands on manpower, National Guard a necessary resource. Need to maintain strength of active
forces. Discussion includes provisions to return
Guard units to states, costs of equipping a Guard
unit, and discussion of parallel with British tradition of keeping part of a force at home while
another part of the force serves in the field.

Gen. Abendroth, National Guard Association:
Support for Pentagon proposal as long as called-up
guardsmen are returned to home units.

*Military and Naval Construction* (May, June 1952)

Dep. Sec. Foster, Defense Department: Problems
of equipping and supplying military forces, and
provision of adequate facilities. Number of new
Air Force facilities.

JOINT COMMITTEES OF HOUSE AND SENATE


JOINT ATOMIC ENERGY COMMITTEE


*Amending the Atomic Energy Act* (February, March 1952)

Gordon Dean, Atomic Energy Commission:  Program
changes, divisions of research and development,
military application, etc.
    Discussion of clearances; discussion of authori-
zation and appropriation processes.


JOINT DEFENSE PRODUCTION COMMITTEE


*Progress Report:  Office of Defense Mobilization*
(January 1952)

    Quarterly reports of Office of Defense Mobiliza-
tion on the allocation of strategic materials.


*Progress Report:  Defense Production Act* (October
1952)

    Henry Fowler, Office of Defense Mobilization:
Need to maintain momentum of mobilization, economy
sound, high levels of employment, orderly allocation of materials.
    Discussion of allocation decision making, wage
and price controls, rise in inflation.

SENATE COMMITTEES

## APPROPRIATIONS COMMITTEE

*Senate Appropriations FY 53:  DOD Appropriations*
(June 1952)

Sec. Lovett, Defense Department:  Economic
impact of the defense budget--62.2% of total budget, 3.5-million-man services, consideration in
preparing budget and formulating military requirements.

Discussion of 143-wing Air Force, length of lead
time for modern weapons, procurement practices,
adequacy of budget, Mig performance.

Breakdown of budget by service and bureau.

Asst. Sec. Bendelsen, Army:  Army programs for
FY 1953, Army reclamation program, "war on waste."

Sec. Kimball, Navy:  Sound management in the
Navy.

Sec. Finletter, Air Force:  Air Force request,
Air Force wing build-up, strengthening of Air Defense Command.

Cost comparisons--World War II and modern.

Vice Adm. Fox, Navy:  Navy procurement program,
new obligational authority by cost category.

Sec. Lovett, Defense Department:  Defense budget
procedures, Soviet budget.

Sec. Pace, Army:  Army preparedness program, effect of Korea.

Sec. Kimball, Navy:  List of twenty priorities
of the Navy, discussion of effect of House cut.

Gen. Bradley, Army:  Need to maintain sound
economy, 1954 period of greatest danger, Soviet
military superiority, Soviet modernization, industrial capacity.

Discussion of Far East, Soviet strength.

Gen. Collins, Army:  Korean situation, need for
Army mobility.

Adm. Duncan, Navy:  Cold War, importance of Far

East, necessity of naval support role, carrier is first priority.

Gen. Vandenberg, Air Force:  Importance of strategic air power, Air Force expansion program, U.S. Air Force superior to Soviet.

Asst. Sec. McNeil, Defense Department:  Appropriation and expenditures, reconciling the budget, formulation of budget ceiling.

Frederick Lawtton, Bureau of the Budget:  Bureau's role in defense budget process.

Statements of three service comptrollers on fiscal management.

Gen. Twining, Air Force:  Expansion of air power, Soviet air power, quality of units, "air strength gap," nature of air war, role of Strategic Air Command.

Asst. Sec. Gilpatrick, Air Force:  Air Force aircraft procurement.

Adm. Fechteler, Navy:  Role of the Navy, anti-submarine warfare capability, Navy role in "brush fire" wars, discussion of carrier request.

Gen. Shepherd, Marine Corps:  Readiness of Marines, basic missions.

Lt. Cmdr. Leahy, Navy:  Need for new "Forrestal" class carrier.

Testimony of veterans' groups on reserve matters and universal military training.

ARMED SERVICES COMMITTEE

*Manpower Utilization:  Task Force of the Preparedness Subcommittee* (January 1952)

Maj. Gen. Hershey, Selective Service:  Discussion of Army physical requirements, other services "skimming" superior candidates.

*National Security Training Corps Act* (February 1952)

James Wadsworth, National Security Training Commission:  Universal military training under civilian control, role of inspectors, schedules of
induction, need for program in light of Communist
aggression.

Lt. Gen. McLain, National Security Training Commission:  Inequities of present service system,
training corps in tradition of America, outline of
training.  Will revitalize Reserves and help ROTC.

Discussion of character building, religion and
moral safeguards in National Security Training Commission.

Dr. Compton, National Security Training Commission:  National Security Training Commission as a
long-run deterrent, Fort Knox experiment, foreign
experiences and ability of Commission to protect
morals of inductees.

Discussion and testimony of Reserve, farm, religious, educational, and peace groups on National
Security Training Commission.


*Armed Forces Reserve Act* (May 1952)

Granville Ridly, American Legion:  Need to im-
plement universal military training, disgrace of
recalling World War II veterans for Korea, supports
measure that would make Reserve call-ups dependent
on congressional approval.

Discussion of universal military training.

Rufus Wilson, Veterans of World War II:  Need
for a priority system of recall, for universal military training, and for adequate Reserve program.

Testimony of other veterans' groups to insure
program would make veterans safe from recall.

Maj. Gen. Walsh, National Guard Association:
Opposition to Reserve legislation, need for universal military training and draft, difficulty of National Guard to maintain authorized strength.

Brig. Gen. Evans, Reserve Officers Association:
Brief history of Reserve forces, need for manpower
source other than Reserves.

Testimony of other Reserve spokesmen on Reserve act.

Maj. Gen. Hershey, Selective Service: Restricted supply of manpower, need for Reserve incentives, support for universal military training.

Asst. Sec. Rosenberg, Defense Department: Need for congressional approval of universal military training, importance of small standing Army and well-trained and equipped Reserve.

Discussion of provisions of bill.

Testimony of several spokesmen in support of proposed act.

Appendix: "History of U.S. Military Policy toward Reserve Forces."

## Mutual Security Act of 1952 (May 1952)

Sec. Lovett, Defense Department: Discussion of defense build-up, background of FY 1953 defense budget, present level to continue for FY 1954.

Military requirements for U.S. assistance to Europe, first priority to Korea, discussion of congressional cuts in military assistance.

Sec. Acheson, State Department: Possibility of a European army, role of Germany, threat facing free world, prospects for NATO, a United States of Europe, developments in the Middle East and Far East.

Gen. Bradley, Joint Chiefs of Staff: Adequacy of defense programs, 137-wing stretch-outs, danger to economy of supporting large military force over an extended period.

Discussion of military waste, construction of foreign bases.

Sec. Finletter, Air Force: Discussion of Air Force opposition to development of private jet airliners, NATO air strength and line of command.

## Military and Naval Construction (June 1952)

Gen. Sessuis, Air Force:  Responsibility of Air
Force Air Research and Development Command.


FOREIGN RELATIONS COMMITTEE


*Mutual Security Act of 1952* (March, April 1952)

Ambassador Harriman, State Department:  Main
features of program, European build-up.

Sec. Acheson, State Department:  European unity,
two-front struggle against communism.

Sec. Lovett, Defense Department:  SHAPE, current
strength of NATO, development of NATO structure,
general discussion of specific nation program.

Gen. Bradley, Joint Chiefs of Staff:  Priorities
of assistant allocation, continuous supervision of
program by military.

Sec. Lovett, Defense Department:  F-86 and Mig
comparisons, procurement costs; discussion of defense budget process, military waste.

Gen. Gruenther, SHAPE:  SHAPE, Military Assistance Program activities, Soviet military strength,
comparisons of U.S. and Soviet airpower.

Gen. Olnsted, Defense Department:  Military Assistance Program organization, fiscal matters, offshore procurement, discussion of slow deliveries.

Testimony of private citizens supporting and
opposing military and economic assistance.

# 1953 CONGRESSIONAL HEARINGS

## 83rd Congress, First Session

ARMED SERVICES COMMITTEE

*Hearings on Amendment to Require Services to Report Active-Duty Personnel Requirements for the Next Fiscal Year to the Armed Services Committee* (1953)

Rep. Short, Chairman, Armed Services Committee: Morale problems of officers in the services, difficulty in promotion.

Vice Adm. DuBose, Navy: Section 634 (Davis Amendment) effect on Navy. Problems of setting limitations on the numbers of officers in the service.

Discussion of lack of promotion and adverse effect on Navy.

Maj. Gen. Wensinger, Marine Corps: Explanation of why there is a large number of high-ranking officers in Marine Corps.

Discussion of changing structure of Marine Corps since World War II.

Maj. Gen. Lee, Air Force: Air Force opposition to a percentage limitation of officers, changes in Air Force, and need for larger officer corps.

Discussion of Air Force adoption of Davis Amendment, discussion of "top heavy" Air Force officer structure.

Brig. Gen. Powell, Army:  Army operations in Korea, need for large officer corps.

Discussion of Army rotation policy, changing structure of Army, need for officers in integrated commands, in NATO, and for advisory groups.  Fallacy of judging officer requirements on troop strengths.


*Hearings on Operation Smack* (February 1953)

Hearings on Korean War operation allegedly staged for observers which resulted in the rout of U.N. forces.

Gen. Collins, Army:  Operation Smack normal military ground-air attack, maneuver not planned for outside observers.

Discussion of Army publicity activities.


*Hearings on Statement Made by Gen. James A. Van Fleet* (March 1953)

Hearings include testimony and discussion by General Van Fleet on Korean War stalemate.

Gen. Van Fleet, Army:  Republic of (South) Korea contribution in Korea, equipment and conditions of 8th Army, U.S. firepower and mobility.

Discussion of Army morale and effect of stalemate, discussion of "no win" Korean policy.


*Review of Promotions of Officers in the Armed Services* (March, April, May, June, July and August 1953)

Testimony by service personnel and Defense Department staff on congressional investigations of services' temporary promotions and large number of officers as compared with World War II.

*Hearings on Reserve Officer Personnel Act* (May, June, July 1953)

Lengthy testimony by service representatives and Reserve officers on Reserve promotion, personnel, and force level implications of Reserve program. Discussion of maintaining Reserve strength, adequacy of training, mobilization capability.

*Hearings to Provide Certain Construction and Other Authority for the Military Departments in Time of War* (June 1953)

Hearings to extend emergency authorization of government-constructed, privately-operated defense industries.

John Houston, Munitions Board: Need to build up reserve supply of capacity for production, role of industry in Cold War, and importance of keeping defense industry infrastructure intact.

Discussion of potential waste tooling problems, plant obsolescence.

*Subcommittee Hearings on HR 2331: Limitation of Ready Reserve Force* (June 1953)

Adm. McQuistien, Defense Department: Problem of 1.5 million ceiling on Reserve strength, need to repeal Reserve ceiling.

Gen. Maas, Reserve Officers Association: Support of Administration position, discussion of realistic Reserve ceiling.

*Hearings to Authorize the Loan of Submarines to Italy* (July 1953)

Vice Adm. Good, Navy: Weakness of Italian submarine fleet, Italy's NATO mission, need for anti-submarine warfare operations in Mediterranean.

Discussion of successful loan of aircraft to France, Italian politics, technicalities of calling back ships if necessary, discussion of lend-lease experience with Soviet Union.

FOREIGN AFFAIRS COMMITTEE

*Mutual Security Act Extension* (March, April, May, June 1953)

Maj. Gen. Olmsted, Defense Department: Japanese mutual defense aid program, South Korean program; general problem in Asia economic, not military.
   Discussion of Red China recognition, aid to National China.
   Asst. Sec. Nash, Defense Department: NATO strength, need to meet goals, organization and administration of NATO.
   Harold Stassen, Mutual Security: Success in economic development, total split on defense, percentage of gross national product.
   Sec. Dulles, State Department: Threat of Soviet domination, Europe vital for security, NATO must be strengthened.
   Communist aggression in Indochina, pressures in the Near East, Japan rearmament, United States cannot abdicate worldwide responsibilities.
   Sec. Wilson, Defense Department: Mission of forces in Europe, NATO strength, threats to Thailand and Laos.
   Discussion of NATO military aid, military aircraft program, technical cooperation.
   Gen. Bradley, Joint Chiefs of Staff: Soviet threat continues, NATO countries making as great an effort as can be expected.
   Discussion of Soviet-NATO balance.
   Gen. Stewart, NATO: Soviet TU-4 threat, Communist party in France, size of budget, training program.

Gen. Ridgway, Army:  Soviet military threat,
size and deployment.  Expresses confidence in SHAPE
and NATO.
Discussion of NATO administration.
Gen. Taylor, Air Force:  Comparison of U.S.,
French, and British fighter-interceptor aircraft
and costs.
Cmdr. Danforth, Navy:  Navy antisubmarine warfare program.
Testimony by various religious and political
groups pro and con act extension.


GOVERNMENT OPERATIONS COMMITTEE


*Military Supply Management Program Subcommittee* (May,
June 1953)

John Houston, Munitions Board:  Organization of
supply management, procurement, distribution, cataloguing, transportation, and production.
Discussion of supply studies and Alaueden project.
Under Sec. Johnson, Army:  Army supply system,
stock control, contracting and surplus disposal.
Discussion of joint and single agency supply and
purchasing.
Lt. Gen. Cook, Air Force:  Air Force logistics,
necessity of single service purchasing, procurement
of aircraft.
Under Sec. Thomas, Navy:  Navy procurement, supply problems, scope of Navy supply system.
Asst. Sec. McNeil, Defense Department:  Fiscal
management in the Defense Department, budgeting and
accounting in the Defense Department, use of stock
funds, single service procurement.

*Reorganization Plan No. 6 of 1953* (June 1953)

Dep. Sec. Keyes, Defense Department: Need to
reorganize the Office of the Secretary of Defense
and give Chairman of the Joint Chiefs managing
duties of the Joint Chiefs staff, importance of assistant secretary for finance, manpower, research
and development, and International Security Affairs.

Discussion of details of reorganization proposal, centralizing the Defense Department.

Robert Johnson, Johnson & Johnson: Danger of
proposed plan, too much power for Chairman and
Joint Chiefs staff--"German general staff."

Discussion of military control of economy.

Ferdinand Eberstadt: Folly of building up power
of Joint Chiefs Chairman at expense of service
chiefs.

T. K. Finletter, former Secretary, Air Force:
Danger of single, monolithic defense establishment.

Adm. Cooke (Ret.), Navy: Need for flexibility
of Joint Chiefs, proposal will create rigidity.

Robert Burke, Reserve Officers Association:
Need for assistant secretary for Reserves.

Nelson Rockefeller, Committee of Defense Organization: Activities of committee, background of
proposal, organization of Defense Department and
Joint Chiefs of Staff.

Joseph Dodge, Bureau of the Budget: Proposal
would create clearer lines of authority, more efficiency and improved planning.

Testimony of retired military leaders on reorganization.


*Survey of Military Supply Management and Surplus
Property Disposal Practices* (October, November 1953)

Testimony concerns specific logistical programs
of three services.

SENATE COMMITTEES

APPROPRIATIONS COMMITTEE

*DOD Appropriations, FY 54* (May, June 1953)

Sec. Wilson, Defense Department: Revised budget
estimates, armed forces strength in divisions,
groups personnel, FY 1954 program, Air Force goals,
reduction in wing goal to 120.
Discussion of budget wing reduction, NATO
strength, revised budget requests, status of funds.
Sec. Anderson, Navy: Navy strength, fleet modernization program, need for modern aircraft.
Sec. Stevens, Army: Korea, ammunition situation, combat effectiveness, Reserve program.
Gen. Collins, Army: Army readiness, high morale, rotation policies, atomic artillery.
Robert Woodbury, Defense Department: Communist
army clothing.
Sec. Talbott, Air Force: Atomic aircraft research and development, Air Force FY 1954 program,
discussion of Air Force aircraft cut, length of
lead time.
Gen. Vandenberg, Air Force: 143-wing strength
essential, Communist airpower impressive, discussion of Joint Chiefs approval in reduction, bomber
lead time.
Statements by service representatives on specific appropriations.
Gen. Vandenberg, Air Force: Extended discussion
of Air Force policies, procurement, Air Force war
in Korea, role of Strategic Air Command, use of nuclear weapons, target studies, pilot training, Mig
effectiveness.
Sec. Wilson, Defense Department: Air Force
strength, 143-group controversy, lead time problems.
Asst. Sec. McNeil, Defense Department: Budget
formation, review, military input, discussion of

B-47 bomber reduction, comparisons of Eisenhower and Truman budgets.

Asst. Sec. Hannah, Defense Department: Office of Secretary of Defense responsibilities, personnel management, number and cost of Army bands.

Maj. Gen. Honnin, Army: Transfer of obligations from Army services, tank research, costs, superior effectiveness of T-48 over T-46 or T-47.

--*Part 2* (June, July 1953)

Gen. Shepherd, Marine Corps: Marine Corps statistics, strength, appropriations, growth of Reserves, aircraft reduction.

Statements by Reserve, National Guard, National Rifle Association, and other special interest spokesmen.

Hamilton Long: Present U.S. lack of long-range nuclear bombing capability, need for immediate investigation--U.S. seen in terrible danger.

ARMED SERVICES COMMITTEE

*Ammunition Supplies in the Far East* (March 1953)

Gen. Van Fleet (Ret.), Army: Republic of (South) Korea army, general situation in Korea, need for military victory in Korea. Alleged ammunition shortages experienced by American forces.

Sec. Wilson, Defense Department: Improvement of the rate of ammunition production.

Sec. Stevens, Army: Current Army capability in ammunition production.

Gen. Collins, Army: Ammunition reserve unsatisfactory but improving, difficulty of defining "shortage," superiority of U.S. firepower in Korea.

*ARO Incorporated* (March 1953)

   Sec. Talbott, Air Force: Feasibility of atomic
aircraft development, need to keep ARO research and
development facilities operational.


*Ammunition Shortages in the Armed Services, Prepared-
ness Subcommittee #2* (April 1953)

   Gen. Van Fleet (Ret.), Army: Army ammunition
supplies seriously depleted at various points during Korean War. Need to stockpile great amount of
ammunition.
   Lt. Gen. Almond (Ret.), Army: Agreement with
General Van Fleet, problems in Korean War--Army
turning down requests for greater supplies.
   Robert Lovett, former Secretary, Defense Department: Deterioration of U.S. military posture prior
to Korean War, military shortages were ably han-
dled, some shortages of "critical rounds."
   Shortages of ammunition not due to funding
shortages but to certain supply problems.
   Discussion of Rockefeller Committee. Report on
organization of the Defense Department.
   Frank Pace, former Secretary, Army: Korean
shortages due to setting up supply operations, dra-
matic increase in need for ammunition and need for
competent supply personnel.
   Sec. Stevens, Army: Munitions industry well or-
ganized, sufficient ammunition capability.
   Discussion concerning ammunition production,
mobilization capability.
   Lt. Gen. Decker, Army: Office of Secretary of
Defense budget ceilings, effect of Korean build-up
on Army, Army budgeting procedure, planning methods.
   Discussion of Army comptroller's role and procurement practices.
   Lt. Gen. Palmer, Army: Army logistic and supply
processes, Korean build-up, disagreement with Van
Fleet's claims of shortages.

Gen. Collins, Army:  Praise for Army Ordnance Corps, organization of the Department of the Army and conduct of the Korean War, specifically the role of State Department.

## NACA Construction Program (April 1953)

Hugh Dryden, National Advisory Committee for Aeronautics:  Need for new test wind tunnels.

## Joint Chiefs of Staff Nominations (May 1953)

Adm. Radford, Joint Chiefs of Staff:  Procedures of the Joint Chiefs, role of Chairman.  Discussion of overlapping service missions.

Gen. Ridgway, Army:  NATO and Warsaw Pact relative strengths and view of size of defense budget.

Adm. Carney, Navy:  Discussion of speaking out if American security imperiled by budget cut.

Gen. Twining, Air Force:  Discussion of size of Air Force, effect of budget cuts.

## Aircraft Procurement, Preparedness Subcommittee No. 1 (June 1953)

Asst. Sec. McCone, Air Force:  Air Force procurement of the C-119 aircraft, Defense Department attempt to broaden industrial base for defense procurement.  Explanation of awarding contract to Fairchild Aircraft.

Discussion of possible political leverage and details of contract-letting and procurement.

Lt. Gen. Cook, Air Force:  Air Force relations with Kaiser-Frazer Co., procedures of source selection and subcontracting practices.

M. F. Mautner, Air Force:  Type of contract awards and cost of aircraft.

Sidney Solomon, Kaiser-Frazer Co.:  Cost of aircraft, company profits.

Henry Kaiser, Kaiser-Frazer Co.: False impressions caused by Fairchild, costs of C-119 production, discussion of extravagant contracts.


*Implementation of Title IV--NSA of 1947, Preparedness Subcommittee No. 3* (November 1953)

Ferdinand Eberstadt: National Security Agency of 1947 attempt to establish uniform budgeting procedures in the service, specifics of Title IV, obstacles to achieving greater efficiency in the Defense Department. Questions adequacy of reporting procedures as required by the act.

Discussion of increasing Defense Department comptroller's authority.

Robert Lovett, former Secretary, Defense Department: Secretary's dependence on "facts," need for Title IV provisions.

Discussion of Defense Department comptroller's duties and need for strong financial management.

Franz Schneider: Defense Department biggest business in the world, problems of inefficiency due to over-centralization.

Sec. Stevens, Army: Army auditing study, reorganization of Quartermaster Corps.

Sec. Anderson, Navy: Problems of Navy financial organization, duties of Navy comptroller, need for scrutiny of decentralized operations.

Asst. Sec. White, Air Force: Activities of Air Force comptroller, need for independent civilian review.

Sec. Wilson, Defense Department: Experiences in General Motors in auditing, implementation of Title IV. Need for military experience in financial areas.

Testimony of service comptrollers and descriptions of their activities.

FOREIGN RELATIONS COMMITTEE

*General Gruenther on NATO* (April 1953)

Gen. Gruenther, Army:  Organization of NATO, Soviet military capabilities, Mig-15 capabilities, T-4.  Role of France in NATO and Soviet strategy in Indochinese and Korean conflicts.

*Mutual Security Act of 1953* (May 1953)

Sec. Dulles, State Department:  Strength through mutual defense, role of NATO, threats in other regional areas, leadership of United States.

Harold Stassen, Foreign Operations Administration:  Overall review of Mutual Security program, size, economy factors.

Sec. Wilson, Defense Department:  Recent NATO conference, appraisal of NATO, equipment deliveries, regional review.

Breakdown of FY 1954 program, geographic breakdown, NATO joint aircraft program.

Gen. Bradley, Joint Chiefs of Staff:  NATO build-up, special weapons, guided missiles, Soviet economic strength.

Maj. Stewart, Military Assistance Program: Defense Department responsibilities, funding, training program, equipment transfers.

Asst. Sec. Jerregan, State Department:  Situation in Near East, South Asia, and Africa.

Asst. Sec. Robertson, State Department:  U.S. objectives in Far East--Korea, Red China, and Southeast Asia.

Asst. Sec. Cabot, State Department:  Latin American program, administration of Point 4 program.

Gen. Ridgway, Army:  Administration of Military Assistance Program, SHAPE command, Soviet strength, FY 1954 objectives.

Testimony of private citizens and groups on Mutual Security Act.

GOVERNMENT OPERATIONS COMMITTEE

*Investigations Conducted by Sen. Joe McCarthy: Communist Infiltration among Army Civilian Workers* (September 1953)

*Investigations Conducted by Sen. Joe McCarthy: Communist Infiltration in the Army* (September 1953)

*Investigations Conducted by Sen. Joe McCarthy: Army Signal Corps--Subversion and Espionage* (October, November, December 1953)

*Investigations Conducted by Sen. Joe McCarthy: Subversion and Espionage in Defense Establishments and Industry* (November 1953; January 1954)

*Investigations Conducted by Sen. Joe McCarthy: Korean War Atrocities* (December 1953)

# 1954 CONGRESSIONAL HEARINGS

## 83rd Congress, Second Session

HOUSE COMMITTEES

ARMED SERVICES COMMITTEE

*Hearings to Extend Emergency Powers of Civil Defense Administrator* (1954)

Val Peterson, Civil Defense:  Threat of Soviet attack, nuclear weapons and new Soviet bomber capability.

*Hearings to Establish Officer Limitations in the Services (Daws Amendment)* (January 1954)

Gen. Powell, Army:  Impact of officer limitations on officer morale, paradoxes in proposed amendment.
Discussion of inflexibility of plan, promotion methods.
Adm. Holloway, Navy:  Need for temporary promotions to maintain qualified manpower.
Discussion of officer levels, difference between statutory officer limits and appropriations limits.
Gen. Nelson, Marine Corps:  Need for long-range planning for officer levels, problems of force attrition if Daws amendment adopted.
Gen. Lee, Air Force:  Air Force officer levels,

air crew ratios, long-range air wing strengths, discussion of pilot shortages.

*Air Strip Paving Materials, Subcommittee on Defense Activities* (February 1954)

Discussion concerns cost problems of air strip construction of heavily used jet air strips. Debate between asphalt and concrete industries.

*Hearings on Award of Noncompetitive Destroyer Contract at Bethlehem Yard* (February 1954)

Sec. Anderson, Navy: Reasons for selecting a noncompetitive negotiational contract.
Discussion of Navy shipbuilding procurement program.
Rear Adm. Leggett, Navy: Bethlehem need for contract, other bidder--Bath--has not suffered as badly.

*Hearings to Authorize Construction of Naval Vessels* (March 1954)

Rep. Short, Chairman of the Armed Services Committee: Statement on build-up of Soviet navy, Soviet naval bases, shipbuilding program.
Rear Adm. Manseau, Navy: Nuclear powered Nautilus, guided missile cruiser, need for new nuclear submarine and Forrestal attack carrier. Growing dependence of private shipyards on naval construction.
Discussion of prerogatives of Armed Services Committee vis-à-vis Appropriations Committee, need for military briefings for Armed Services Committee members, Russian submarine threat.

*Hearings on Air Force Reserve Program* (April 1954)

Maj. Gen. Hall, Air Force: Need for greater Air
Force Reserve effort; effect of Korean call-up.
Proposed changes in Air Force Reserve organization.
Discussion of expanded Reserve, pilot shortages.
Gen. Burvell, Air Force: Volunteer Air Reserve
program, members of Reserve officers on active
duty.
Gen. Wilson, Air National Guard: Make-up of Air
National Guard, missions, training requirements.

*Military and Naval Construction* (April, May 1954)

Discussions include construction of five new
bases for Strategic Air Command and increasing importance of strategic air power.

*Hearings to Authorize Long-Term Charter of Tankers*
(May 1954)

Sec. Thomas, Navy: U.S. commitments, need for
ocean transportation capability, world movement of
petroleum to foreign bases. U.S. Navy contribution
to maintaining and expanding U.S. tanker fleet.
Proposal for private construction of private tankers to be chartered by the Navy Operation of Military Sea Transportation Service.
Discussion of contracting methods, profits to be
realized by private companies, explanation of the
industrial fund concept.
Adm. Denebrink, Navy: Rapid decline of U.S.
tanker fleet since World War II, aging, foreign
program expansion, U.S. tanker fleet falls short of
military requirement.
Discussion of national ownership in foreign
countries, practice of U.S. tankers registering in
foreign countries.
Daniel Strohmeir, Bethlehem Steel: Need for
Navy tanker plan to forestall closure of U.S.

shipyards, need for private shipbuilding capability.

Marvin Coles, attorney:  Navy practice of tanker
charter normal, discussion of fairness of cost.

Gordon Duke, shipbuilder:  Private shipbuilding
cheapest means of shipbuilding, impact of shipyard
failures on local economies.

*Hearings to Provide for Two Additional Secretaries
for the Respective Services* (June 1954)

Sec. Wilson, Defense Department:  Need for service secretary for financial management, another
with a flexible assignment.

Discussion of Secretary Wilson's cost cutting
program, discussion of management in the Defense
Department.  Discussion of necessity for assistant
secretary for research and development.

Rep. McCormack:  Need for assistant secretary
for research and development, importance of research and development.

FOREIGN AFFAIRS COMMITTEE

*To Control the Exportation and Importation of Arms,
Ammunition, and Implements of War* (February 1954)

Jon Elliot, State Department:  Need to revise
Neutrality Act, problem of imported munitions coming into country.

*Mutual Security Act of 1954* (April, May, June 1954)

Sec. Dulles, State Department:  Soviet plans of
domination, isolationism no longer viable, need for
strong NATO; discussion of situation in Middle
East, Latin America, Japan and Indochina.

Discussion of Dien Bien Phu, Navarre plan, situation in Guatemala, Chinese shelling of islands.

Harold Stassen, Foreign Operations Administration: Size of aid program, regional breakdown, program by function.

Discussion of administration in specific regional areas.

Asst. Sec. Merchant, State Department: Administration of NATO.

Maj. Gen. Stewart, Defense Department: Military Defense Assistance Program locations, screening process, organization--summary of military assistance program by function.

Asst. Sec. Byroade, State Department: Military assistance to Middle East, India, and Pakistan--progress scene.

Dep. Asst. Sec. Drumwright, State Department: Situation in Far East, Japan, Philippines, aid to France for Indochina, situation in Laos, Thailand, Burma.

Tracey Voohees, Defense Department: Offshore procurement procedures.

Lt. Col. Dodge and Gen. Marquat, Army: Republic of (South) Korea training and readiness.

Testimony from numerous government witnesses on regular economic development programs, India, Latin America, etc.

Arthur Gardiner, State Department: Threat in Middle East, Military Assistance Advisory Group programs, discussion of Israel, Iraq, Egypt, and Syria.

Testimony of outside witnesses on political and administrative aspects of mutual security program.


GOVERNMENT OPERATIONS COMMITTEE


*Organization and Administration of Military Research and Development Programs, Subcommittee* (June 1954)

Asst. Sec. Quarles, Defense Department:  Defense
Department research and development, extent of coordination and organization.
   Discussion of U.S. research, interservice competition, role of civilian scientists in research and
development program, morale problems.
   Asst. Sec. Smith, Navy:  Organization of research and development in the Navy, Navy mission
and striking power.
   Discussion of organization, research and development spending.
   Bruce Eaton, Navy:  Naval research activities,
administration, nature of military control of research activities.
   Trevor Gardner, Air Force:  Air Force research
and development program, role of RAND Corp., research and development administration.
   Maj. Gen. Maude, Army:  Lincoln project administration, scientist morale.
   John Marchettu, Defense Department:  Military
management of research and development.
   Testimony by other government scientists on military management and problems of research and development.

*Operations of U.S. in France, Spain and Germany* (November 1954)

   Elin O'Shaughessy, State Department:  Activities
of U.S. agencies in West Germany, rearmament program, nature of NATO agreements, role of Germany.

JOINT COMMITTEES OF HOUSE AND SENATE

JOINT DEFENSE PRODUCTION COMMITTEE

*Proportion of Government Contracts Awarded to Small
Business Concerns* (March 1954)

Asst. Sec. Thomas, Defense Department:  Small
business policies of Defense Department, enthusias-
tic government support, need for fair procurement
practices, amounts awarded to small businesses--38%
of contracts.

Wendell Barnes, Small Business Administration:
Small Business Administration's study of military
procurement, need for competitive bidding, general
procurement information.


SENATE COMMITTEES


APPROPRIATIONS COMMITTEE


*DOD Appropriations for FY 1955* (1954)

Sec. Wilson, Defense Department:  "New Look"--
emphasis on nuclear weapons, economies in use of
manpower, maintenance of ready Reserves and
strengthened continental air defense.  Development
of New Look doctrine, 137 air wing goal, decrease
in manpower.

Discussion of shipbuilding programs, manpower
management.

Asst. Sec. Hannah, Defense Department:  Reserves
policy, military turnover, morale in armed services.

Adm. Radford, Joint Chiefs of Staff:  Nature of
Communist threat, need for long-range planning,
continental defense, emphasis on combat readiness.

Statements by service department heads on programs.

Statements by service chiefs submitted for record; did not testify.

ARMED SERVICES COMMITTEE


*Long-Term Charter of Tankers by Navy* (March 1954)

   Sec. Anderson, Navy: Need for sufficient tanker
force, private industry not willing to build.  Discussion of tanker capacity required.
   Vice Adm. Denebrink, Navy: Description of world
tanker fleet, declining U.S. numbers, need for petroleum transport.
   Hoyt Haddock, Congress of Industrial Organization: Problem of U.S. citizens operating foreign
flag ships, need for strong U.S. tanker capability.
   Testimony of U.S. shipbuilders and operators in
support of proposal.


*Reserve Officer Personnel Act of 1954, Part 1* (April
1954)

   Asst. Sec. Hannah, Defense Department: Need for
fair and effective Reserve officer promotion sys-
tem; need for larger, more effective Reserves.
   Discussion of promotion rules, differences in
Reserve and National Guard procedures.
   Maj. Gen. Walsh, National Guard Association:
Strength of National Guard, support for measure,
minor amendments.
   Charles Boyle, Reserve Officers Association:
History of Reserve legislation, problems with tem-
porary promotion procedures.
   Franklin Orth, Army: Inequities of present sys-
tem of promotion.
   Statements by other Reserve and National Guard
spokesmen on proposed plan.


*Military and Naval Construction Authorization, Sub-
committee on Real Estate and Military Construction of
the Committee on Armed Services* (June 1954)

Sec. Talbott, Air Force:  Build-up to 137 wings requires reactivation of World War II bases.

*Two Additional Assistant Secretaries for Army, Navy, and Air Force* (June 1954)

Sec. Wilson, Defense Department:  Need for specialized advice in areas of financial management and need for service flexibility for additional secretaries.

Discussion of pay, size of military departments, duties of service comptroller.

Sec. Thomas, Navy:  Need for fiscal management, and need for an assistant secretary of Navy for Air.

Discussion of latter assistant secretary's duties, specialization required for modern U.S. Navy.

Sec. Stevens, Army:  Department of the Army overcome with management responsibilities, additional secretary will make civilian control effective.

Sec. Talbott, Air Force:  Importance of Air Force research and development.

Discussion of authorization and duties of comptroller.

*Essentiality to the National Defense of the Domestic Horological Industry, Preparedness Subcommittee #6* (June, July 1954)

Statements by congressmen and representatives of watchmaking company on importance of timepieces to defense effort.

*Antarctic Expedition* (July 1954)

Capt. Ronnie, American Antarctic Association: Soviet threat in the Antarctic, strategic importance of the area, scientific significance.

FOREIGN RELATIONS COMMITTEE

*Statements of Sec. Dulles and Adm. Radford: Foreign Policy and Its Relation to Military Progress* (1954)

Sec. Dulles, State Department: Threat of communism, Communist tactics, the New Look, NATO, and Pacific treaties, responsibilities of Congress and the Executive.

Discussion of U.S. retaliation policy, presidential warmaking powers.

Adm. Radford, Joint Chiefs of Staff: Soviet goals, New Look depends on airpower, clarification of massive retaliation.

*Mutual Security Act of 1954* (June 1954)

Sec. Dulles, State Department: NATO progress, status of European Defense Community base agreement with Spain, discussion of regional areas. Problems with Indochina.

Harold Stassen, Foreign Operations Administration: Regional programs, Foreign Operations Administration role, reduced costs of mutual security program.

Adm. Radford, Joint Chiefs of Staff: Types of aid, administration of Indochina area, support for self-defense concept in Asia, European situation, discussion of offshore procurement.

Asst. Sec. Merchant, State Department: European political situation.

Gen. Russell, Military Assistance Advisory Group: Military Defense Assistance Program activities, new weapons program, Advisory Group locations, military assistance, screening process, quantity of selected major items and values.

Dep. Asst. Sec. Drumwright, State Department: Far East situation.

Asst. Sec. Byroade, State Department: Middle East and African situations.

**Asst. Sec. Holland, State Department:**  Latin
American assistance.


*The Southeast Asia Collective Defense Treaty* (November 1954)

**Sec. Dulles, State Department:**  Need for collective security pact in Asia, pact protects against both armed attacks and subversion, differences within NATO.

Discussion of subversion threat, obligations under Article IV, para. 2.

# 1955 CONGRESSIONAL HEARINGS

## 84th Congress, First Session

HOUSE COMMITTEES

ARMED SERVICES COMMITTEE

*Hearings on Authorization for National Advisory Committee for Aeronautics* (1955)

Hugh Dryden, National Advisory Commission on Aeronautics: History of National Advisory Commission on Aeronautics, need for test facilities, Army and Air Force jet and missile projects.

*Briefing on National Defense* (January 1955)

Sec. Wilson, Defense Department: Modification of Reserve and National Guard, growth of NATO and other alliances, rejection of preventative war, nuclear deterrence, continental air defense--Nike, Early Warning Line, establishment of Continental Air Defense Command. Expansion of fighter interceptors, retaliatory capability, replacement of B-36 with B-52, an additional carrier, Honest John missiles, active-duty strengths, aircraft inventory, Communist intentions and American response, stability of defense budget.
Discussion of importance of strong economy, size

of the budget, discussion of Formosan defense, military aid.

Adm. Raborn, Joint Chiefs of Staff: Feast and famine problem of defense budget, multi-sided Soviet threat, importance of air defense, impossibility of returning to pre-World War II level of defense.

Sec. Talbott, Air Force: 137-wing program, bomber replacement program, air defense, Air Force enlistment and inventory control.

Discussion of base housing.

Gen. Twining, Air Force: Air Force missions, strengths, airlift capability, missile developments.

Sec. Thomas, Navy: Operating forces, carrier procurement, logistic performance.

Discussion of maintaining a floor on ships, use of carriers, U.S. fixed air bases.

Sec. Stevens, Army: Need for combat-ready reserve, enlistment problems, limited war and increasing possibility of war.

Discussion of Army strength, Reserve readiness, need for larger Army in extended global war.

Gen. Ridgway, Army: Communist threat, need for readiness, Army's unique capabilities, balanced force concept, need for Reserve readiness.


*Hearings to Extend Universal Military Training* (February 1955)

Mr. Blandford, Armed Services Committee Counsel: Explanation of draft.

Sec. Wilson, Defense Department: Importance of retaining qualified military personnel, need to continue draft.

Asst. Sec. Burgess, Defense Department: Explanation of extension, armed forces strength without induction, induction and reserve forces. Discussion of details of draft law, mental and physical requirements, comparative draft lengths.

Maj. Gen. Hershey, Selective Service: Inequalities in draft law, draft deferments.

Asst. Sec. Wilbur, Army: Induction of specialists, necessity of draft.

Maj. Gen. Booth, Army: Necessity in nuclear era
of keeping large Army force in being. Need to make
Army more attractive.

Asst. Sec. Pratt, Navy: Navy and Marine Corps
plans to maintain strengths without draft.

Asst. Sec. Smith, Air Force: Attempts to maintain four-year specialists, necessity of Army draft
to maintain Air Force strength.

C. M. Boyer, Reserve Officers Association: Support for draft extension, need for permanent legislation.

Seaborn Collins, American Legion: Military defense should be based on large reserve units and
not on large standing army.

Rep. Henshaw: Need for more scientists, engineers, and technicians in military, drop in school
enrollment, discussion of programs in Soviet Union,
China, and Europe.

Ralph Chaney, California Institute of Technology: Need to keep scientists and engineers in private research pursuits.


*Hearings on Navy Aircraft Procurement Program, Sub-
committee for Special Investigations* (February 1955)

Sec. Thomas, Navy: Explanation of naval aircraft procurement cutback, slippages in contracts
for new aircraft, "fly before buy," new Navy procurement program.

Discussion of aircraft obsolescence, practices
of opening production lines for older aircraft.

Capt. Dietrich, Navy: Navy approach to procurement and contracting methods, discussion of uncertainty in aircraft production.

Asst. Sec. Fogler, Navy: Ability to expedite
aircraft production in war time, Navy mobilization
planning.

J. H. Smith, Navy: Explanation of advanced
tooling capabilities of new aircraft--F4D, Cougar

3, FJ3.  Discussion of armaments for naval attack
aircraft.

Discussion of Soviet Air Show, Soviet airlift
capability.


*Hearings on Career Incentive Act of 1955, Subcommittee #2* (February, March 1955)

Sec. Wilson, Defense Department:  Need to increase military pay and benefits to attract qualified military personnel, particularly technicians.

Adm. Radford, Joint Chiefs of Staff:  Complexity of modern equipment, need for higher pay.

Charles Hook, Hook Commission:  Statements to Commission by Secretary of Defense and chiefs of three services supporting request for higher pay scales, and by commanders of specific commands--Strategic Air Command, submarine forces--for need to retain specialists.


*National Reserve Plan, Subcommittee #1* (February, March 1955)

Sec. Wilson, Defense Department:  Program to strengthen Reserve and National Guard, creation of ready reserve, six-month training program.

Discussion of details of plan, draft problems.

Adm. Radford, Joint Chiefs of Staff:  Need for Reserve combat readiness.

Sec. Stevens, Army:  Need for ready reserve, discussion of Army manpower, need for increased training.

Gen. Ridgway, Army:  Need for better training, the six-month training concept.

Sec. Thomas, Navy:  Naval and Marine Reserve strength, support for plan.

Gen. Twining, Air Force:  Importance of maintaining Air Force readiness.

Maj. Gen. Hershey, Selective Service:  Complacency cannot happen again, need for mobilization capability.

Asst. Sec. Burgess, Defense Department: Details
of Reserve plan, discussion of enlistment rates,
necessary force levels.

Large number of witnesses include spokesmen from
Reserve, National Guard, religious and civic groups
discussing position on Reserve plan.

## Authorization of Construction and Conversion of Naval Vessels (March 1955)

Sec. Thomas, Navy: Navy shipbuilding program—
5th Forrestal carrier, new jet aircraft on carriers, guided missile cruisers and destroyers.

Discussion of supercarriers, costs, vulnerability to nuclear attack.

Adm. Duncan, Navy: Problem of block obsolescence, Soviet submarine threat, importance of carrier.

Discussion of Naval loan carriers, problem of
carrier vulnerability, Soviet naval size.

Rear Adm. Leggett, Navy: Navy program, shipbuilding value, results of Bikini tests.

## Alleged "Waste" in the Armed Services, Hearings before Subcommittee for Special Investigations, Part 1 (April 1955)

John Hollister, Commission on Organization of
Executive Branch: Role of Hoover Commission, discussion of Readers' Digest story on "waste."

## Air Force Procurement of Rocket Launchers, Subcommittee for Special Investigations (April, July 1955)

Col. Trapp and Col. Soukup, Air Force: Service
standardization, Air Force rejection of rocket
launchers.

Adm. Harrison, Navy: Naval procurement of rocket launchers, pricing, exchange of information

between services, Navy evaluation of contract performance.

   Irving Babbitt, Century Industry:  Navy contract, waste and inefficiency in contract, negotiation with services.

   Gen. Mitchell, Air Force:  Air Force procurement program, relations with other services, cost controls.

*Military Public Works* (May, June 1955)

   Asst. Sec. Floete, Air Force:  Long-range planning for military construction, requirements for protective construction (against enemy attack), study of airfields, hangars, and fueling systems.

FOREIGN AFFAIRS COMMITTEE

*Mutual Security Act of 1955* (May, June 1955)

   Sec. Dulles, State Department:  Meeting of NATO Council, NATO a going concern, Manila Pact, Columbus Plan, disarmament progress.

   Discussion of administration, allies' expenditure on defense.

   Harold Stassen, Foreign Operations Administration:  European recovery, European defense expenditures, FY 1956 program by function, importance of development.

   Discussion of Soviet bloc "economic warfare," importance of "Free Arc of Asia."

   Asst. Sec. Allen, State Department:  Middle East and India, importance of development, particularly Indian development.

   Gen. Gruenther, Army:  Soviet strength, bomber development, discussion of German addition of forces, the introduction of tactical nuclear weapons in NATO.  Discussion of Soviet submarine threat.

Asst. Sec. Sebald, State Department:  ANZUS, other bilateral treaties, Bandung Conference--Asia most vulnerable and important area of U.S. security interests; Vietnam, Laos, and Cambodia--nature of Military Defense Assistance Program in Far East.

Adm. Radford, Joint Chiefs of Staff:  Military aid crucial to defense, successes of aid, discussion of U.S. troop-ally support trade-offs, possible U.S. manpower problem, extent of Russian foreign assistance.

Col. Critz, Defense Department:  Aid to Middle East; Arab-Israeli situation; Greece, Turkey, and Iran.

Asst. Sec. Holland, State Department:  Latin American economic and military aid, progress in development, Communist threats.

Testimony by private citizens on various aspects of aid program, primarily economic aid.

## GOVERNMENT OPERATIONS COMMITTEE

*Civil Defense Atomic Shelter Tests, Part 1* (April, May 1955)

Robert Constine, Atomic Energy Commission:  Commission's nuclear effects research, full-scale field experiments, shelter tests and results.

Dr. Harris, Los Alamos Laboratory:  Medical experiments, radiation effects on people and food.

Luke Vortman, Scandia Corp.:  Nuclear effects on physical structures, discussion of different shelter designs.

Dr. White, Los Alamos Laboratory:  Nuclear effects on environment.

Gerald Gallagher, Federal Civil Defense Administration:  Status of federal shelter program, different shelter designs, tests and results.

Dr. Johnson, Johns Hopkins University:  Cost trade-offs between active and passive defense

system, need for strong offensive systems, proposals for a minimum civil defense posture.  Effect of intercontinental ballistic missiles on warning time; civil defense must be directed toward intercontinental ballistic missile threat.
Discussion of high costs of civil defense.


--*Part 2: Reorganization Plan*

William Tinan, Bureau of the Budget:  Proposal to converge Federal Civil Defense Administration with Office of Defense Mobilization, how reorganization would operate; creating greater planning effectiveness.
Leo Hoegh, Federal Civil Defense Administration: Current Federal Civil Defense Administration responsibilities, changes under proposal.


*Navy Jet Aircraft Program, Subcommittee on Military Operations* (October 1955)

James Eckhart, Government Operations Committee Staff:  Navy aircraft crashes related to engine failure, history of committee's investigation—Westinghouse and McDonnell Aircraft.
Rear Adm. Russell, Navy:  Westinghouse engine development, contract award and testing procedures.
W. M. Crickenberger, Navy:  Westinghouse contract termination.
Lt. Cmdr. Smith, Navy:  Navy testing procedures.
J. S. McDonnell, McDonnell Aircraft:  McDonnell program, engine selection, contract conditions.
W. W. Smith, Westinghouse:  J-40 engine development.

JOINT COMMITTEES OF HOUSE AND SENATE

JOINT ATOMIC ENERGY COMMITTEE

*AEC-FCDA Relationship, Subcommittee on Security*
(March 1955)

Val Peterson, Federal Civil Defense Administration: Discussion of security classifications on
fallout data which have obstructed civil defense
work. Need for American public to be well informed
on impact of atomic weapons.
Lewis Strauss, Atomic Energy Commission: Commission's declassification practices, problems with
"scare" effects concerning effect of nuclear weapons. Discussion of fallout danger.

*Health and Safety Protections and Weather Effects As-
sociated with Atomic Explosions* (April 1955)

Lewis Strauss, Atomic Energy Commission: Nevada
testing, H-bomb tests at Bikini, press reports sen-
sationalizing effects of nuclear explosions, radiation received equal to one chest x-ray. Discussion
of reckless predictions of genetic harm coming from
nuclear weapons, United States must continue testing to stay ahead of the Soviet Union.
Dr. Bugher, Atomic Energy Commission: Nevada
radiation too slight to cause biological harm, Commission's findings during Castle series H-bomb
tests, areas of uncertainty in biological research.
Merril Eisenbid, Atomic Energy Commission: Commission's fallout monitoring system, ability of
Commission to predict heavy fallout before it could
be dangerous.
Dr. Wexber, Weather Bureau: Influences of nuclear explosions on weather, no proven connection.

JOINT DEFENSE PRODUCTION COMMITTEE

*Progress of Defense Mobilization Program* (April 15, 1955)

Dr. Fleming, Office of Defense Information: Mica expansion program, preparations for administering government during an emergency, production and material controls following an atomic attack, mineral planning, stabilization measures, manpower, transportation, and telecommunications.

Government responsibilities in strengthening mobilization base and linkage with military manpower planning.

Discussion of "war game" technique of planning and policies toward specific industries and economic sectors.

SENATE COMMITTEES

APPROPRIATIONS COMMITTEE

*DOD Appropriations for FY 56* (1955)

Dep. Sec. Anderson, Defense Department: Military requirements, present service strengths, reductions in FY 1956 budget, Strategic Air Command build-up, additional carrier, continental defense and early warning.

Discussion of balanced concept, economy in defense, need for more accurate fiscal forecasting, problems in research and development duplication.

Adm. Radford, Joint Chiefs of Staff: Need for "stabilized" defense spending and long-range planning and technical developments.

Sec. Thomas, Navy: Navy personnel, increase in Navy aircraft, major procurement--5th Forrestal carrier.

Discussion of Formosa situation, guided missile research, sealift capability.

Adm. Carney, Navy: Soviet navy, possibility of drawn out sea war with U.S.S.R., performance of Nautilus, fleet modernization.

Gen. Shepherd, Marine Corps: Marine Corps missions and budget straightforward, aircraft procurement, ballistic missile development, Russian air strength and Type 39 and Type 37 bomber development; need for expansion of airpower, continental air defense, airlift capability.

Gen. Twining, Air Force: Guided missile research, Air Force readiness, B-52 pilot training costs.

Under Sec. Finucane, Army: New Army programs, missile research, military strength, readiness, manpower reduction, concept of "brush fire" war.

Gen. Ridgway, Army: World situation, Army missions, adequacy of forces, importance of research and development.

Statements by service comptrollers and service bureau and command representatives on financial aspects of specific programs.

Brig. Gen. Kilsy, Army: Evolution of a major weapons system.

Statements by Reserve, National Guard, National Rifle Association officials and other special interest groups.

Adm. Carney, Navy: Shift to nuclear submarines.

Gen. Taylor, Army: Need for increased air support for Army missions, flexible mobile forces; Army research and development most urgent requirement--modernization to meet local aggression.

Discussion of NATO, trouble in Taiwan.

Sec. Gates, Navy: Concept of balanced Navy, naval personnel, operating forces, new weapons procurement.

Adm. Burke, Navy: Nuclear Navy, advantages of nuclear power, research and development, aircraft procurement, Soviet submarine threat, House reductions.

Discussion of Navy and Air Force strategic missions.

Gen. Pate, Marine Corps: Marine readiness, combat unit reorganization.

Sec. Douglas, Air Force: Deterrence, size of structure of Air Force from 137 wing to 128 wing, Bomarc program, F-101, F-102, F-104, F-105, and F-106 programs, missile programs, Sage air defense system, production of B-52's.

Gen. Twining, Air Force: Threat of total war, missile development, B-45 retirement, B-52 conversion, jet tanker program, bomber dispersal, ground alert, reduction in Air Force wings.

Discussion of missile costs, carrier vulnerability, Air Force-Army duplication, adequacy of airlift.

Asst. Sec. Francis, Defense Department: Active force strengths, operating forces, regular officer increases, necessity for trained manpower.

Asst. Sec. McNeil, Defense Department: FY 1956 budget by major categories, general and specific fund appropriation, procurement policies, research and development policies, contracting methods.

Dep. Sec. Quarles, Defense Department: Defense research and development, complexity of weapons, increase in costs, ballistic missile development, FY 1956 research and development budgets. Discussion of KC-135 development.

Statements by service representatives on financial management, specific command spending.

Maj. Gen. Wilson, Air Force: Description and breakdown of Air National Guard strength and deployment.

Perry Shoemaker: Analysis and support for House cut of FY 1956 budget.


*Supplemental Appropriations Bill 1956* (June 1955)

Asst. Sec. Garlock, Air Force: Air Force construction, need for 137-wing force, B-52 introduction, need for adequate base facilities.

ARMED SERVICES COMMITTEE


*Civil Defense Program, Subcommittee on Civil Defense*
(February, March 1955)

Willard Libby, Atomic Energy Commission:  Effects of atomic radiation, scientific evidence of
fallout, precautions taken in testing.
Dr. Bugher, Atomic Energy Commission:  Radiation
diseases, expense in Japan, discussion of radiation
and atomic blasts generally.
Arthur Fleming, Office of Defense Mobilization:
Need for protective construction from blast and
fallout, necessity of federal, state, and local
action.
Discussion of civil defense financing and government management of shelter programs.
Willard Libby, Atomic Energy Commission:  Effect of nuclear blasts, discussion of what constitutes an effective shelter.
Val Peterson, Federal Civil Defense Administration:  Importance of problem, possibilities of surviving atomic blasts.  Discussion of community
services required after nuclear blast and hope that
Reserve forces could aid in civil defense effort;
need for federally sponsored shelter program.
Francis DuPont, Commerce Department:  No construction of special highways for national defense.
Discussion of urban evacuation, viability of evacuation team.


*--Part 2* (March, April, May, June 1955)

Joseph Clark:  Need for federal government to
take more active lead in civil defense.
Maj. Zeidler, Army:  Need for large evacuation
programs, massive federal assistance.
Gov. Herter:  Need for long-term planning, role
of National Guard in an emergency.
Witnesses include other mayors, governors, and

representatives of various groups testifying on
need for increased civil defense effort.

*National Advisory Commission Committee for Aeronautics Construction Program* (March 1955)

Dr. Dryden, National Advisory Commission on Aeronautics: Research on nuclear propulsion systems,
development of the F-102.

*National Defense Facilities Act Amendments (for Reserve Forces)* (April 1955)

Asst. Sec. Floete, Defense Department: Defense
Department installation construction proposal.
Asst. Sec. Milton, Army: Army support for increased construction for services.
Testimony of Reserve spokesmen in support of
proposal.

*Military Public Works Costs, Subcommittee on Real Estate and Military Construction* (May, June 1955)

Witnesses include Office of the Secretary of Defense and service representatives on construction
planning and construction practices.

*National Reserve Plan* (July 1955)

Raymond Walters, American Council of Education:
Need to change six-month Reserve obligation to conform to students in college.
George Riley, AFL: Need for larger Reserve
forces, must combat low rate of participation.
Edmund Claxton, National Association of Manufacturers: Need to maintain scientific and technological expertise in private enterprise.
Testimony of other business and professional

association representatives to keep technical talent deferred.

Seaborn Collins, American Legion: Need to strengthen Reserve, compulsory six-month training.

Testimony from farmers', peace, and religious groups opposing compulsory six-month reserve training.

Col. Boyer, Reserve Officers Association: Need for strengthened, better equipped Reserve.

Adm. Radford, Joint Chiefs of Staff: Need for 2.9-million forces Reserve, ready and experienced.

Discussion of deficiencies in Reserves and problems of amendments offered to change Defense Department proposal.

Gen. Taylor, Army: Army mobilization needs, discussion of six-month training plan.

Gen. White, Air Force: No Air Force need for compulsory reserves.

Gen. Shepherd, Marine Corps: Six- to eight-month duty compulsion.

Asst. Sec. Burgess, Defense Department: Defense Department manpower needs; need for increased readiness and increased strength; discussion of age of induction, length of obligation.

Maj. Gen. Hershey, Selective Service: United States can afford a large active-duty force, need for large Reserve program, need to remove inequalities between Reserve and National Guard status.


FOREIGN RELATIONS COMMITTEE


*The South-East Asia Collective Defense Treaty, Part 2* (January 1955)

Hamilton Fisk: SEATO a mistake, possibility of another Korean episode, land war in Indochina would cost the United States many lives.

Agnes Waters: Asia not worth American defense.

Gen. Gruenther, Army: NATO accords on West Germany.

--(March 1955)

   Gen. Gruenther, Army:  Organizational set-up of
NATO, Soviet land forces, satellite forces, German
contribution to NATO.


*Mutual Security Act of 1955* (May 1955)

   Sec. Dulles, State Department:  History of program, the Administration's request, achievements of
program, discussion of Communist threat in Asia,
Europe, and Latin America.  Statistics of status of
program.
   Harold Stassen, Foreign Operations Administration:  European expenditures and U.S. aid, FY 1956
program by function, technical assistance, results
of Marshall plan, decline of Communist influence.
   Adm. Radford, Joint Chiefs of Staff:  Military
assistance part of national security, importance of
economic assistance.
   Asst. Sec. Hensil, Defense Department:  Contribution of allies to defense, Military Defense
Assistance Program administration, role of International Security Affairs.
   Rep. Powell:  Bandung Conference not anti-white
or anti-West, interested in democracy.
   Asst. Sec. Sebald, State Department:  Far East
situation, nation-by-nation analysis.
   Asst. Sec. Allen, State Department:  Middle East
and South Asia situations.
   Asst. Sec. Sparker, State Department:  Assist-
ance to Latin America, political stability in Latin
America, Communist subversion, role of Export-
Import Bank.


GOVERNMENT OPERATIONS COMMITTEE


*Investigations Conducted by Sen. Joe McCarthy:*

*Communist Infiltration of Defense Plants* (May 1955)


*Investigations Conducted by Sen. Joe McCarthy: Harold Talbott, Secretary of the Air Force (Business Activities)* (July 1955)

# 1956 CONGRESSIONAL HEARINGS

## 84th Congress, Second Session

HOUSE COMMITTEES

ARMED SERVICES COMMITTEE

*Extension of Government Operation of Defense Plants:*
*Subcommittee on HR8709* (1956)

Gen. Englis, Army: Need for government to operate industrial enterprises that private concerns
cannot or will not operate; large costs of capital
equipment to build modern weapons systems.
Discussion of service investment in privately-
owned defense enterprises, number of obsolescent
plant facilities.

*Inspection Tour of Overseas Bases: Special Subcom-*
*mittee Report* (1956)

Discussion of military and civilian government
in Okinawa and the Ryukyu Islands.

*Reserve Forces Legislation: A Legislative History of*
*the Reserve Forces Act of 1955, Subcommittee #1*
(1956)

Includes President's message on national

security, legislative developments, Senate and
House hearings, and concluding observations.


## *Review of Reserves Program* (January 1956)

Asst. Sec. Burgess, Defense Department: Progress of Reserve program change, integration of congressional changes, problems with new program.
Increase in Army enlistment.


## *Aircraft Production Costs and Profits: Subcommittee for Special Investigations* (February, March 1956)

Extensive hearings on costs and profits of defense contractors in aircraft industry. Witnesses
include representatives from Chance Vought, Cor-
vair, Douglas, Fairchild, Boeing, Grumian, Lockheed, and North American. Government witnesses
include representatives from Air Force, Navy, General Accounting Office, and Government Renegotiation Board.


## *Military Public Works* (February, March 1956)

Asst. Sec. Kelleher, Air Force: Discussion of
Sage system and explanation of functions.
Roscoe Turner, American Legion: Problem of pilots leaving Air Force, need for better housing.
Maj. Gen. Blade, Air Force: Explanation of Continental Air Defense Command and Sage, new devices,
and weapons systems management.


## *Review of Reserve Program by Subcommittee #1* (May 1956)

Asst. Sec. Burgess, Defense Department: Report
of National Security Committee, six-month reserve
proposal, elimination of National Guard and Reserve

pay differential, Critical Skills Program.

Discussion of training, service compliance with new program, ability to meet force levels, and Reserve equipment.

Asst. Sec. Milton, Army:  Army Reserve program, recruiting progress, and publicity program.

Discussion of enlistments indoctrination.

Granville Ridley, American Legion:  Need for universal military training and support for six-month training program.

Discussion of American Legion's recruitment publicity program.

Brig. Gen. Lindeman, Army:  Army publicity, lag in recruitment, Reserve groups, and Army age bracket.

Asst. Sec. Pratt, Navy:  Success of Navy and Marine reserves, Navy and Marine drilling, and publicity.

Maj. Gen. Erickson, National Guard Association:  Actual strength of Reserves compared with requirements, problem of maintaining strength, source of enlistments.

Asst. Sec. Smith, Air Force:  Air Force Reserve step-up in training, totally manned at programmed strength, use of publicity.

Maj. Gen. Hall, Air Force:  Manning, aircraft, instructors, and Air Force Reserve airlift capability.

Maj. Gen. Wilson, Air National Guard:  What the Guard consists of, training, aircraft, and facilities.


*Hearings on Armed Services Regular Officer Augmentation* (May 1956)

Asst. Sec. Burgess, Defense Department:  Need for increasing Army and Air Force general officers. Problems of officer instability, need for permanency of status and security.

Discussion of high turnover and low morale. Discussion of Air Force "officer hump."

*Hearings on Civil Air Patrol Compensation* (May 1956)

Maj. Gen. Beau, Air Force:  Size of Civil Air
Patrol, missions, relations with Air Force.
    Discussion of Soviet pilot training, large num-
ber of pilots.

*Study of Armed Services Procurement Regulations* (June
1956)

    Witnesses include James Nash (Defense Depart-
ment), Edwin Fisher (General Accounting Office),
and service representatives testifying on practice
of not examining late bids for procurement contracts.

*Hearings on Plan to Provide for an Assistant Secreta-
ry for R&D for Each of the Military Departments* (June
1956)

    Asst. Sec. Robertson, Defense Department:  Reor-
ganization Plan No. 1.  Technical activities of
each of the services, magnitude of Defense Department research and development.  Importance of research and development to national security, role
of new assistant secretary.
    A. R. Jones, Bureau of the Budget:  Background
of plan to improve supervision and coordination of
service research and development.
    Discussion of need for new assistant secretary.
    Sec. Brucker, Army:  Problems faced by Army in
current research and development programs.
    Sec. Gates, Navy:  Increase in research and de-
velopment responsibilities in Navy.
    Sec. Quarles, Air Force:  Level of research and
development operations in Air Force, need for full-
time secretary to handle research and development.
    Dep. Sec. Robertson, Defense Department:  Dis-
cussion of legislative approach to creating new
posts, role of Hoover Commission.

*Hearings on Authorization of Loan of Naval Vessels to Certain Friendly Nations* (June 1956)

Vice Adm. Good, Navy:  History of naval loan, discussion of naval programs in China, Japan, and Korea.

FOREIGN AFFAIRS COMMITTEE

*Mutual Security Act of 1956* (March, April, May 1956)

Under Sec. Hoover, State Department:  New Soviet economic warfare, importance of mutual security program, need for economic development.
Discussion of Soviet trade patterns.
John Hollister, International Cooperation Administration:  Outlines of military assistance, program by program.
Asst. Sec. Gray, Defense Department:  U.S. alliance pattern, Military Assistance Advisory Group program, need for advanced weapons for allies, military program by size and region.
Gen. Gruenther, NATO:  NATO effort, Soviet pressures, needed NATO improvement, Soviet air defense improvement.
Dep. Asst. Sec. Ellrick, State Department:  NATO and Soviet tactics, size of aid apportionment and expenditures.
Dr. Moyer, State Department:  Far East mutual security program, size and regional breakdown, discussion of Korea, Indonesia, role of Sukarno.
Gen. Lemnitzer, Army:  Korean forces--size, readiness; size and capability of free world forces in Asia.
Asst. Sec. Holland, State Department:  Latin American economic and military aid programs, Guatemala situation.
Adm. Radford, Joint Chiefs of Staff:  Success of latest Soviet disarmament propaganda, Soviets

building up strength, regional view of Soviet threat.

Asst. Sec. Allen, State Department: Middle East and South Asia, Soviet threat of infiltration. Independence of new states in Africa, Soviet aid tactics. Discussion of Aswan Dam, situation in Middle East.

Testimony of private groups on aid program.


GOVERNMENT OPERATIONS COMMITTEE


*Civil Defense for National Survival* (January, February 1956)

Dr. Frederick Libby, Atomic Energy Commission: Effect of nuclear blasts, extent of fallout, medical problems.

Discussion of effect of winds on fallout, strontium 90 count, effectiveness of shelters.

Dr. Hill, M.I.T.: Need for defense, capability of Sage system, effectiveness of early warning systems, need for federally sponsored civil defense effort.

Dr. Berkner, Office of Civil Defense: Civil defense part of deterrent effort, need to maintain industrial capability after an attack.

Discussion of likely targets in United States, shelter effectiveness, proposed cabinet post for civil defense.

Willard Bascon: Results of studies, Distant Early Warning line, need for early warning.

Dr. Earnest Tuve, Carnegie Institute: Need for large civil defense effort, findings of Killian Commission.

James Killian, M.I.T.: Need to mobilize resources for both military and national defense, large shelter program and early warning systems.

Discussion of Soviet scientific and educational efforts.

--*Part 2* (February, March 1956)

Charles Fairman, Harvard Law School:  Pattern of
government following a nuclear attack, Ure declara-
tion of martial law.
    Adm. Radford, Joint Chiefs of Staff:  Primary
mission of armed forces to defeat enemy forces,
civil defense primarily civilian leadership.  Supports civilian leadership for civil defense.
    Discussion of current civil defense readiness
and Defense Department role in civil defense.
    Gen. Twining, Air Force:  Air Force preparation
in civilian emergencies; Army possesses greatest
responsibility.
    Adm. Burke, Navy:  Civilian defense basically a
local and civilian problem; opposition to creation
of an Office of Civil Defense.
    Gen. Taylor, Army:  Coordination of service civ-
il defense responsibilities, opposition to placing
civil defense responsibilities within the Defense
Department.

--*Part 3* (March 1956)

Dr. James Machta, Weather Bureau:  Weather as a
factor during an atomic attack, Weather Bureau net-
works, fallout patterns.
    C. D. Curtis, Bureau of Public Roads:  Highway
civil defense requirements, traffic control.
    Otto Nelson, New York Life Insurance Company:
"Nonmilitary defense" a deterrent, need for large
federal program.
    Further testimony of private citizens on civil
defense program and government witnesses on current
state of civil defense efforts.

--*Part 4* (April, May 1956)

Arthur Fleming, Office of Defense Mobilization:
U.S. mobilization base, creation of damage

assessment centers, dispersion of industries, further studies of civil defense.

Under Sec. Morse, Agriculture Department:  Emergency flood program, biological research.

Asst. Sec. Siciliano, Labor Department:  Manpower mobilization.

Val Peterson, Federal Civil Defense Administration:  Difficulty of civil defense, effect of nuclear blasts, role of federal and state authorities.  Need for all-out citizen participation for civil defense.

Discussion of federal-state-local cooperation, need for early warning systems, adequate shelters.

Benjamin Taylor, Federal Civil Defense Administration:  Shelter program, identification and modification.

--*Part 5* (May, June 1956)

Testimony of state and city civil defense administrators and government officials in Baltimore, Detroit, Syracuse, New York, Milwaukee, and Washington, D.C.

--*Part 6* (June 1956)

Hearings held in San Francisco and Los Angeles: testimony by civic leaders and government administrators.

--*Part 7* (June 1956)

S. A. Anthony, Civil Defense Research Association:  Civil defense work of Research Association.

Walter Cronin:  Civil defense a federal responsibility, need for cabinet level agency or inclusion in the Defense Department.

Murray Levine:  Need for strong economy after nuclear attack.

Testimony by medical groups and American Legion on civil defense.

*Air Force and Navy Rocket Launcher Procurement* (May 1956; February, March, April 1957)

Extended discussion of cost overruns and delayed delivery of rocket launcher. Testimony by Air Force representatives (Air Material Command), General Accounting Office, and representatives from private contractors.

*Budget and Accounting Subcommittee* (May, June 1956)

Asst. Sec. McNeil, Defense Department: Defense Department views on drills to provide central reporting functions in the Bureau of the Budget and establishment of periodic agency performance reports.
Discussion of special Bureau of the Budget problems in assessing budget.

*Reorganization Plan No. 1 of 1956 (New Offices in the Army, Navy and Air Force) Subcommittee* (June 1956)

Rep. Vinson: New secretary for research and development for each of services and for financial management.
Acting Sec. Robertson, Defense Department: Details of proposal, discussion of Hoover Commission recommendations, service research and development efforts.
A. R. Jones, Bureau of the Budget: Plan will lead to greater efficiency and monetary savings.
Dr. Kelly, Hoover Commission: Need for civilians in service with research and development backgrounds.

JOINT COMMITTEES OF HOUSE AND SENATE

JOINT ATOMIC ENERGY COMMITTEE

*Shortage of Scientific and Engineering Manpower: Subcommittee on R&D* (April, May 1956)

Frederick Libby, Atomic Energy Commission: Shortage of scientists and engineers, gains in Soviet Union, atomic energy program difficulties, lack of adequate high school programs, need for fellowships, research programs.

Discussion of proposed fellowship program, university nuclear energy programs, competence of Soviet scientists.

Dr. Trytten, National Academy of Scientists: Cold war of the classrooms, U.S. complacence in education, Soviet approaches to schooling, size of technical manpower pool.

Dr. Kelly, National Science Foundation: Shortages in engineers, activities of the Foundation.

Dr. Meyerhoff, Scientific Manpower Commission: United States only graduating 50% of needed engineers, needs of industry and the military.

Testimony of educators in high school and college on how to attract students to science careers.

Rear Adm. Rickover, Navy: Navy's training program, Soviet educational system, proposals for strengthening U.S. education.

JOINT DEFENSE PRODUCTION COMMITTEE

*Defense Mobilization Programs* (April 1956)

Arthur Fleming, Office of Defense Mobilization: Development of methods to calculate bomb damage to compute expected bomb damage.  Need to determine

essential military end term that must be produced
during the first phase of an attack.

Discussion of sizes of stockpiles, metal prices,
alternate mobilization plans.

## JOINT ECONOMIC COMMITTEE

*Defense Essentiality and Foreign Economic Policy*
(June 1956)

Dr. Daid, Labor Department: Manpower policy,
need for technical skills, relationship between
technology and changes in occupational structure.

Raymond Vernon, Harvard Business School: Civilian dislocation in wartime, effect on industry.
The mobilization base in nuclear war.

Dr. Bidwell, Council of Foreign Relations: Case
study of watch industry.

Number of witnesses representing watch industry
discussing technology for trade and war.

## SENATE COMMITTEES

## APPROPRIATIONS COMMITTEE

*DOD Appropriations for FY 57* (1956)

Sec. Wilson, Defense Department: Loss of officers to private industry; reports of Soviet military superiority untrue; U.S. strength in airpower,
B-52 production at six-per-month, naval role in nuclear weapon delivery, continental defense, Nike,
Falcon, and Sparrow programs, research and development efforts adequate.

Discussion of effect of budget ceiling, aircraft

production, NATO aid, Rockefeller report, effect of weapon lead time on budget.

Adm. Radford, Joint Chiefs of Staff: Problem of military turnover, budget procedure, intercontinental ballistic missile development.

Sec. Brucker, Army: Principal missions of the Army, regional analyses, size of Army request, total Army personnel, Reserve forces. Guided missile program--Jupiter project.

Discussion of Army turnover.

Gen. Taylor, Army: Army deterrent role, Communist bloc forces, division strengths, need for Army versatility, missile program, contribution of German scientists.

Discussion of Nike-Talos competition.

Sec. Thomas, Navy: FY 1957 Navy request, role of carriers, Skywarrior and Skyhawk programs, new guided-missile ship.

Discussion of adequacy of budget, Navy nuclear-weapon delivery capability, nuclear submarine programs.

Adm. Burke, Navy: New Navy procurement, block obsolescence, Soviet naval threat, submarine-launched ballistic missile research, "New" Soviet navy composition.

Gen. Pate, Marine Corps: Security forces, amphibious warfare, Reserve.

Sec. Quarles, Air Force: 137-wing goal, B-52, F-102, F-101 and F-104 production, Thor, Atlas, Titan programs, Sage system, and procurement practices.

Gen. Twining, Air Force: Navy carrier over-rated, Air Force possesses prime strategic mission, importance of early warning system, Air Force research and development, nuclear aircraft research.

Discussion of Soviet troop reduction, B-52 procurement.

Asst. Sec. Burgess, Defense Department: Defense Department manpower, enlistments, and inductions.

Asst. Sec. Furnas, Defense Department: Defense Department research and development, private

research, discussion of duplication, missile programs in existence, service expenditures.

Asst. Sec. McNeil, Defense Department: Total
obligational authority for all programs, factors in
budget increase, major procurement items, expenditures by major budget category.

Statements by service representatives on appropriation for respective areas.

Statements by Guard, Reserve, National Rifle Association, and other private interest groups.

Gen. Blake, Air Force: Air defense status, Sage
system, possibility of antiballistic missile.

Gen. Le May, Air Force: Current U.S. supremacy
is on wane, increased Soviet capability, need for
better trained personnel, importance of tankers,
need to speed up B-52 procurement, airpower greatest deterrent to war.

Gen. Twining, Air Force, and Adm. Burke, Navy:
Discussion of service duplication in missile pro-
gram, service missions:  Nike, Talos, Distant Early
Warning Line program.


ARMED SERVICES COMMITTEE


*Study of Airpower:  Subcommittee on the Air Force*
(April 1956)

Gen. Smith (Ret.), Army:  Soviet industrial potential after World War II, Soviet industrial
policy, need for increased American scientific
training.

Gen. Bradley (Ret.), Army:  Contribution of airpower in military history, role of atomic and hy-
drogen bombs, need of airpower to deter war.

Discussion of nuclear deterrence, Soviet-
American military balance, Soviet intentions.

Adm. Carny (Ret.), Navy:  Need for airpower in
all services.  Soviet lead in airpower and submarine strength.

Discussion of need for scientists.

Gen. Spaatz (Ret.), Air Force: How nuclear weapons have changed war, need for large manned bomber fleet.

Discussion of implication of ballistic missiles.

Gen. Le May, Air Force: Strategic Air Command's deficiency in trained manpower, Soviet air force better rewarded. Need for larger bomber force to achieve air superiority, inability of intercontinental ballistic missile to replace bomber. Soviet heavy bombers will outnumber U.S. force by 1958.

History of Strategic Air Command, roles and missions, organization and types of aircraft and description--basing, flying formation, bombing tactics, ability of bombers to penetrate enemy defenses, and bombing accuracy.

Discussion of warning and communications systems, budgetary cuts, use of war games.

Col. Hanlon, Air Force: Strategic Air Command bombing and targeting procedures, weapons allocation, strategic planning administration.

Maj. Gen. McConnell, Air Force: Capabilities of Strategic Air Command bombers to reach Soviet targets, and capabilities of Bison-Bear Soviet bombers to reach United States.

Discussion of service coordination of nuclear attacks against Soviet Union.

Maj. Lukeman, Air Force: Strategic Air Command mission after 1958, need for secure bomber force, launch-on-warning tactics, air alerts. Need for more bombers and improved early warning systems.

Gen. Le May, Air Force: KC-135 tanker program, Strategic Air Command operation and maintenance costs; discussion of B-52 production schedule and existence of a bomber gap.

Gen. Partridge, Air Force: History of Air Force air defense efforts, growing strength of Soviet bombers and submarines, probable Soviet targets. Organization of Continental Air Defense Command, function and means of identification and interception.

Discussion of specific weapons systems--F-86,

F-89, F-94, F-101, F-102, and Falcon.  Discussion
of air defense missiles and Sage control system.
Discussion of ballistic missile defense and improvements in technology.

Threat of Soviet intercontinental ballistic missile frightening, shortage of trained air defense
personnel.

Discussion of Soviet radar system and deficiencies of U.S. air defense system.  Discussion of
possibility of Soviet one-way bomber attack.

Lt. Gen. O'Connel, Air Force:  Air Force personnel, ROTC programs, competition with private industry for personnel, declining reenlistment rates.

Discussion of career uncertainty in the Air
Force and effect of Office of the Secretary of Defense budget limitations.

Maj. Gen. Washbourne, Air Force:  Air Force construction program, concept of 1954 as "critical
year," budget cuts a major problem.

Discussion of budget procedure and inadequacy of
existing air bases.


--*Part 6*


Lt. Gen. Irvine, Air Force:  Air Force contracting procedures, facilities and manpower shortages.

Discussion of B-52 and KC-135 programs and Air
Force cargo plane capabilities.

Discussion of Soviet production efficiency, the
need to shorten U.S. lead times.


--*Part 7*


Gen. Weyland, Air Force:  Tactical Air Command
missions, number of Tactical Air Command wings and
major support commands.  Tactical Air Command reenlistment problems, need for better equipment and
increased tanker support.

Discussion of Soviet tactical air capabilities,
capabilities of Soviet fighter pilots.

Lt. Gen. Putt, Air Force: Revolution of technology in airpower, need for large research and
development expenditures, United States losing
technological margin to the Soviet Union, need for
more basic research.

Discussion of research and development contracting, determination of U.S. requirements. Discussion of Killian Report recommendations and Defense
Department budgetary ceilings.

Discussion of Soviet jet and missile technology,
possibility of Soviet breakthroughs.

Discussion of nuclear bomber slowdown, radar research, missile research. U.S. advantage in intercontinental ballistic missiles; and FY 1957
shortage in research and development funds.

Organization of Air Force ballistic missile program and authority and management.

Lt. Gen. Gavin, Army: Developments in Army organization and tactics, readiness for small wars.
Army strategies in nuclear theater operations, attempt to gear Army to changes of missiles.

Discussion of Army air defense missile programs.

Maj. Gen. Medaris, Army: Army ballistic missile
program, development of the Redstone and Jupiter
missiles, substantial progress.

Discussion of uses for Jupiter intermediate-
range ballistic missile, differences in Army and
Air Force missile programs.

Richard Hough, Bell Laboratories: Ballistic
missile defense, need for basic research.

Discussion of system complexity and state of the
art.

Werner von Braun, Army: Jupiter missile program, integration with Navy, superiority over Air
Force program. History of U-2, discussion of intercontinental ballistic missile development.


--Part 10


Maj. Gen. Howze, Army: Need for Army aviation
capability, observation and air support,

particularly interested in helicopter capability,
Soviet advances in helicopters, and troop mobility.


## --Part 11

Rear Adm. Clark, Navy: Navy missile programs,
Terrier, Talos-Nike comparisons. Size and composition of carrier aircraft, use of missiles. Discussion of Regulus program, launching missiles from
submarines.
Vice Adm. Combs, Navy: Role of naval airpower,
description of forces and new equipment. Role of
antisubmarine warfare.
Brig. Gen. Salmon, Marine Corps: Functions of
Marine aviation, aircraft in use. Discussion of
relations with naval aviation.
Discussion of role of seaplanes.
Vice Adm. Combs, Navy: Eisenhower "stable economy" in relation to defense needs, impact of unification on Navy.
Discussion of carrier vulnerability and strategic uses of Naval airpower.
Capt. Martineau, Navy: Short of trained naval
manpower, need for more career officers. Pay must
be comparative with industry.
Rear Adm. Griffin, Navy: Navy budgets inadequate, Soviet threat severe, need to continue 15-
ship carrier fleet.
Vice Adm. Libby, Navy: Joint Chiefs planning.
Rear Adm. Bennett, Navy: Navy research and development funds, Army-Navy intermediate-range ballistic missile development program.


## --Part 13

Trevor Gardner, Defense Department: Astounding
Soviet research and development progress, effect of
U.S. dollar ceilings.
Discussion of missile development slowdowns,
need for better management.

--*Part 14*

Lt. Gen. Powers, Air Force:  Organization of Air Force Research and Development Command.

Maj. Gen. Schriever, Air Force:  Air Force ballistic missile program, Ramo-Wooldridge management, need for intercontinental ballistic missile--Atlas and Titan projects.


--*Part 15*

Dr. James Killian, White House Staff:  Soviets advanced in military technology, weakness of science motivation in United States.  Importance of basic research, need for increased government funding.

Discussion of Killian Report, Soviet pace of producing engineers.


--*Part 16*

Maj. Gen. Bergquist, Air Force:  Air Force forces in NATO, NATO decision making and line of authority.

Gen. Taylor, Army:  Increasing likelihood of small wars, comparisons of Soviet conventional capability.  Need for larger FY 1958 Army budget, improved airlift.

Discussion of assignments of roles and missions, role of Joint Chiefs in defense budget.

Sec. Brucker, Army:  Responsibility of service secretary, establishment of force levels, discussion of Army budget process, Army budget "minimum austere" level.

Discussion of unification, Army and Air Force intermediate-range ballistic missile competition.

--*Part 18*

    Adm. <u>Burke</u>, <u>Navy</u>: Navy alone could survive
atomic attack, carrier task force strategy, and
Navy missile program.
    Discussion of antisubmarine warfare capability,
carrier vulnerability, transferring Air Force tactical air missions to naval air.
    Discussion of interservice competition, role and
mission assignments.
    Sec. <u>Thomas</u>, <u>Navy</u>: Roles and missions of the
Navy, contribution of carriers, atomic submarine
program.
    Discussion of rising Soviet naval capabilities,
introduction of guided missiles to fleet.

--*Part 19*

    Adm. <u>Radford</u>, <u>Joint</u> <u>Chiefs</u> <u>of</u> <u>Staff</u>: Communist
threat to world security, current defense program
sound, indirect participation of Joint Chiefs in
fiscal aspect of the budget.
    Discussion of responsibilities of the Chairman
of the Joint Chiefs of Staff, possibilities of interservice conflict over missile development, discussion of differences of opinion with the Defense
Department.
    Disagrees with Air Force request for more B-52s
and increased research and development.

--*Part 20*

    Gen. <u>Twining</u>, <u>Air</u> <u>Force</u>: Importance of intelli-
gence, threat of general nuclear war, increased
spending to adjust to growing Soviet capabilities.
    Discussion of B-52 procurement, tanker ratios,
and question of cuts in Air Force budget. Sees
carrier-based air force more expensive than land-
based air force.

*--Part 21*

    Sec. <u>Quarles</u>, <u>Air Force</u>: Need for economical methods, United States possesses largest strategic capability, discussion of Air Force research and development ceiling.

    Strategic Air Command mission given top priorities, prediction of continued U.S. strategic superiority.

*--Part 22*

    Sec. <u>Wilson</u>, <u>Defense</u> <u>Department</u>: Airpower important, diversity of Communist threat. Military strength cannot imperil economic strength. United States cannot support forces for all contingencies. Role of Strategic Air Command of primary importance, future importance of intercontinental ballistic missiles.

    Discussion of budget cutbacks, stoppages, fiscal policies used in determining budget policies.

    Predicts Soviet liberalization; differences in interpretation of intelligence data; argues United States ahead in general military strength.

    Discussion of executive and congressional prerogatives in national security, vulnerability of carriers, strength of Soviet air force. Discussion of B-52 acquisition rate.

*--Part 23*

    Gen. <u>Twining</u>, <u>Air Force</u>: Soviet air force larger, same number of Bears as B-52s. Predicts that Soviets will soon have superior air force.

    Discussion of relative strategic balance, Soviet technological progress.

*Assistant Secretary for R&D for Each of the Three Military Departments* (July 1956)

Dep. Sec. Robertson, Defense Department: Discussion of Defense Department proposal, coordination of research and development work, discussion
of research and development defense management,
cost of Nike and Talos, problems of research and
development duplication.

FOREIGN RELATIONS COMMITTEE

*Control and Reduction of Armaments, Subcommittee,
Part 1* (January 1956)

Harold Stassen, State Department:  U.S. Geneva
disarmament position, Eisenhower Open Skies proposal.
Discussion of aerial reconnaissance capabilities,
technological changes affecting disarmament, the
Soviet position.
Discussion of changes in U.S. and Soviet positions, conventional disarmament, the prevention of
surprise attack.

*--Part 2* (February 1956)

Sec. Dulles, State Department:  Difficulties of
disarmament, cannot proceed until insecurity dis-
appears, inspection the key to disarmament.

*--Part 3* (March 1956)

Sen. Flanders:  Need for complete and universal
disarmament, moral evil of communism, discussion of
graduated deterrence.

--*Part 4* (March 1956)

Sec. Wilson, Defense Department: Disarmament policy, need for inspection and control system.
Discussion of detection, inspection, possibility of arms control.

--*Part 5* (April 1956)

John Gibson, Boston University: Approaches to disarmament.
Walter Leuson, Boston University: Military problem of intelligence, photographic inspection, ground inspection, intercontinental ballistic missile detection.
Laurence Fuchs, Brandeis University: Deficiencies of present disarmament proposals, establishing a world police force, proposal for comprehensive disarmament.
Donald Stone, Springfield College: Self-interest concept of disarmament, importance of trust.
Louis Sohn, Harvard University: Need for strong U.N., international inspection, disarmament by stages.
Robert Reno, attorney: Need for international police force.
Charles Corvell, M.I.T.: International corps of inspectors, scientific and engineering committee conference on inspection.
W. Barton Leach, Harvard University: Arms race secrecy, weapons specialization, disarmament problems, manpower, geographic and weapons system differences.
Walt Rostow, M.I.T.: Soviet military policy, Soviet defense expenditures, post-Stalin policy.
Carl Friedrich, Harvard University: Effect of disarmament on European alliance.
Duncan MacDonald, Boston University: Changing warfare methods, weapons development, aerial inspection.

David Cavers, Harvard University:  Problems of
enforcement, legal procedures.

Max Millikan, M.I.T.:  Long-run purposes of U.S.
policy, strategy of Communists.

Russell Johnson, Friends Committee:  Economic
impact of disarmament.

Samuel Atkinson, Boston University:  U.S. proposals must be publicly plausible.

Thomas Mahoney, Northeastern University:  Advocates international enforcement.

Mark Shaw, Democracy Unlimited:  Danger of arms
race, need for revised priorities.

Mrs. Paul Johnson:  Need for intelligence in
disarmament, prayer for disarmament.

John Pearlman:  Need to understand Russian view-
point.


--*Part 6* (April 1956)

Thomas Murray, Atomic Energy Commission:  Validity of deterrence, proposals for limited ceilings
on size of stockpiles, size of individual weapons.

Discussion of different targeting strategies,
nuclear proliferation.


--*Part 7* (June 1956)

Ambassador Stassen, State Department:  London
negotiations, inspection requirements, importance
of aerial inspection prior to missile development.

Discussion of announced Soviet force reductions.


--*Part 8* (June 1956)

Kenneth Boulding, Friends Committee:  Adjustment
of economy to disarmament, size and expense of defense establishment.

Charles Price, Federation of American Scientists:  Need to halt intercontinental ballistic

missile testing, establish U.N. police force.

Norman Thomas: Need for universal disarmament, balance of terror unsafe.

J. David Singer, Vassar College: Arms create tensions, should be transferred to U.N.

Mrs. J. Pomerance, World Peace and Disarmament: Need to shift arms spending to foreign economic development.

Number of private citizens and representatives of religious groups expressing concern over arms race.


--*Part 9* (June 1956)

Testimony by individuals and representatives from peace and religious groups advocating disarmament.


--*Part 10* (December 1956)

Hearings held in St. Louis, Missouri--peace and religious groups advocating disarmament.


*Situation in the Middle East* (February 1956)

Sec. Dulles, State Department: Tripartite agreement of 1950, Soviet arms shipments, possibility of Israeli-Egyptian arms race.

Under Sec. Hoover, State Department: Saudi-Arabian arms request, Soviet attitude toward Middle East, discussion of effect of Baghdad Pact.

Discussion of Russian offensive in Middle East, role of United States in Israeli security.


*Mutual Security Act of 1956* (April, May 1956)

Gen. Lemnitzer, Army: Military situation in Far East, Republic of (South) Korea army, situation in Okinawa.

Sec. Dulles, State Department: Military assistance, national insurance policy, region by region threats, new Soviet tactics, foreign aid program from Soviets.

John Hollister, International Cooperation Administration: FY 1957 request by function, military and technological assistance programs.

Asst. Sec. Allen, State Department: Situation in Middle East and South Asia, strategic areas, important resources.

Asst. Sec. Holland, State Department: Latin American program, technological assistance crucial, communism in Guatemala.

Sec. Wilson, Defense Department: Need for free-world weapons modernization, International Security Affairs responsibilities.

Adm. Radford, Joint Chiefs of Staff: Soviet advanced weapons, NATO, SEATO problems.

Discussion of Soviet air strength, size of defense budget.

Discussion of inserting military aid into defense budget.

Tracy Voorhees, Defense Department: Navy's Pacific command, situation in Southeast Asia, collective security treaties.

Walter Reuther, United Auto Workers: Struggle for democracy cannot be won by arms alone, Communist appeal to Asians, danger of overemphasis on military, need for multilateral economic aid.

Testimony of other groups on aspects of nonmilitary aid.

Asst. Sec. Robertson, State Department: Situation in Far East.

Dep. Asst. Sec. Elbrick, Defense Department: European affairs, NATO military problems, discussion of Allies' cutbacks.

Col. Critz, Defense Department: Offshore procurement practices.

Gen. Gruenther, Army: Improvements in NATO since 1951, German contribution, Soviet naval and air power.

# 1957 CONGRESSIONAL HEARINGS

## 85th Congress, First Session

HOUSE COMMITTEES

ARMED SERVICES COMMITTEE

*Full Committee Hearings to Authorize Secretary of Air Force to Establish and Develop Certain Installations for National Security Purposes* (1957)

Floyd Bryant, Defense Department and Sec. Douglas, Air Force: Discussion of Sage system, Distant Early Warning line, Strategic Air Command dispersal and alert system, and ballistic missiles.
Gen. Rentz, Air Force: Air Force intercontinental ballistic missile program and location.

*Hearings on Boeing Airplane Company--Ford Motor Company--Purchase Order Subcontract, Subcommittee for Special Investigations* (1957)

Hearings on alleged excessive profit-taking by Ford Motor Company on subcontract for Boeing for construction of B-47 wings.
Lawrence Powers and William Newman, General Accounting Office: General Accounting Office report of Air Force laxity in supervising Boeing contract and failure to follow procurement regulations;

discussion of "realistic price" of B-47, Boeing
pricing techniques.


*Investigation of Reduction in Force Programs for Re-
serve Officers, Subcommittee #1* (1957)

Sec. Gates, Navy:  Naval Reserve reductions, Reserve levels.
William Francis, Defense Department:  Defense
Department decision to reduce Reserve forces, discussion of releasing Reserve officers.
Adm. Halloway, Navy:  Effect of reduction on officer levels.
Sen. Thurmond:  Injury to Reserves by Defense
Department decision.
Sec. Smith, Air Force:  Effect of Air Force reduction, personnel morale, discussion of reducing
pilot levels, cost of training B-47 and B-52 pilots.
Sec. Jackson, Navy:  Naval reduction, selection
of older officers, importance of Navy ROTC.


*Military Posture Briefing* (January 1957)

Sec. Brucker, Army:  Presentation of new Army
flag to Committee.
Sec. Wilson, Defense Department and Adm. Radford, Joint Chiefs of Staff:  Difficulty of increasing military budget to meet Joint Chiefs'
requests, discussion of Suez Crisis, Hungarian invasion, service strengths, enlistment rates, increase in B-52 acquisition, discussion of saving
manpower with more powerful weapons.
Sec. Brucker and Gen. Taylor, Army:  Service
strengths, 7th Army strength, other military deployments and commitments.
Discussion of Hungarian invasion, tank procurement, Jupiter intermediate-range ballistic missile.
Discussion of need for increased mobility and firepower.

Sec. Thomas and Adm. Burke, Navy:  Atomic propulsion, need for carriers, nuclear submarines,
discussion of using submarines as missile launchers.  Growing Soviet naval capacity.

Gen. Pate, Marine Corps:  Marine status, need
for limited war capability.

Sec. Quarles and Gen. Twining, Air Force:  128-
wing force, Air Force strength, B-52 production,
Thor program, Sage system, discussion of Air Force
air support capability.

*Review of the Reserve Program:  Hearing before Sub-
committee #1* (February 1957)

Asst. Sec. Jackson, Defense Department:
Strengthening Reserve components, six-month active
program for reservists, growth of nonactive Reserves, opposition to six-month plan from National
Guard.

Asst. Sec. Burgess, Defense Department:  "Take
6" program, Reserve strengths, discussion of welfare, health, safety, and morals of National Guard.

Sec. Brucker, Army:  Army Reserve strengths, mobilization capacity.

Gen. Taylor, Army:  Need for trained and active
Reserves, need for six-month training program.

Gen. Erickson, National Guard Association:  National Guard program, service levels and construction.

Gen. Hershey, Selective Service:  Size of draft
pool, need for ready reserve.

Sec. Thomas, Navy:  Navy and Marine Reserve,
basic mission, merchant marine academy.

Sec. Quarles and Gen. Twining, Air Force:  Need
for quick air-nuclear capability, size of Air Force
Reserve, Air National Guard, Reserve strengths.

*Study of Armed Services Procurement Act (Title 10)*
(February, March, April 1957)

Witnesses include Defense Department and service
procurement officials and representatives of defense contractors to discuss section of procurement
bill which allows government to let contracts without competition.  Over 50 witnesses, including military regional procurement officers, on procurement
practices.

*Full Committee Briefing on Navy Shipbuilding Program*
(March 1957)

Sec. Gates and Adm. Burke, Navy:  Long-range
shipbuilding projections, nuclear navy-air-sea power, request for first nuclear carrier, Marine helicopter assault ship, nuclear missile carrying
submarines.
Discussion of carrier fleet, need for guided
missile frigates, antisubmarine warfare capabilities.
Rear Adm. Mumma, Navy:  Nuclear navy, cost reduction program.

*Hearings on Establishment of Federal Civil Defense*
*Administration, Subcommittee* (March 1957)

Val Peterson, Civil Defense Administration:
Need for civil defense preparedness, federal-state
program, shelter identification, survival lists,
time constraints.
Rep. Hobfield:  Effect of nuclear blasts, organization of civil defense.
George Riley, AFL-CIO:  Federal government
should supervise civil defense, need for federal
rules for civil defense workers.

*Full Committee Hearing to Authorize Transfer of Naval*
*Vessels to Friendly Foreign Countries* (May 1957)

Adm. Burke, Navy:  Loan of Reserve vessels,

allies' naval capability, training program for foreign navies, discussion of German, Danish and Nor-
wegian naval capability.

*Military and Naval Construction* (May, June 1957)

Committee discussion of Air Force strength,
137-, 128-wing strengths, and criticism of White
House budget stringency.

*Hearings on Promotion of Naval Officers, Subcommittee*
(July 1957)

Extensive testimony and discussion of naval officer levels, statistics and historical comparisons.

*Hearings on Size of National Guard, Subcommittee*
(July 1957)

Discussion of Defense Department's and Army's
interpretation of Armed Services Committee's
400,000-man floor for the National Guard, and six-
month training period.

*Aircraft Engines Production Costs and Profits, Sub-
committee for Special Investigations* (July, August
1957)

Edmund <u>Aldous</u>, Roy <u>Hurley</u>, and George <u>Hill</u>, Curtis <u>Wright</u>: Curtis Wright production, profit and
taxation record, cost of aircraft engine production; less profits under military contract than on
sales to private concerns; cost reduction program.
Discussion of contracting procedures, relations
with subcontractors, jet engine costs, and production delays.
Testimony includes a number of letters from
James Douglas, Secretary of Air Force.

*Hearings on Air Force Contract AF33--General Motors--Buick, Oldsmobile, Pontiac Assembly Division, Subcommittee for Special Investigations* (July, August 1957)

Hearings on General Accounting Office funding of General Motor's excessive profit on IE-84F aircraft production.

Lawrence Powers, General Accounting Office: General Accounting Office studies, discussion of General Motors inefficiency, refusal of General Motors to open books.

John Gordon, General Motors Corp.: General Motors defense profits below private business, delay problems, contracting mistakes, questions General Accounting Office statistics.

Discussion of Air Force and General Motors inconsistencies.

Gen. Thurmond, Air Force: Air Force contracting procedures, typical problems.

Air Material Command Staff representatives discussing negotiation details, differences over contract interpretation.

## FOREIGN AFFAIRS COMMITTEE

*Economic and Military Cooperation with Nations in the Middle East* (January 1957)

Sec. Dulles, State Department: Growing Communist threat in the Middle East, need for military assistance.

Discussion of internal subversion in Iran, Saudi Arabia, Lebanon, and elsewhere.

Adm. Radford, Joint Chiefs of Staff: Interests in Middle East, Soviet geographical problems in intervening directly in Middle East, threat is subversion.

Dean Acheson, former Secretary, State Department: Eisenhower policy vague, gives President too much authority.

Discussion of Suez Canal policy, alternative approaches to Middle East.

Other witnesses testifying on general aspects of U.S. policy toward Middle East.

*Mutual Security Act of 1957, Part 1* (May 1957)

Sec. Dulles, State Department: Major foreign aid programs, success of collective security.

Gen. Norstad, NATO: NATO, SHAPE programs, missions of NATO forces, strength of Soviet forces, progress in Geneva build-up.

Discussion of status of Forces Treaty.

Asst. Sec. Sprague, Defense Department: Continuing threat of communism, role of military assistance, emphasis on new weapons to meet Soviet force modernization, increasing strength of free world, shift in geographic emphasis—Middle East and Asia—breakdown in regions and programs.

Discussion of threat, security agreements, strategic materials.

Adm. Stump, Navy: Growth in Asian defense effort, Communist ideological warfare.

Dep. Sec. Quarles, Defense Department: Soviet threat never greater, need for $1.9 billion program, fear of Soviet technological advances.

Adm. Radford, Joint Chiefs of Staff: Need to hold deployment of forces to a minimum, need for strong allied forces and bases, particularly for strategic bomber force.

Asst. Sec. Rountree and Adm. Bligh, Defense Department: Middle East, African and Indian aid, importance of Near East to NATO, growth in forces.

Brig. Gen. Guthrie, Army: Military Assistance Program, need for force modernization, Soviet threat in Europe.

GOVERNMENT OPERATIONS COMMITTEE

*Defense Cataloguing and Standardization Programs*
(January, March 1957)

*Availability of Information from Federal Departments
and Agencies: DOD, Part 8* (March 1957)

Charles Coolidge, Committee on Classified Information: Report of Coolidge Committee on government
security regulations.
Discussion throughout hearings of Defense Department guided missile program, particularly Army-
Air Force rivalry.

JOINT COMMITTEES OF HOUSE AND SENATE

JOINT ATOMIC ENERGY COMMITTEE

*Authorizing Legislation, Subcommittee on Legislation*
(April, June 1957)

K. E. Fields, Atomic Energy Commission: Dis-
tinction between military and civilian responsibilities.
Adm. Rickover, Navy: Depletion of fossil fuels,
need for large atomic power plants.

*The Nature of Radioactive Fallout and Its Effects on
Man, Subcommittee on Radiation, Part 1* (May, June
1957)

Extensive testimony by Atomic Energy Commission
scientists, military researchers, and private scientists on effect of nuclear explosions, wind and

fallout patterns, and long-range biological effects.


## JOINT DEFENSE PRODUCTION COMMITTEE


*Reducing Our Vulnerability to Attack* (June 1957)

Gordon Gray, Office of Defense Mobilization:
Threat of massive attack, concentration of economic
strength, identification of targets, damage assessment, vulnerability of economic resources. Reducing vulnerability, dispersion, protection through
shelters, relocation, preparation for emergency
government and individual management.


## SENATE COMMITTEES


## APPROPRIATIONS COMMITTEE


*DOD Appropriations FY 58* (1957)

Sec. Wilson, Defense Department:  House reductions, development of the budget, management problem of duplication, substantial manpower reduction,
proposed budget adequate for defense.
Discussion of missile and aircraft programs.
Adm. Radford, Joint Chiefs of Staff:  Air Force
program stoppage, unobligated funds surplus, effect
of rising costs.
Discussion of military service unification, augmentation of Reserves, Army-Air Force intermediate-
range ballistic missile competition, the Cordiner
report, international threats.
Sec. Brucker, Army:  FY 1958 Army strength, num-
bered Army breakdown, region and weapons armament,

Army missile development, list of research and development projects, Army manpower and personnel.
Discussion of service missions.


*Supplemental Defense Appropriations Bill: FY 58*
(1957)

Sec. McElroy, Defense Department:  Acceleration
of missile research and development, Strategic Air
Command alert facilities, bomber dispersal, and
Sage construction.
Discussion of B-52 production, Strategic Air
Command readiness, Snark production, Polaris development.
Sec. Brucker, Army:  Pershing missile, Sputnik
launch, Army airlift capability and adequacy of
size of Army.
Sec. Gates, Navy:  Polaris acceleration capabilities.
Adm. Burke, Navy:  Capability of Polaris.
Sec. Douglas, Air Force:  Intercontinental ballistic missile acceleration, Strategic Air Command
alert and tanker redeployment, Sage acceleration.
Gen. Le May, Air Force:  Need for both offensive
and defensive systems, combined use of bombers and
missiles.


ARMED SERVICES COMMITTEE


*Nominations* (February, March, April 1957)

Leo Hoegh, Office of Civil Defense:  Discussion
of effect of 10-megaton bomb and slighting of civil
defense.


*National Stockpile* (July, August 1957)

Gordon Gray, Office of Defense Mobilization:
Different probable war scenarios, description of
vital materials, means to meet potential shortages.
    Discussion of Defense Materials Program and pro-
curement practices; discussion of need for large
stockpile inventory in light of current strategic
conditions and nature of war.


*Military Pay* (August 1957)

    Ralph Cordiner, Defense Advisory Committee on
Professional and Technological Compensation:  Challenge of Communist technology, problems of excessive turnover, low incentives, need for manpower
development, including special pay for proficiency.
    Other witnesses include Reserve personnel and
members of Advisory Commission on military pay proposals.


*Nomination of Neil McElroy* (August 1957)

    Sec. McElroy, Defense Department:  Discussion of
Pentagon waste, use of competitive procurement
practices.


*Inquiry into Satellite and Missile Programs, Pre-
paredness Investigation Committee, Part 1* (November,
December 1957)

    Dr. Teller, California Institute of Technology:
Relationship of nuclear weapons and intermediate-
range and intercontinental ballistic missiles.
Destructive capabilities of missiles and Soviet
progress in booster construction.
    Discussion of why United States is behind Sovi-
ets, lack of funding.  Need to create invulnerable
retaliatory capability and importance that Russians
understand it.  Dr. Teller advocates civil defense
and active defense.  Calls for high priority space

program and incentives for scientists.

Vannevar Bush, M.I.T.: Russian performance in missiles, possibility of Soviet first strike, problems of American complacency, need for centralized missile planning and American support by scientists.

John Chipman, M.I.T.: Boundaries of metallurgy, Soviet advances in metallurgy, need for more rigorous science and technical programs. Russian emphasis on steel production.

James Doolittle: Soviets ahead in some aspects of missiles, United States in others. Need to overhaul U.S. educational system and increase defense spending—air defense, Strategic Air Command and Tactical Air Command, as well as missiles. Comparison of U.S. and Soviet schools.

Dr. Hagh, Vanguard Project: Description of Vanguard Project, how satellite is orbited and tracked.

Discussion of Vanguard launching schedule and information to be gained.

Sec. McElroy, Defense Department: Reassessment of U.S. missile program, authorization of both Thor and Jupiter missiles. Discussion of Army and Air Force development projects, intercontinental ballistic missile development, bottlenecks in program and contracting problems.

Discussion of role of guided missile Director and his authority. Discussion of budget ceilings and Russian claims of overall military superiority.

Dep. Sec. Quarles, Defense Department: Underestimation of U.S. strength dangerous, U.S. in overall lead in missile development.

Discussion of Soviet booster lead and supposed B-52 cutbacks. Discussion of increased funding and missile management in the Defense Department.

William Holaday, Defense Department: Clarification of Director's functions, Soviet technical infrastructure and need to reform U.S. science education. Discussion of Atlas program, need for increased research and development funds. Discussion of why Army Jupiter-C not used prior to Soviet Sputnik launch.

Sec. Brucker, Army: Army "went all out" in Jupiter program, Nike serious, Army satellite program, history of Army ballistic missile program.

Discussion of 200-mile range limitation and Thor competition.

Maxwell Taylor, Army: Army interest in missiles, conventional armament programs suffering, Soviet tactical missiles superior.

Gen. Gavin, Army: Soviet army capabilities, including guided missiles, strong. No U.S. counterpart to Soviet 350-mile missile. Need for military advice to Secretary of Defense.

Maj. Gen. Medaris, Army: Army ballistic missile program, Jupiter development program, need for long-term funding programs.

Werner von Braun, Army: History of U-2, current impediments in missile program, control of outer space important, Soviet space program.

Discussion of what keeps a satellite up.

William Martin, Army: Army management of development program.

Adm. Burke, Navy: Importance of control of the seas, importance of nuclear vessels, research and development in antisubmarine warfare and Polaris program.

Rear Adm. Bennet, Navy: Navy organization of research and development, Vanguard project discussed.

Rear Adm. Weakly, Navy: Navy antisubmarine warfare capability, 24-hour duty, Soviet submarine threat.

Rear Adm. Clark, Navy: Navy missiles—Regulus and Terrier programs.

Rear Adm. Raborn, Navy: Polaris program—solid fuel breakthrough, progress at a fast pace.

Discussion of "blank check" for Polaris.

Prof. Livingston, Harvard University and Defense Department: Defense management, problems of lead time; different approaches to development, lead time, concurrency. Supports "weapons system" Manhatten Project approach.

Sec. Douglas, Air Force: Air Force outer space

exploration, intercontinental and intermediate-range ballistic missile programs, Ramo-Wooldridge role. Need for additional funds, X-15 program and uses.

Discussion of lead time in missile production, Snark program, role of Strategic Air Command in deterrence and air defense missions.

Gen. Le May, Air Force: Strength of Strategic Air Command, need for manned bombers. Supports dispersal and 15-minute warning. Sees increased Soviet threat and need for more pilots.

Discussion of B-52 production cutback and attempts to keep Gaither Report secret.

Lt. Gen. Pitt, Air Force: Air Force missile program, missile program over-bureaucratized, discussion of B-58.

Lt. Gen. Irvine, Air Force: Soviet diversity of weapons, ability to build complex weapons. Air Force does not need Army Jupiter intermediate-range ballistic missile.

Maj. Gen. Schriever, Air Force: Air Force's first intercontinental ballistic missile division assigned to command.

Nelson Rockefeller: Study of Rockefeller project, technology lag, illustrates American complacency. Need for new strategy, increased defense spending, economy could stand it.

David Sarnoff, R.C.A.: Discussion of Rockefeller Report, suggestion of administrative streamlining and increased defense spending.

Robert Gross, Lockheed Aircraft: Need to preserve interim U.S. strength before missiles enter inventory, complexity of present procurement practices, complexity of administration in the Pentagon.

Dan Kimball, Aero-Jet General: Procurement or bottlenecks, absolute necessity that United States procure sizeable number of missiles before Soviets.

Lawrence Hyland, Hughes Aircraft: Proposal for Defense Department reorganization, need to coordinate research and development and procurement.

Roy Hurly, Curtis Wright: Overhaul procurement

operations, procurement policies discourage flexibility, long-run planning.

Thomas Lanphier: Need for B-58 program, lack of urgency due to ignorance of peril.

Donald Douglas, Douglas Aircraft: Need for more advanced cargo aircraft, need for more work on antiballistic missile.

George Fitch: Disarmament should be submitted to international court.

Lester Groves: History of Baruch plan, possibility of proliferation, problem of stockpiling.

Benjamin Cohen: Types of disarmament, partial measures, regional approach, problem of arms traffic.

Dr. Hans Morgenthau, University of Chicago: Proliferation problem, need for multilateral control.


--*Part 12* (January 1958)

Thomas Finletter, former Secretary, Air Force: Airpower safeguard of security, partial disarmament dangerous.

Warren Weaver: Effects of nuclear weapons becoming better known, disarmament increasingly important.

John Elliot: Arms trade more active, disarmament increasingly complex.

Albert Hill, Institute for Defense Analysis: Detection of tests, surprise attack, Open Skies proposal.


--*Part 13* (March 1958)

William Martin, Federal Reserve Board: Economic impact of reduction in arms spending.

Seymour Harris, Harvard University: Effect of arms spending reduction on economy.

Henry Hazlitt, *Newsweek*: No adverse effect on economy.

Harlan Cleveland, Maxwell School:   Relation of
arms spending to prosperity.


--*Part 14* (February 1958)

Ambassador Stassen, State Department:   Disarmament in Europe, inspection problems.


--*Part 15* (March 1958)

Index.
W. F. Libly, Atomic Energy Commission:   Underground testing, test suspensions, detection.


--*Part 16* (March 1958)

Dr. Brown, California Institute of Technology:
Consequences of arms race, effects of test suspen-
sion.
Brig. Gen. Starbird, Atomic Energy Commission:
Tests to improve warheads, reduction of fallout,
effects of test suspension on missile development.


--*Part 17* (April 1958)

Dr. Teller, California Institute of Technology:
Possibility of detecting tests low, need for inspection.
Dr. Oreor, Columbia University:   Detection of
tests technically possible.
Dr. Hans Bethe, Cornell University:   Danger of
proliferation, detection of tests.
Lewis Strauss:   Why testing continued, size of
stockpile, fallout a matter of concern.

FOREIGN RELATIONS COMMITTEE

*President's Proposal on the Middle East* (January, February 1957)

Sec. Dulles, State Department: Communist threat in Middle East, economic crisis, Communist infiltration, 1950 Tripartite Agreement, Baghdad Pact, Communist arms shipment to Middle East, possibility of U.S. troop involvement.

Adm. Radford, Joint Chiefs of Staff: No fear of overt Soviet involvement; Middle East arms race, Soviet military assistance, importance of Suez Canal, location of oil pipelines and location of Soviet military bases.

Elmore Jackson, Friends Council: Regional approach to aid Middle East.

Rep. Kersten: Creation of national military units composed of Iron Curtain escapees.

Rep. Fisk: Proposal would give President "blank check to make war," opposition to foreign "handouts."

W. C. Daniel, American Legion: Support for Eisenhower Doctrine, danger of Communist expansion.

Kenneth Burkhead, American Veterans Committee: Support for aid proposal.

Rabbi Bernstein, American Zionist Committee: Doctrine necessary; does not go far enough.

Statements by private citizens pro and con the Eisenhower Doctrine.

*--Part 2* (February 1957)

Herbert Hoover, Jr., State Department: Oil income from Middle East.

Ambassador Wadsworth, State Department: Saudi Arabian attitude toward resolution, Yemen conflict.

Joseph Green, State Department: Situation in Jordan, dubious about effect of Eisenhower Doctrine.

Ambassador Byroade, State Department:  Support
for resolution, Suez Canal seizure, Aswan Dam.
Ambassador Caffery, State Department:  Middle
East only understands power, importance of resolution.


*Mutual Security Act of 1957* (May, June 1957)

Sec. Dulles, State Department:  Disarmament unlikely, necessity of military aid, need for deterrent power.
Asst. Sec. Hollister, International Cooperation
Administration:  Summary of mutual security program, functional breakdown.
Asst. Sec. Sprague, International Security Affairs:  Soviet threat, role of Military Assistance
Program, size of the free world, defense expenditures, changing regional emphasis toward Asia.
Sec. Wilson, Defense Department:  Collective defense effort.
Adm. Radford, Joint Chiefs of Staff:  Military
posture required, Communist threat, impact of new
weapons on Military Assistance Program.
Asst. Sec. Rubottom, State Department:  Latin
American program, sales of military equipment.
Asst. Sec. Ellrick, State Department:  European
aid program, achievements of NATO, aid to Yugoslav-
ia.
John Hollister, International Cooperation Administration:  Status of military assistance personnel
throughout world.
Statements by private witnesses on non-military
aid.


*--Part 2* (June 1957)

Gen. Norstad, NATO:  Organization of NATO, NATO
bases, air defense, British cost sharing program.

GOVERNMENT OPERATIONS COMMITTEE

*Budgeting and Accounting, Subcommittee* (June 1957)

 Asst. Sec. McNeil, Defense Department: Defense
Department management problems, reforms since Hoover Commission, authorization and appropriations
processes. Research and development process lead
times, engineering changes, spares and work after
delivery.

*Supply Waste and Excesses in the Northeast Air Com-
mand, Subcommittee on Investigations* (August 1957)

# 1958 CONGRESSIONAL HEARINGS

## 85th Congress, Second Session

HOUSE COMMITTEES

ARMED SERVICES COMMITTEE

*Investigation of National Defense Missiles* (January, February 1958)

Sec. McElroy, Defense Department: Sputnik launches, capability of U.S. strategic forces, limited war capabilities, importance of research and development--costs of modern weapons systems.

Major deployments, U.S. troop strengths, U.S. commitment.

Establishment of Advanced Research Projects Agency--role of Strategic Air Command, Thor, Jupiter, Polaris, and Atlas programs, speed up, personnel problems.

Discussion of funding restrictions, status of missile programs, management of programs, Soviet programs.

Gen. Twining, Joint Chiefs of Staff: Need for more bombers and missiles, service allocations of missile roles.

Discussion includes consideration of impact of interservice rivalry on missile development.

Dep. Sec. Quarles, Air Force: Air Force missile responsibilities, Atlas, Titan, and Snark programs, other smaller missile programs, the Matador,

Falcon, Genie, Rascal, Bomarc; discussion of Zeus-
Wizard competition, adequacy of technical expertise, bomber development, nuclear and chemical
bomber plans, Soviet ability in new technological
breakthrough.

William Holaday, Defense Department:  History of
Defense Department guided missile program and management, discussion of missile management and role
of budget criteria in decision making.

Sec. Brucker and Gen. Lemnitzer, Army:  Army
missile program, history of missile development,
discussion of interservice rivalry, Nike-Zeus system, Army ability to insert satellites into orbit.

Gen. Lemnitzer, Army:  Smaller Army missiles,
Honest John, Pershing, Army nuclear planning, nuclear war scenario.

Gen. Daley, Army:  Army missile program, discussion of Vanguard decision, decisions concerning
missile management.

Gen. Gavin, Army:  Changes in Army firepower,
need for mobility and firepower.  Discussion of
Army budget requests, Defense Department ceilings,
Eisenhower budget process.

Discussion of General Gavin's frustrations with
the Defense Department--decision making and strategic doctrine.

Dr. Martin, Army:  Technical approaches to weapons research and development, impact of rivalry
management of weapons programs.  Discussion of Army
difficulties in attaining research and development
funding, competence of Office of the Secretary of
Defense assistant secretaries and staff.

Maj. Gen. Traib, Army:  Army Nike-Zeus program.

Sec. Gates and Adm. Burke, Navy:  Naval mission
and requirements, discussion of naval missile programs, need for more Polaris money for acceleration, need for antisubmarine warfare research and
development.

Adm. Burke, Navy:  Naval needs increasing, growing Soviet threat, fleet capabilities, need for
modern aircraft carriers, naval role in low-level
strategic bombing.

Asst. Sec. Norton, Navy: Vanguard program, discussion of costs and management.

Adm. Raborn, Navy: Polaris program, management.

Sec. Douglas and Gen. Le May, Air Force: Air
Force missile and bomber program; Atlas success,
Titan development, X-15 experiments and military
uses for space. Need for larger B-52 force, maintaining manned bomber force with missiles.

Gen. White, Air Force: Air Force mixed force
concept, discussion of air defense, ballistic missile defense, Distant Early Warning system; Air
Force management of intermediate range and intercontinental ballistic missile programs, costs.

Gen. Schriever, Air Force: Air Force management, new weapons development, contracting techniques.

Gen. Putt, Air Force: Air Force space program,
Dynasoar program, X-15 results, satellite intelligence, Super Hustler concept.

*Hearings on Proposed Reduction of the National Guard*
(February 1958)

Sec. Brucker, Army: Need for National Guard
readiness, modern organization.

Gen. Taylor, Army: Combat readiness, plan for
reduction, reorganization of Guard. Discussion of
Reserve strengths, danger to nation in current international situation.

Gen. Woolnough, Army: Missions of Army Reserve,
training required, pentomic army concept, discussion of training and ROTC.

Gen. Erickson, National Guard Association: National Guard enlistment rates, deployments, need to
maintain strength.

Discussion of enlistment problems and cost of
maintaining Guard at 400,000.

Maj. Gen. Harrison, National Guard Association:
Recommendation of "floors" for Reserve and National
Guard strengths, criticism of Defense Department
six-month Reserve policy, discussion of enlistment
problems.

Gen. Rich, Utah National Guard: Organization of typical National Guard unit, community relations, financial squeeze.

Col. Carleton, Reserve Officers Association: Need for strengthening Army Reserve, need for 700,000-man floor.

Other witnesses include governors and congressmen describing National Guard organization and problems in respective states.


*Hearings on Investigation of National Defense Establishment: Procurement and Utilization of Scientists, Engineers, and Technical Skills, Special Subcommittee #6* (March 1958)

Rear Adm. Cronin, Navy: Naval industrial relations, salaries of technicians, labor market, naval training.

Discussion of the need for higher pay, practices of Bureau of Naval Procurement.

Rear Adm. Dormin, Navy: Navy's technical needs in the future, Navy ROTC programs, retention of technicians.

Brig. Gen. Conway, Army: Army research and development programs, need for scientific exchange among services.

Gus Lee, Defense Department: Manpower utilization plans, size of technician pools, personnel practices to obtain and retain skilled technicians and scientists.

Maj. Gen. Carmichael, Air Force: Air Force need for technicians, technical schools, Air Force ROTC programs, cooperation with National Advisory Committee for Aeronautics.

Discussion of making service programs attractive.


*Hearings to Authorize Construction of Modern Naval Vessels* (March 1958)

Adm. Felt, Navy: Authorization of 20,000 tons

of amphibious and landing ships; concept of amphibious assault ship, use of Marines, need for
limited-war capability--Suez expdrience, antisubmarine warfare program.

Discussion of tonnage authority, costs of shipbuilding, carrier air.

Adm. Mumma, Navy: Landing ship dock concept,
use of helicopters, discussion of laid-off shipbuilders, and military failure in Suez.

Adm. Rose, Navy: Talos and Terrier Program,
antisubmarine warfare program, fleet modernization
program; discussion of U.S. and Russian naval
strategies.

*Hearings on Investigation of National Defense Estab-
lishment: Regulations and Procedures of Classification and Dissemination of Information, Subcommittee
#6* (March, April, July 1958)

Murray Snyder, Defense Department: Defense Department information procedures, congressional
access to information, role of Office of Public
Affairs.

Discussion of General Accounting Office prerogatives.

Maj. Gen. Stoke, Army: Army public information
procedures, role of local commanders in information
dissemination.

Brig. Gen. Reynolds, Joint Chiefs of Staff: Declassification procedures.

Edmund Burnett, Army: Army research and development disclosures.

Rear Adm. Kirkpatrick, Navy: Naval information
program, classification programs.

Maj. Gen. Luckman, Air Force: Air Force information services, need for good morale.

Robert Killer, Office of the Secretary of Defense: Procedures for releasing auditing figures,
discussion of "need to know" philosophy, General
Accounting Office prerogatives, role of Comptroller
General in legal terms.

Edwin Fisher, General Accounting Office:  Accounting Office's legal responsibilities, discussion of Defense Department practices of evasion.

*Investigation of National Defense:  Phase II, Subcommittee #4* (March, April, July 1958).  [Hearings on Military Air Transport Service.]

Asst. Sec. Sharp, Air Force:  Objectives of Military Air Transport Service, cost-ceiling programs.
Discussion of Air Force subsidy of private air carriers, need for Military Air Transport Service exercises, mobilization capability.
Gen. Smith, Air Force:  Size of Military Air Transport Service, aircraft in operation, allocation to Strategic Air Command, ability to airlift troops to Europe, Civil Reserve Air Force program.
Gen. Donnelly, Air Force:  Wartime airlift requirements, role of Tactical Air Command and Strategic Air Command, discussion of size of Military Air Transport Service and role of Civil Reserve Air Force.
Robert Turner, Air Transport Association:  Role of private carriers in Civil Reserve Air Force, importance to Military Air Transport Service.

*Hearings on Reorganization of the DOD* (April, May 1958)

Charles Coolidge, Defense Department:  Legal opinion of Defense Secretary's authority--supreme power and authority of Secretary over Defense Department, meanings of National Security Act; role of services and Congress.
Sec. McElroy, Defense Department:  Need for Defense Department reorganization, history of National Security Act; concept of functional, unified command; nuclear threat and need for clear response and coordinated chain of command; discussion of roles of service chiefs of staff, problems of transition,

locus of strategic planning, missile program.

Gen. Twining, Joint Chiefs of Staff: Concept of operational unified commands, need for service coordination and flexibility.

Discussion of proposed increase in Joint Chiefs' staff, organization of the Department of the Army, discussion of Army missile program, effect of proposed reorganization.

Adm. Burke, Navy: Need for organization, dynamic management in the Defense Department, role of the service chief in Defense Department, problems of single service unification, and need to maintain service autonomy.

Discussion of unified co-mands in military regions, role of Congress, role of Marines within unified command, role of Chief of Naval Operations, and Joint Chiefs' staff responsibilities.

Gen. Pate, Marine Corps: Marine role in unified commands, discussion of duplication with Army missions.

Gen. Bradley (Ret.), Army: Experience of unified commands in World War II, need for reorganization, discussion of role of Office of the Secretary of Defense agencies in new plan, and coordination with military.

Adm. Radford, Joint Chiefs of Staff: Situation of Cold War, need for central administration, discussion of Joint Chiefs' responsibilities, possibility of harming the Marine Corps, need for separate services.

Perkins McGuire, Defense Department: Supply and logistics under proposed reorganization, need for uniform policies standardization, problems of parochialism.

Discussion of legal authority of Defense Secretary, ability of Secretary to function as single management, complexity of supply problems.

Murray Snyder, Defense Department: Defense Department public affairs, increased need for information, Defense Department classification problems.

Discussion of size of military public affairs, potential conflict between Defense Department and services on information policies.

Asst. Sec. Sprague, Defense Department: International Security Affairs' responsibilities, development of defense positions, use by Secretary.

Discussion of role of State Department, potential conflict with services, military assistance role.

Gen. White, Air Force: Need for quick weapons systems development, advantages of unified command, discussion of potential conflict between chiefs and unified commanders.

*Hearings on Military and Naval Construction* (May, June 1958)

Asst. Sec. Bantz, Navy: Naval construction, Bureau of Yards and Docks program.

Gen. Rentz, Air Force: Strategic Air Command program for bomber and tanker relocation, warning line, alert facilities.

*Hearings on Naval Ship Loan Program* (June 1958)

Adm. Rittenhouse, Navy: Need to defend sea lanes, responsibilities of allies, discussion of Ship Loan program details.

*Hearings on Armed Services Procurement Regulations and Departmental Implementation, Subcommittee for Special Issues* (July 1958)

Courtney Johnson, Army: Army procurement procedure, local procurement boards, procurement training.

Discussion of procurement waste, procurement regulation.

Brig. Gen. Engler, Army: Details of Army procurement organization.

Col. Treasy, Air Force: Air Force procurement structure, training programs.

FOREIGN AFFAIRS COMMITTEE

*Mutual Security Act of 1958* (February 1958)

Brig. Gen. Guthrie, Army:  Military Assistance
Advisory Group functions and operations, discussion
of its administration.
Asst. Sec. Sprague, Defense Department:  Discussion of Military Assistance Advisory Group delivery
of weapons--intermediate-range ballistic missiles,
advanced aircraft, new missiles, discussion of Hobfield Report.
Sec. Dulles, State Department:  Soviet economic
penetration, requirements for deterrence.
Discussion of Middle East doctrine; discussion
of foreign aid inefficiency.
Sec. McElroy, Defense Department:  Necessity of
program.
Discussion of deterrence, role of forward-based
attack carriers, Strategic Air Command, and intercontinental ballistic missile development and need
for intermediate-range ballistic missile bases.
Gen. Twining, Joint Chiefs of Staff:  Military
potential of allies greatly improved.
Discussion of capacity of NATO.
Asst. Sec. Sprague, Defense Department:  Accomplishments of Military Assistance Program, status
of funds, FY 1959 program.
Capt. Robbins, Defense Department:  Military aid
in Far East, Chinese threats, U.S. agreements, major items in Far East program, strategic importance
of Far East, discussion of specific nation programs.
Asst. Sec. Palmer, State Department:  Events in
Africa, Soviet threat, countries participating in
program (Ethiopia and Libya).
Asst. Sec. Rountree, State Department:  Middle
East and South Asia--Baghdad Pact, countries participating in aid programs.
Testimony by representatives from private groups
and congressmen in support of and opposition to

specific proposals in aid bill.

Gen. Norstad, Air Force:  Purpose of NATO, the 1954 plan, possibility of limited war.

Discussion of NATO atomic stockpile, national contributions.

Col. Hanford, Army:  Latin American regional aid, strategic materials, countries and expenditures, U.S. military training missions.

Summary statements on country programs under mutual security program.


GOVERNMENT OPERATIONS COMMITTEE


*Use of Defense Support Funds for Economic and Social Purposes, Subcommittee* (January 1958)

C. Douglas Dillion, State Department:  Defense support necessary for political stability, history of program, expansion to include all non-military aid received by a country also receiving military assistance.

Discussion of aid level determination.

James Smith, International Cooperation Administration:  Military aid creates economic status, instability alleviated by defense support.

John Holcombe, International Security Affairs: Relationship of defense support to Military Assistance Advisory Group and to Vietnam, Military Assistance Advisory Group mission in NATO countries.

Discussion of Military Assistance Advisory Group policy.


*Military Air Transportation, Subcommittee* (January, February 1958)

Stuart Tipton, Air Transportation Association: Need for large airlift capability, reliance on civil air carriers, phase down of Military Air

Transport Service, Civil Reserve Air Force proposal
for airlift expansion.

Discussion of costs, role of Military Air Transport Service, airlift duplication.

Maj. Gen. Doyle (Ret.), Air Force: Role of independent airlines, phase down of Military Air
Transport Service.

Testimony from airline representatives on need
for civilian owned and operated system of military
air transportation.

Maj. Gen. Yount, Army: Army transportation requirements, discussion of Army government and private aircraft usage.

Asst. Sec. Sharp, Defense Department: Objectives of Military Air Transport Service--size
related to Defense Department's airlift needs for a
general war. Military Air Transport Service training and operations go beyond civilian carriers.

Discussion of whether Civil Reserve Air Force
would meet military requirements.

Further testimony by Air Force personnel on operations and costs of Military Air Transport Service.


*Research and Development, Part 1* (January, February
1958)

Alan Waterman, National Federation of Scientists: Place of the United States in world scientific activity, Soviet efforts, United States still
paramount in basic research.

Discussion of Soviet science and science education, weaknesses in U.S. research. Federal role in
encouraging research, rocket development, role of
universities in basic research.

Peter Schenk, Air Force Association: Need for
drastic reorganization of military research and development, decentralized research and development,
increased expenditures, relaxed security.

Discussion of Advanced Research Projects Agency's role in research and development, over-
bureaucratization.

L. V. Berker, Association of Universities:  Need greater secondary school emphasis on science and mathematics, need greater federal support.

C. C. Funas, University of Buffalo:  Current role of United States in science, Soviet achievements, need for larger government science effort.

Ivan Getting, Raytheon Corp.:  Technological race, need for government support.

Brig. Gen. Starbird, Atomic Energy Commission: History of Atomic Energy Commission's nuclear testing, research requirements, cooperation with Defense Department.

Lt. Gen. Gaun, Army:  U.S.S.R.-U.S. missile race, continuation of Cold War.

Discussion of possibility of surprise attack, Army research and development, the Jupiter program, U.S.S.R.-U.S. conventional strength.

Dr. Houde, Purdue University:  Management of research and development programs, Army research and development programs, Soviet intercontinental ballistic missile efforts.

Dr. Turkeuch, Princeton University:  Soviet scientific advances, government and science.


--*Part 2*

Asst. Sec. Norton, Navy:  Navy research and development expenditures, extent of research, study contracts, new aircraft, other research programs.

Asst. Sec. Horner, Air Force:  Air Force accomplishments, organization, bomber and missile programs.

William Martin, Army:  Army research and development spending, new projects, organization.

Asst. Sec. Foote, Defense Department:  Defense Department research and development expenditures, research duplication, intercontinental ballistic missile programs, basic research.

## JOINT COMMITTEES OF HOUSE AND SENATE

### JOINT ATOMIC ENERGY COMMITTEE

*Amending the Atomic Energy Act of 1954, Subcommittee on Agreements for Cooperation* (January, February, March, April, May 1958)

Lewis Strauss, Atomic Energy Commission: Amending act to provide for greater sharing of information and utilization of nuclear facilities.

Discussion of attempts to guard against proliferation, aimed at countries already possessing nuclear capability.

Adm. Rickover, Navy: U.S.-British submarine cooperation, concern that exchange might hamper U.S. defense efforts.

Discussion of U.S.S.R. reactor programs, possibility of secrets falling into Soviet hands.

Gen. Starbird, Army: U.S.-NATO cooperation, discussion of cooperation under proposed measure-- supplying both military personnel and materials for nuclear weapons.

Statements by representatives of religious and peace groups opposed to amendments.


*Physical Research Program, Subcommittee on R&D* (February 1958)

Dr. Seaborg, University of California: Importance of basic research to practical applications, allegation that basic research not adequately funded.

Testimony of scientists on overall state of the field; projected applications for nuclear power.


*AEC Authorization Legislation, Subcommittee on Legislation* (May, June 1958)

K. E. Fields, Atomic Energy Commission: Importance of nuclear accelerator research on arms control.

JOINT DEFENSE PRODUCTION COMMITTEE

*Mobilization Programs of Office of Civil Defense and Defense Mobilization* (1958)

Leo Hoegh, Defense Department: Merger of two agencies, duties; proposal for federal-state program will not create great bureaucracy. States have acted on requests, federal funding delayed by Congress. Examples of state action.
Discussion of fallout shelter costs.

*Adequacy of Preparedness Programs to Meet Nuclear Attack and Limited Scale War* (July 1958)

Leo Hoegh, Office of Civil Defense Mobilization: Responsibilities of Office of Civil Defense Mobilization, requirements for survival. Federal survival studies and federal-state matching programs.
Discussion of medical care, information dissemination, warning system requirments. Discussion of federal-state interface.
H. B. McCoy, Commerce Department: Mobilization planning in the Commerce Department, need for flexibility in administration of civil defense programs, need to maintain Commerce Department's civil defense responsibilities.
Discussion of civil defense duplication, impracticality of civil defense schemes.
Under Sec. Morse, Agriculture Department: Food stockpiles, Department of Agriculture rural expansion program.

SENATE COMMITTEES

APPROPRIATIONS COMMITTEE

*DOD Appropriations for FY 59* (1958)

Sec. McElroy, Defense Department: Budget formulation, increase in military personnel, additional
funds in budget due to Polaris, Titan, B-52G and
KC-135, Strategic Air Command conversion, Snark
missile, B-58 delivery, intermediate-range ballistic missile production, Fleet Ballistic Missile
program, Regulus, nuclear attack carrier, Bomarc,
antiballistic missile.

Gen. Twining, Joint Chiefs of Staff: House cut
restoration required.

Sec. McElroy, Defense Department: Congressional
action on budget, adequacy of research and development, Polaris tests, Institute for Defense Analysis
role, Sputnik launch, limited-war capability, discussion of Army reduction.

Sec. Brucker, Army: Jupiter, intermediate-range
ballistic missile, Army pentomic division conversion, need for mobility, antiballistic missile
research--Nike-Hercules, Nike-Zeus, solid-fuel Pershing missile.

Discussion of decline in manpower, Reserve,
Guard programs.

Gen. Taylor, Army: Army airlift must be modern-
ized, development and use of tactical nuclear weapons, operational units, worldwide deployment of
major units, need for strategic Army forces.

Sec. Gates, Navy: Soviet surface and submarine
menace, operating forces, Polaris increase, Regulus
II, second nuclear carrier denied, antisubmarine
warfare.

Discussion of research and development programs,
availability of scientists, nuclear powered carrier.

Adm. Burke, Navy: Soviet "creeping aggression,"

Soviet threat in Mediterranean, antisubmarine warfare capabilities, missions of carriers, world
merchant fleet by flag and tonnage.

Gen. Pate, Marine Corps: Operating forces, use
of helicopters in operations, need for new landing
craft.

Dep. Sec. Quarles, Defense Department: Research
and engineering program, role of Advanced Research
Projects Agency, research and development expenditures, scientist recruitment, manned satellites,
atomic aircraft, antiballistic missile development.

Asst. Sec. Foote, Defense Department: Weapons
Systems Evaluation Group, procurement procedures.

William Holaday, Guided Missiles: Total program
costs, air-breathing missiles, Polaris, management
problems.

Roy Johnson, Advanced Research Projects Agency:
Advanced Research Projects Agency role, antiballistic missile research, military reconnaissance satellites, space mission.

Asst. Sec. McNeil, Defense Department: House
cuts, requested restorations, justifications, Military Assistance Program, major functional cost categories, summary of expenditures by service and
category.

Sec. Douglas, Air Force: House cut, need for
balance between aircraft missile procurement, Minuteman, Hound Dog programs, Strategic Air Command
dispersal.

Gen. White, Air Force: Soviet airpower, Air
Force capabilities, Distant Early Warning line,
tactical forces.

Discussion of unit cost of B-52G, Snark production, B-70 development, B-58 introduction.

Sen. Allott: Need for greater research and development expenditures.

Statements by service heads on proposed funding.

Adm. Rawson, Navy: Navy research and development, Terrier, Tartar, Talos and Sidewinder programs, Polaris research.

Sen. Jackson: Need for more B-52B's, importance
of manned bombers, role of the Hound Dog, high priority of KC-135's.

Maj. Gen. Webster, Air Force: Retaliatory
forces, missile--Hound Dog, Quail, Rascal, Minuteman, B-70.
   List of missile programs, characteristics, guidance, launch characteristics.
   Statements by civil air carriers on adequacy of
airlift; Civil Reserve Air Force proposal.


ARMED SERVICES COMMITTEE


*FY 1958 Supplemental Military Construction Authoriza-
tion (CAF)* (January 1958)

   Asst. Sec. Bryant, Defense Department: Missile
construction and missile detection systems--Sage
and Distant Early Warning line. Discussion of Advanced Research Projects Agency responsibilities.
   Sec. Douglas, Air Force: Need to maintain bomber readiness--warning, alert facilities, and
dispersal. Discussion of tanker dispersal, intermediate-range ballistic missile emplacement, ballistic missile detection.
   Lt. Gen. Putt and Lt. Gen. Rentz, Air Force:
Distant Early Warning line and Sage, discussion of
possibilities of antiballistic missile and negotiations with allies concerning intermediate-range
ballistic missile emplacement.
   Robert Techert, Office of the Secretary of Defense: Legal status of new agency for space, discussion of administration of Vanguard program.


*Inquiry into Satellite and Missile Programs, Pre-
paredness Investigation Committee, Part 2* (January
1958)

   Rear Adm. Rickover, Navy: Problems of defense
management, need for services to possess own scientific expertise. Need to train students in scientific expertise.

Discussion of Admiral Rickover's conflicts with
other service personnel.  Discussion of the
submarine-launched ballistic missile concept, need
for competent people in defense establishment.

Lt. Gen. Gavin, Army:  Discussion of Gavin's retirement, objection to "deterioration of military
forces."

Discussion of need for larger Army forces
equipped with tactical nuclear weapons.

Gen. White, Air Force:  Discussion of air defense capability--F-108 and Bomarc missile.  Discussion of sufficiency of bomber and tanker force.

Maj. Gen. Schriever, Air Force:  Air Force on
schedule in Thor research and development, satis-
faction with the project.  Discussion of Atlas and
Titan program, Titan hardness.  Prediction of reconnaissance satellites.

Maj. Gen. Medaris, Army:  Jupiter program, role
of Von Braun group, Jupiter program ahead of schedule.  Difference in Army and Air Force development
approaches.

Asst. Sec. Merton, Navy:  Regulus program, Polaris solid fuel program.

George Bunker, Martin Co.:  Titan contract,
progress on Titan program, discussion of Titan
delays.

Mervin Kelly, Bell Laboratories:  Bomarc program, Talon-Nike controversy, possibilities of
ballistic missile defense.

Gen. Twining, Joint Chiefs of Staff:  Restate-
ment of position on U.S.-Soviet military balance,
United States in superior position.  Discussion of
the manned bomber program and major missile programs.

Witnesses include defense contractors on status
of their respective programs.

Gen. LeMay, Air Force:  KC-135 procurement, need
for maintaining manned bombers.  Question of intercontinental ballistic missile reliability.

Lt. Gen. Putt, Air Force:  Soviet intermediate-
range ballistic missile capability, introduction of
Dynasoar program, slow pace of nuclear rocket research.

Sec. McElroy, Defense Department:  Discussion of mobility of Jupiter, submarine gap, capability of airlift and status of Nike-Hercules.

Discussion of interservice duplication, need for Pentagon reorganization, future of Snark program.

--*Part 3* (April, July 1958)

Sec. McElroy, Defense Department:  Increase in FY 1959 authority, increase in Atlas, Thor, and Jupiter programs, establishment of Advanced Research Projects Agency, progress in intercontinental ballistic missile detection.

Discussion of decision on future of B-52's, capability of airlift and Army unhappiness and important emphasis on Polaris.

Dep. Sec. Quarles, Air Force:  Acceleration of KC-135 program.

Gen. Twining, Joint Chiefs of Staff:  Comparison of Soviet and American military strength.

Discussion of methods of comparison.

*Naval Vessels* (May 1958)

Adm. Burke, Navy:  Need of allies for antisubmarine warfare loan ships, Latin American in particular.

Discussion of European and Latin American naval activities and capability of vessels being loaned to allies.

*Military Construction Authorization for FY 1959* (May June, July 1958)

Maj. Gen. Schriever, Air Force:  Air Force missile program, industrial team concept, important milestones in development.

Col. Lombard, Air Force:  Location of missile facilities.

*Department of Defense Reorganization Act of 1958*
(June, July 1958)

Sec. McElroy, Defense Department: Need for unified command, office of Director, Defense Research
and Engineering, and clarification of Secretary of
Defense's responsibilities. Need to establish Secretary's clear-cut control over three military departments and safeguards for continued service
existence. Need to do away with service duplication and rivalry.

Discussion of Thor-Jupiter competition, congressional authority in defense, need to coordinate
missile development and role of Director of Defense
Research and Engineering and Advanced Research
Projects Agency.

Gen. White, Air Force: Provision for unified
and specified combatant commands, necessity that
Defense Secretary's command clear. Need to cut
down Pentagon duplication in U.S. development.

Discussion of Strategic Air Command's role in
reorganization, planning function of the Joint
Chiefs and congressional prerogatives.

Adm. Burke, Navy: Importance of defense organizations, role of services as administrative units;
supports Joint Chiefs' role of major strategic
planner.

Discussion of Joint Chiefs of Staff organization, Navy organization.

Ferdinand Eberstadt: Need to make proposed legislation more specific; disturbing tendency toward
centralization, will create more inefficiency.
Criticizes growth of Office of the Secretary of Defense and congressional weakness in defense issues.

Discussion of utility of unified commands, experience in World War II, questions of Joint Chiefs
of Staff organization.

Gen. Gates (Ret.), Marine Corps: Proposal over-
steps separation of powers between Congress and the
Executive, dangerous "blank check" philosophy in
defense organization, dangers of overcentralization
and unification.

Otto Nelson, Chamber of Commerce: Generally
supports reorganization, but disagrees with retention of service secretaries; need to supply Secretary of Defense with necessary flexibility and
control.

Discussion of Secretary of Defense's prerogatives under reorganization.

Statements from various Reserve and National
Guard groups opposing legislation as putting too
much power in the Secretary.

Sec. McElroy, Defense Department: Discussion of
U.S. decisions and service assignments, role of
Congress in U.S. decisions.

Descriptions of how Defense Department is organ-
ized, flow of command and decision-making processes.
Discussion of Soviet tactics, Khrushchev's "We will
bury you" speech. Discussion of Armed Services
Committee's role in defense budget—manpower, equipment, and construction.

Gen. Taylor, Army: Necessity of unified commands for strategic planning, and augmentation of
Joint Chiefs of Staff.

Discussion of plan's effect on Army, Reserve,
and National Guard. Discussion of Army and Air
Force—defense competition.

Gen. Pate, Marine Corps: Fear of role of Marines in reorganization, need for congressional
control over roles and missions of services.

Discussion of Joint Chiefs' decisions to reduce
the size of Marine Corps.

Adm. Carney (Ret.), Navy: Limited support for
concept of unified commands, proposed legislation
goes too far.

Discussion of unified planning in World War II.

Gen. Spaatz (Ret.), Army Air Force: Excessive
waste in Defense Department, need to vest full executive authority in the Secretary of Defense.

Discussion of U.S. assignments and Nike-Talos
controversy.

Adm. Radford, Joint Chiefs of Staff: Need for
increased research and development coordination,
support for unified command concept.

*Amending Civil Defense Act* (July 1958)

Leo Hoegh, Federal Civil Defense Administration:
Need to strengthen civil defense, 50-50 federal-
state sharing plan.

*Construction of Naval Vessels* (July 1958)

Vice Adm. Combs, Navy:  Need for amphibious
ships and conversion, discussion of Marine airlift.
Rear Adm. Mumma, Navy:  Size of many shipbuilding authorizations, tonnage in various categories.

FOREIGN RELATIONS COMMITTEE

*Review of Foreign Policy, 1958, Part 1* (February,
March 1958)

Gen. Twining, Joint Chiefs of Staff:  United
States strong enough to deter attack.  Polaris system going ahead, comparison of forces, Soviet
forces growing in effectiveness, B-52 replacement,
nuclear attack submarines, century-series fighter.
Discussion of education impact of U.S. military
strength, Soviet education, possibility of limited
war, training costs for Air Force personnel, status
of Jupiter-C program.

*--Part 2* (May 1958)

Asst. Sec. Robertson, Defense Department:  Far
East situation, Communist economic offensive, SEATO
accomplishments.
Maj. Gen. Willoughby (Ret.), Army:  Geopolitical
position of U.S.S.R., Communist expansion, naval
strength in Pacific.
Appendix:  Location of U.S. and Soviet army

divisions; cost per unit of divisions in NATO, SEATO; location of U.S. and Soviet divisions in the Far East.

*--Part 3*

Ambassador Merchant, State Department: Ballistic missile early warning system, start negotiations with Canada.

*--Part 4*

Asst. Sec. Elbrick, Defense Department: U.S.S.R. relations, political unity in Europe, West German sentiment against intermediate-range ballistic missile bases.

James Warburg: Proposal of U.S.-Soviet troop withdrawal in Germany.

Sec. Dulles, State Department: Basic goals of United States and Soviet policy, collective defense agreement, no risk of accidental nuclear war.

*MSA of 1958* (March, April 1958)

Sec. McElroy, Defense Department: Communist threat, alliance system, need to improve NATO, U.S. programs in India and Pakistan, the purpose of defense support.

Discussion of intermediate-range ballistic missile placement in England, balance of payments problem.

Asst. Sec. Sprague, Defense Department: Criticisms of military assistance, accomplishments of Military Assistance Program, extent of allies' contribution. Functional breakdown of Military Assistance Program.

Adm. Stump, Navy: Importance of military assistance in Far East, Military Assistance Advisory Group in Vietnam, Communist strength in Far East.

Sec. Dulles, State Department: Soviet economic
offensive, different elements of aid program.
Region-by-region situations. Country-by-country
contribution to the common defense.

Discussion of adequacy of economic aid.

Gen. Norstad, NATO: History of NATO, NATO organization, nuclear strike forces, NATO airfields.

Asst. Sec. Rountree, State Department: Middle
East, South Asia, and Africa; major developments
and components of aid program.

Asst. Sec. Robertson, State Department: Far
East; developments and aid program, military
strength, strategic interests.

Asst. Sec. Jandrey, State Department: Europe;
developments, aid program.

Asst. Sec. Rubottom, State Department: Latin
American situation, aid program.

Testimony of private witnesses on foreign aid
program.

## GOVERNMENT OPERATIONS COMMITTEE

*Disapproving Reorganization Plan No. 1 of 1958, Sub-
committee for Civil Defense* (June 1958)

William Finan, Bureau of the Budget: Integration of Office of Defense Mobilization and Federal
Civil Defense Administration, overlapping responsibility, creation of Office of Defense and Civil
Mobilization in Executive Office.

Discussion of responsibilities, current status
of organization, nature of new organization.

Gordon Gray, Office of Defense Mobilization:
History of Office of Defense Mobilization, present
bureaucratic difficulties, changes in concept of
"mobilization."

Leo Hoegh, Federal Civil Defense Administration:
Need for integration.

Walter Halstead, Civil Defense Council: Plan is

vague, government indifferent to civil defense problems.

# 1959 CONGRESSIONAL HEARINGS

## 86th Congress, First Session

HOUSE COMMITTEES

ARMED SERVICES COMMITTEE

*Hearings on Bill to Construct Amphibious Warfare Vessels and Landing Craft* (1959)

    Vice Adm. Beakly, Navy:  Need for assault ship (LPH) and amphibious transport dock (LPD).  Improvement in antisubmarine warfare.
Discussion of hydrofoil technology.

*Hearings to Extend Draft Law* (January 1959)

    Asst. Sec. Finucane, Defense Department:  Defense Department draft policies, enlistment rates, volunteers and inductees.
    Rev. Taylor:  Opposition to the draft.

*Military Posture Briefing* (February 2, 1959)

    Sec. McElroy, Defense Department:  Nation remains strong, moving faster with Polaris and intercontinental ballistic missiles, better utilization of manpower.  Importance of acquisition, Atlas, Titan, and Minuteman bomber programs.  Importance

of Strategic Air Command, lessons of Lebanon experience, need for new carrier.  Air defense needs.

Discussion of missile gap, creation of Director
of Defense Research and Engineering, changes in
budget formulation.  Discussion of Army strength,
Reserve strength, missile gap, budget stringency,
Nike-Zeus.  Discussion of prerogatives of assistant
secretaries of defense.

Gen. Twining, Joint Chiefs of Staff:  Soviet capabilities, prospects for limited war, degree of
risk in budget, carrier request, discussion of history of intercontinental ballistic missile program.

*Military and Naval Construction* (March 1959)

Bill to authorize construction at military installations.

*Weapons System Management and Team System Concept in
Government Contracting, Subcommittee for Special Investigations* (April, May, June, July, August 1959)

John Atwood, North American Aviation:  North
American's achievements, organization, complexity
of modern systems, history of contracting since
World War II, operation procedures, competitions,
contracts, relationship with services.

Robert Gross, Lockheed Aircraft:  Discussion of
Lockheed, approaches to weapons system management,
"system" team approach, defense profits.

J. V. Marsh, General Dynamics Corp.:  The weapons system concept, development of intercontinental
ballistic missiles.

Philip Taylor, Air Force:  Air Force approach to
development, role of Ramo-Wooldridge in intercontinental ballistic missile development, Air Force
management techniques in source selection.

Cecil Milne, Navy:  Navy procurement policies,
contracting procedures, role of General Accounting
Office.

George Bunker, Martin Company: Mace contract, Air Force-Martin cooperation, Titan development, cost-plus-fixed fee contracting.

*Amendments to Reserve Officers Personnel Act, Subcommittee #3* (May, June, July 1959)

Discussion of amendment to Reserve Officers' Act to accelerate Reserve promotions. Witnesses include active, reserve, and retired officers.

*Special Subcommittee on Utilization of Military Manpower* (May, July, August 1959, February 1960)

Witnesses and testimony include wide range of military, government, and private witnesses discussing military distribution and allocation of manpower, military rotation, civilian contractual services, comparative federal compensation.

*Adequacy of Transportation in Support of the National Defense Effort in the Event of Mobilization* (July, August 1959)

Sec. Allen, Commerce Department: Highway transportation history, during World War II and recent developments, national system of defense highways.
Theodore Hardeen, Defense Air Transportation Administration: Mobilization capacity in air industry, air carrier inventory.
Discussion of civilian reserve fleet, manpower needs.
Hermann Bretsch, Federal Aviation Administration: Mobilization capacity.
Leo Hoegh, Office of Civil Defense Mobilization: Plans for mobilization during a nuclear attack, need to maintain all transportation systems.
Kenneth Tuggle, Interstate Commerce Commission: History of Interstate Commerce Commission and

defense, role of railroads and motor carriers, oil
pipelines; and discussion of nationalization during
war emergency.

Perkins McGuire, Defense Department: Defense
Department Supply and Logistics, military requirements in emergency, military traffic management.

Maj. Gen. Besson, Army: Military Traffic Management Agency, mobilization requirements.

Capt. Lewellen, Navy: Logistical requirements,
Navy planning.

Col. Hedlund, Air Force: Airlift requirements,
planning, LOGAIR system, role of Military Air
Transport Service.

Maj. Gen. Morris, Military Traffic Management
Agency: Role of agency, civil-military comparisons, discussion of major transportation systems.

Vice Adm. Gano, Military Sea Transportation
Service: Need for ocean transportation, NATO pool
of shipping.

Lt. Gen. Tunner, Military Air Transport Service:
Military Air Transport Service role, equipment,
capacity in war time.

Maj. Gen. Cooper, Federal Aviation Administration: Plan for national air cargo fleet, discussion of military-industrial relationship.

Stuart Tipton, Air Transport Association: Need
for private air cargo capability, discussion of
separate Military Air Transport Service and private
roles.

Number of witnesses from private sector transportation associations and concerns testifying in
favor of government subsidies for increased transportation systems.


*Employment of Retired Military and Civilian Personnel
by Defense Industries, Committee for Special Investigations* (July, August, September 1959)

Lengthy testimony by defense contractors and retired service personnel in industry. Witnesses
include Admiral Rickover discussing contractor

pressure and Senator Javits presenting legislation
to restrict military personnel from serving with
defense industry.


FOREIGN AFFAIRS COMMITTEE


*Mutual Security Act of 1959* (March 1959)

Sec. Herter, State Department: Economic challenge of the Soviets, need for development.
Discussion of International Cooperation Administration management, size of aid package.
Sec. McElroy, Defense Department: Importance of
military aid, successes in Nationalist China, Vietnam, and NATO, importance of forward bases for
Strategic Air Command, overseas bases for Army and
Navy.
Gen. Twining, Joint Chiefs of Staff: Discussion
of Dryden Report's recommendation for increased assistance to NATO, size of Free World forces
expense, programming, cost sharing.
Asst. Sec. Irwin, Defense Department: Discussion of Military Assistance Program—alliance structures, management accomplishments in regional
areas.
Testimony of government officials and private
citizens on the economic aspects of developmental
assistance.
Military Assistance Program representative furnished carry-over analyses by category.
Gen. Norstad, NATO: NATO mission, Military Assistance Program vital to NATO effectiveness, NATO
command structures, ability to compel a pause in
European conflict vital.
Discussion of shield strategy, limited war unlikely, need for American commitment to keep
alliance intact. Discussion of current deficiencies and comparative European defense budgets,
and possible Soviet and Warsaw Pact strategies.

Asst. Sec. Saterthwaite, State Department:
Emergence of independent Africa, strategic assets,
Communist threat to Africa.

Rear Adm. Grantham, Defense Department:  Middle
East and South Africa--military interests, regional
programs, Lebanon experience.

Asst. Sec. Snow, State Department:  Latin American program, State Department-Military Assistance
Program, special programs, military expenditures as
percentage of gross national product.

Brig. Gen. Felkes, National Guard Association,
Citizens for Aid Committee:  Military Assistance
Program wasteful, better spent on strategic air
power.

Capt. Howe, Defense Department:  Communist
threat in Far East, Military Assistance Program
activities.

Maj. Gen. Guthrie, NATO:  Military Assistance
Program activities in NATO, specific programs in
NATO.

Adm. Radford (Ret.), Navy:  Report on study of
Military Assistance Program--program is vital, proposed budget minimum.

*Current Situation in the Far East* (July, August 1959)

Asst. Sec. Parsons, State Department:  Situation
in Vietnam, nature of Communist menace, need for
strong Vietnam.

Raymond Moyer, International Cooperation Administration:  Vietnam aid, need for better government
management, Military Assistance Advisory Group
activities.

Ambassador Elridge Durbrou, State Department:
Aid program in Vietnam, disputes "waste" criticism.

Lt. Gen. Williams, Army:  Military Assistance
Advisory Group program, organization of Vietnamese
army.

GOVERNMENT OPERATIONS COMMITTEE

*Organization and Management of Missile Programs, Sub-committee* (February, March 1959)

Sec. Douglas, Air Force: Air Force commands concerned with missile development, intercontinental ballistic missile development—Atlas, Titan programs, Hound Dog development. History of Air Force missile programs.

Discussion of history, missile lead times, Ramo-Wooldridge role, development costs, and management procedures—contract negotiations, bidding, procurement.

James Doolittle, Space Technology Laboratory: Space Technology Laboratory's activities in ballistic missile research and business operations.

Simon Ramo, Ramo-Wooldridge Company: Ramo-Wooldridge's relations with Space Technology Laboratory.

Sec. Brucker, Army: Arsenal approach to research and development, Army missile achievements, Redstone, Jupiter programs, relations with Advanced Research Projects Agency and National Aeronautics and Space Administration.

Maj. Gen. Medaris, Army: Army transfer of missile responsibilities to National Aeronautics and Space Administration—administration, outside contacts.

Discussion of antiballistic missile program.

Asst. Sec. Bantz, Navy: Navy missile and research programs, management, Polaris Office and Special Projects Office.

Dep. Sec. Quarles, Defense Department: Defense Department missile management (history), Killian Committee, interservice duplication, role of U.S. Evaluation Group, Institute for Defense Analysis and Advanced Research Projects Agency.

Dr. Glennan, National Aeronautics and Space Administration: Space Administration's relations with Defense Department, research projects, relations with the Army, ballistic missile defense research.

William Finan, Bureau of the Budget:  Missile contracting, accounting.

Vice Adm. Rickover, Navy:  Problems of bureaucratic interference, major blocks to development, discussion of research and development management, criticism of "committee approach" to research and development programs.  Exhorts managers to stop dead-end projects.


JOINT COMMITTEES OF HOUSE AND SENATE


JOINT ATOMIC ENERGY COMMITTEE


*AEC Authorization Legislation FY 60, Subcommittee on Legislation* (February, March, April, May 1959)

John McCone, Atomic Energy Commission:  Discussion of new projects, new reactor programs.

Gen. Starbird, Atomic Energy Commission:  Discussion of responsibilities of the Atomic Energy Commission and the Defense Department in nuclear weapons procurement, separation of funds.

Vice Adm. Rickover, Navy:  Operations under the North Pole, need to emphasize attack submarines.


*Review of Naval Reactor Program and Admiral Rickover Award* (April 1959)

Vice Adm. Rickover, Navy:  Reasons for large submarines, improvements of new submarines--*Skate, Skyjack*--over the *Nautilus*, nuclear submarines making conventional submarines obsolete.

Statements by various members of the committee congratulating Admiral Rickover on submarine development.

*Fallout from Nuclear Weapons Tests, Special Subcommittee on Radiation,* Vols. I, II, III (May 1959)

Extensive updating since 1957 on fallout in the
atmosphere, with testimony from Atomic Energy Commission and service representatives and from
private scientists on radiation levels and government efforts to monitor radiation.

*Biological and Environmental Effects of Nuclear War,
Special Subcommittee on Radiation* (June 1959)

Eugene Quindlen, Civil Defense:  Effects of
specified attack on United States—263 weapons de-
livered on 224 cities, total of 1,446 megatons.
Numerous witnesses and extensive testimony by
military, civilians, scientists, and doctors on
effect of nuclear weapons, different types of
nuclear blasts, long-range biological effects,
fallout, strontium 90, fallout shelter protection,
radiation sickness.

*Agreements for Cooperation for Mutual Defense Pur-
poses, Subcommittee on Agreements for Cooperation*
(June, July 1959)

I. B. White, State Department:  Atomic cooperation with NATO allies, need for tactical nuclear
capability, Soviet threats to NATO alliance.  Details of proposals for material transfers for
England, Canada, France, Germany, Greece, the Neth-
erlands, and Turkey.
Discussion of whether "nuclear materials are
weapons"; importance of France to Atlantic Alliance.
Herbert Loper, Defense Department:  U.S.-British
nuclear cooperation, nuclear forces in NATO, French
fuel agreement.
Dr. Willard Libby, Atomic Energy Commission:
Canadian agreement.

Philip Farley, White House Staff: The future of U.S. relations with France, De Gaulle's attitudes, necessity of NATO for France's survival.

*Aircraft Nuclear Propulsion Program, Subcommittee on R&D* (July 1959)

Maj. Gen. Keirn, Air Force: The Advanced Nuclear Propulsion program, need for long-range aircraft, attractiveness of a nuclear-powered aircraft. Need to find an economical basis for developing such an aircraft.

Background of 125-A, concept of a continuously airborne strike force (CAMAL).

Discussion of costs, need to move to new testing concepts, Soviet progress in nuclear engine development.

Gen. White, Air Force: Atomic power—new era of development. Range and endurance crucial problems of development. Support for CAMAL concept.

Discussion of technical problems.

Asst. Sec. Taylor, Air Force: No doubt that nuclear aircraft can fly, questions performance.

Under Sec. Bantz, Navy: Navy needs long-range aircraft, but recognizes serious technical problems.

Discussion of nuclear aircraft as an antisubmarine warfare system.

John McCone, Atomic Energy Commission: History of Advanced Nuclear Propulsion project, technical problems, no immediate military or commercial application.

Discussion of problems, comparability to Nautilus program.

Sec. Gates, Defense Department: Nuclear power represents substantial improvement over conventional aircraft, disagrees that Air Force has a "requirement" for CAMAL type aircraft, proposes modest increase in funding.

Dr. York, Defense Department: Technical problems remaining, technical studies done on aircraft,

discussion of whether existing aircraft companies
blocking nuclear flight.


## SENATE COMMITTEES


## APPROPRIATIONS COMMITTEE


*DOD Appropriations for FY 60* (1959)

Sec. McElroy, Defense Department:  "Hard
choices" in budget, ballistic missile program,
Polaris program progress, ballistic missile early
warning system development, Nike-Zeus research and
development, Strategic Air Command dispersal and
ground alert.  Regulus II, Rascal, Corporal, Redstone, F8V-3 cancellations.

Soviet intercontinental ballistic missile
threat, missile gap exaggerated, cautious with
"worst case" estimates; strengthening U.S. air defense capabilities, modernizing Navy, continuing
low-level nuclear aircraft research, Defense Department reorganization, FY 1960 budget adequacy.

Lists of projects cancelled, intercontinental
ballistic missile development status, Army airlift
capability, new conventionally powered carrier,
research and development duplication.

List of limousines used by Defense Department
officials and costs.

Sec. Brucker, Army:  Strategic Army Corps, Soviet strength, Berlin situation, need for modern-
ization--M-60, Scorpion, Pershing, LaCrosse,
Jupiter, Nike-Zeus.  Budget breakdown.

Gen. Lemnitzer, Army:  Army missions, strength
of break-in divisions, battalions and battle
groups, Army Reserves, reduction in Army strength.
Number of helicopters and light planes in Army division.

Sec. Gates, Defense Department:  Breakdown of
FY 1960 budget, austere current force levels.
  Discussion of Polaris program, status (in time),
aircraft inventory, need for new carrier, discussion of overreliance on Polaris.
  Gen. Pate, Marine Corps:  FY 1960 program,
strengths.
  Adm. Russell, Navy:  Force levels, carrier
operations, Polaris program, statement of budget
reservations.
  Discussion of carrier vulnerability.
  Sec. Douglas, Air Force:  Ballistic missile
program--Minuteman, Sage construction, missile
procurement, satellite programs.
  Discussion of bomber vs. missiles, location of
17 Zone of Interior Strategic Air Command bases,
cost of intercontinental ballistic missiles, Thor
sites in England.
  Gen. White, Air Force:  Soviet threat, Air Force
deterrent posture, B-52 penetration capabilities,
tactical air capabilities, airlift capability,
Dynasoar.
  Discussion of hardening, vulnerability of fixed
bases, the B-70 program, "overkill theory."
  Asst. Sec. McNeil, Defense Department:  Changes
in research and development budget format, Advanced
Research Projects Agency role, cancellation deci-
sions.
  Dr. York, Advanced Research Projects Agency:
Extent of agency role, discussion of missile pro-
gram, Bomarc and Nike-Hercules.
  William Holaday, Defense Department:  Missile
deployment, list of missile programs in existence.
  Asst. Sec. McNeil, Defense Department:  FY 1960
budget, service and functional categories, Defense
Department contracting, budget formulation.
  Statement of Air Force service representatives
on requested command appropriations.
  Sec. Douglas, Air Force:  Air Force missile
programs, discussion of missile obsolescence, Thor
capability, Thor-Jupiter controversy.
  Lt. Gen. Shriever, Air Force:  Ballistic missile

program history, organization of missile program,
Atlas and Titan performance, Minuteman development.

Vice Adm. Hayword, Navy: Navy research and development projects, Polaris, defuse capabilities,
antisubmarine warfare research.

Adm. Raborn, Navy: Polaris test success.

Adm. Burke, Navy: House cuts, appeals to Senate, importance of FRAM program, need for nuclear
attack carrier.


## ARMED SERVICES COMMITTEE


*Missile and Space Activities,* Joint Hearings before
*Preparedness Investigating Subcommittee and Committee
on Aeronautical and Space Sciences* (January 1959)

Sec. McElroy, Defense Department and Gen.
Twining, Joint Chiefs of Staff: Description of
U.S. intercontinental ballistic missile program--
installation, vulnerability of U.S. Atlas and Titan
bases, Polaris successes and Regulus cancellation.

Manned bombers viewed as current deterrent
forces, severe questioning of Administration's missile program and adequacy of budget. Projections
of Soviet missile capability.

Gen. Twining, Joint Chiefs of Staff: U.S. capabilities superior to Soviet, questioning of early
warning system.

Adm. Burke, Navy: Joint Chiefs' functional program review, cancellation of certain programs,
problems of block obsolescence--amount cut out of
Navy budget. Navy antisubmarine warfare programs.

Gen. Pate, Marine Corps: Marine limited-war
capability.

Gen. White, Air Force: B-47 replacement urgent-
ly needed but present budget safe. Need for KC-135
tanker to keep Strategic Air Command modern.

Adm. Burke, Navy: Impossibility of winning
general nuclear war. Need for nuclear carrier.

Gen. White, Air Force:  B-47 phase-out plans, replacement with B-52 and B-58.

Maj. Gen. Schriever, Air Force:  Air Force ballistic missile program.  Forces must be designed to respond after first strike.  Discussion of missile development progress.  Advanced Research Projects Agency intervention in missile program, need for intercontinental ballistic missile dispersal and hardening.

Gen. Taylor, Army:  Lack of modernization in Army; Soviets have completely replaced World War II equipment.  Army budget request and cut, need for more mobility in airlift.

Discussion of size of Soviet army.

Gen. Power, Strategic Air Command:  Philosophies and capabilities of Strategic Air Command—major share of U.S. deterrent.  Need for air base hardening and bomber dispersal.  Allowing initiative to the Soviets for the first strike calls for larger U.S. forces.  B-47 not being replaced rapidly enough, need for more B-58's.

Discussion of Hound Dog program.

Keith Glennan, National Aeronautics and Space Administration:  Space, the great adventure.  Soviet propaganda over space exploits.  Space mission has vital military overtones.

Discussion of Space Administration's disappointment in not receiving Army Ballistic Missile Agency talents.  Discussion of Vanguard program and integrated Space Administration-Defense Department rocket program.  Future uses of satellites.

Dr. York, Defense Department:  Activities of Advanced Research Projects Agency and Office of the Director of Defense Research and Engineering, programs for Thor, Jupiter, Atlas.  Possibility of satellite early warning systems, ballistic missile defense and solid fuel propulsion programs.  Defense research management in the Defense Department.

Werner von Braun, Army:  Soviet space exploits, high-thrust capability, need to develop a 1.5 million pound thrust rocket, size of "booster gap."

*Extension of the Draft* (March 1959)

Rep. Curtis: Draft law has disrupted students'
college work, need to make Reserve system work and
hire more civilians in Defense Department.

John Thomas, National Council of Churches: Opposition to extending draft and universal military
training.

Witnesses from a variety of religious, scientific, farm, and labor groups opposed to extension
of the draft.

Asst. Sec. Finucane, Defense Department: Need
to extend draft authority, rising volunteer rates,
but draft essential to Reserve enlistment program.

Discussion of obtaining medical officers, deferments, different service enlistment rates.

Lt. Gen. Hershey, Selective Service: Deferment
system explained, draft necessary to maintain size
of regular and Reserve forces.

Statements by service chiefs of staff in favor
of maintaining draft.


*Major Defense Matters (Emphasis on FY 1960 Budget and
Berlin Situation), Part 1* (March 1959)

Gen. Taylor, Army: Berlin situation, could not
be locally resisted. Capability of the 7th Army.
Army needs equipment and adequate supplies.

Discussion of limited-war tactics, airlift capa-
bilities, use of tactical nuclear weapons.
Recommendation for a 925,000-man army, mission of
Strategic Army Corps.

Gen. White, Air Force: Berlin a political problem, Joint Chiefs' contingency plans, Air Force
airlift capability, discussion of Civil Reserve
Air Force capabilities.

Discussion of effect of fallout during nuclear
war, level of missile funding for FY 1960, ability
of Strategic Air Command to mobilize, and capabilities of interceptors against Soviet bombers.

Further discussions of B-47 obsolescence, no

alternative to all-out nuclear war with Soviets,
U.S. dependence on manned bombers, Air Force opposition to Nike-Zeus.

Adm. Burke, Navy:  Role of Navy in Berlin a supporting role.  Deployment of ships against Soviet
submarines, growing Soviet naval threat.  Aircraft
carriers are mobile, provide supplement to the Air
Force bomber force; limited size of Soviet bomber
force.  Nike-Zeus system has a long way to go.
Problems with antisubmarine warfare, need to mod-
ernize existing ships.

Discussion of Naval missile programs--Regulus,
Polaris--comparisons of cost with Air Force programs.  Possibility of limited warfare.


--*Part 2* (May, June 1959)


Maurice Stans, Bureau of the Budget:  Duties of
the Bureau, outline of defense budget process.
Joint review of budget with services and Office of
the Secretary of Defense.

Need to review budget on a functional basis,
discussion of spending ceilings.

Discussion of Nike-Zeus costs, Atlas costs and
ability of Bureau of the Budget to obtain service
weapons system reports.  Questioning of advisability of procuring large numbers of B-58's.
Discussion of accelerating intercontinental ballistic missile program and of budget deficit.


*Military Construction Authorization* (March, April
1959)


Col. Johnson, Air Force:  Shift from bomb to
missile attacks, need to change air defenses, area
and point defense concepts, need for ballistic missile defense research, list of technological
developments in missiles and warheads.

Col. Farley, Air Force:  Protective defenses for
Air Force missile programs, Strategic Air Command

readiness, bomber and tanker dispersal, 15-minute
readiness, Hound Dog program.

## Construction of Modern Naval Vessels (April 1959)

Vice Adm. Beakley, Navy: Navy shipbuilding program, amphibious LPD and LPH landing crafts. Antisubmarine warfare capability.

## Nomination of Gen. Lyman Lemmitzer to be Chief of Staff of the Army (April 1959)

Gen. Lemnitzer, Army: Background, use of ground
forces in nuclear wars, discussion of two- or four-
year terms for service chiefs, limited-war contingencies.

## Establishing a Bureau of Naval Weapons (July 1959)

W. B. Franke, Navy: Consumer-producer relationship between naval bureau and operations; need for
shortened lead time for new weapons and effective
procurement. Background of Navy research and development, aircraft and missiles. Greater effectiveness of a single bureau over current
proliferation of responsibilities.
Discussion of vested interests within Navy, need
for missile development.

## Military Procurement: Encouraging Competition (July 1959)

Sen. Williams: Era of American superiority
coming to an end, 1947 procurement regulations that
produced leisurely, time-wasting efforts and con-
centrated on equality of opportunities for defense
contractors must be replaced by attempts to procure
weapons systems as quickly as possible. Equality

of opportunity must be sacrificed for motivation.
    Sen. Bridges:  Opposition to negotiated con-
tracts, need for openly advertised, incentive based
contracting processes.
    Asst. Sec. McGuire, Defense Department:  Pro-
posed act would make formal advertising necessary
for weapons contracting.  Discussion of how procurement techniques affect weapons development,
proposed changes would exempt missile development.
    Witnesses include congressmen from defense-
industry regions, defense contractors, and service
procurement representatives.


*Nomination of Dr. Herbert York to be DDRE* (July 1959)

    Herbert York, Defense Department:  U.S. missile
program, early technical problems, Soviet developments.


FOREIGN RELATIONS COMMITTEE


*Treaty of Mutual Cooperation and Security with Japan*
(1959)

    Sec. Herter, State Department:  Need to revise
1952 treaty, summation of treaty, self-defense
forces allowed, no new U.S. responsibilities with
treaty.
    Miss Esther Rhoads, Friends Committee:  Need for
more rapid withdrawal of U.S. forces from Japan.


*United States Foreign Policy* (January 1959)

    Sec. Dulles, State Department:  Sino-Soviet re-
lations, opposes U.S. recognition of China, situation in Berlin.

*Disarmament and Foreign Policy, Subcommittee on Disarmament, Part 1* (January, February 1959)

Dr. Fisk, U.S. Delegation, Geneva Conference: Detection of underground explosions feasible.

Dr. Romney, Air Force: Agreement that seismologists can detect underground tests.

Phillip Farley, State Department: Impact of new data on negotiations, Soviet concessions without substance, Soviet position on inspection.

William Foster, Surprise Attack Conference: Discussion of U.S.-Soviet discussions on surprise attack, possibility of worldwide system to detect surprise attacks.

Adm. Burke, Navy: Need for large, diversified military force, possibilities of limited war, problem of ship obsolescence, danger of Soviet submarine strength. Expression of confidence in Polaris program.

Gen. Taylor, Army: Effects of test suspension on weapons development--would slow down program.

Gen. White, Air Force: Caution necessary in arms control agreements, advantages of nuclear stockpiles, need to bargain from strength.

Discussion of U.S. and Soviet missile programs.

Dr. Bethe, Cornell University: Nuclear test inspection, use of nuclear tests for peaceful projects, United States ahead of Soviet Union in sophistication of nuclear weapons.

*--Part 2* (February 1959)

George Kennan: U.S. disarmament position too rigid, need for balanced U.S. forces before nuclear disarmament can succeed.

Discussion of Soviet position on inspection, a neutralized Germany, relation of force to prevention of surprise attack.

Arnold Wolfers: Berlin problem, arms control in European zone.

Henry Cabot Lodge, State Department:  U.N. disarmament debate, prospects of Geneva convention,
Soviet attitude toward testing suspension.
Asst. Sec. Irwin, Defense Department:  Disarmament functions of International Security Affairs.
NATO and intermediate-range ballistic missile emplacement, Soviet progress in missile development,
discussion of nuclear weapons transfer to allies.
Jerome Frank:  Psychiatric approach to the arms
race.

*Geneva Test Ban Negotiations, Subcommittee on Disar-
mament* (March 1959)

Ambassador Wadsworth, State Department:  U.S.
Draft Articles, new data on difficulty of detecting
underground tests, Soviet demand for veto, Soviet
position on on-site inspection.
Discussion of basis for Soviet objectives,
Soviet propaganda.

*What Is Wrong with Our Foreign Policy?*  (April 1959)

Hans Morgenthau, University of Chicago:  Overemphasis on military commitments, need for more
initiatives, misperceptions in the Middle East.

*Mutual Security Act of 1959* (April, May 1959)

Adm. Felt, Navy:  Pacific Command, Communist
threat, integration of targeting responsibilities
with Strategic Air Command, discussion of Quemoy
crisis.
Sec. McElroy, Defense Department:  Collective
security vital; United States receives long-term
benefits.
Discussion of criticisms of military aid, dangers of overemphasizing programs, Military Assistance Program in dictatorships.

Asst. Sec. Merchant, State Department: NATO
situation, allies' efforts, use of NATO equipment
in France, concept of "Sword and Shield," proposed
FY 1960 programs.

Asst. Sec. Robertson, State Department: Far
East situation, Chinese threat, country-by-country
programs.

Asst. Sec. Saiterthwaite, State Department:
African nationalism, Communist offensive.

Douglas Dillon, State Department: Military aid
to Pakistan; situation in Kashmir.

Asst. Sec. Rubottom, State Department: Latin
American situation, attempted invasion of Panama.

Asst. Sec. Rountree, State Department: Middle
East and South Asia Military Assistance Program,
country-by-country breakdown.

--*Part 2* (May 1959)

Charles Shuff: Support of FY 1960 program, in-
terdependance of economic and military aid.

William Draper, Presidential Committee to Study
Military Assistance Program: Committee findings;
Communist threat worse, need for greater aid.

Alexander Smith, Presidential Committee to Study
Military Assistance Program: Asian independence,
imperative that aid must continue.

Numerous witnesses on future of aid program,
economic aid.

*Testimony of John McCone on Geneva Test Ban Negotia-
tions, Subcommittee on Disarmament* (June 1959)

John McCone, Atomic Energy Commission: Discussion of an agreement ending tests, dangers of proliferation, fallout problem, seismic detection.

*Situation in Vietnam* (July 1959)

Asst. Sec. Parsons, State Department:  Communist
terrorist activities, South Vietnamese army effective, discussion of corrupt aid practices.

Lt. Gen. Williams, Military Assistance Advisory
Group:  Advisory Group's Vietnam operations, discussion of corruption.


--Part 2, Subcommittee on State Department Organization and Public Affairs

Testimony of U.S. Civilian and military officials concerning charges of corruption in Vietnam
aid program.

# 1960 CONGRESSIONAL HEARINGS

## 86th Congress, Second Session

HOUSE COMMITTEES

APPROPRIATIONS COMMITTEE

*DOD Appropriations for 1961, Part 1* (1960)

Sec. Gates, Defense Department:  Importance of retaliatory forces; manned bombers still primary weapon of deterrence.  Soviets enjoy slight missile lead, will disappear by 1962.  United States possesses superior sea power.  Strategy of shifting to more advanced weapons--B-58, Minuteman, Polaris. Advantages of B-70 over missiles.

Discussion of adequacy of missile intelligence gathering and estimation techniques, antimissile program.

Gen. Twining, Joint Chiefs of Staff:  U.S. missile strength, U.S.S.R. strength.

Sec. Franke, Navy:  Method of Navy budget formulation, Navy's antisubmarine warfare program, major procurement--new carrier, missiles.

Adm. Burke, Navy:  Communist threats, Third World instability, importance of naval aviation.

Discussion of nuclear carrier proposals, vulnerability of carriers.

Gen. Shoup, Marine Corps:  Fleet marine forces, personnel strengths and requirements.

Rear Adm. Yeager, Navy:  Navy antisubmarine

warfare programs, new research and development, vulnerability of carrier.

Adm. Burke, Navy:  Polaris program, role in deterrence.

Sec. Sharp, Air Force:  Changes in the Air Force, missile procurement--Atlas, Titan, Minuteman, new satellite programs.

Gen. White, Air Force:  Air Force bomber capabilities, missile programs, early warning systems.

Discussion of pilot reductions, trends in Air Force planning, role of Polaris in retaliatory forces--not vulnerable; possibility of antimissile missile.

Maj. Gen. Friedman, Air Force:  B-70 a breakthrough, funding, advantages over missiles.

Sec. Brucker, Army:  Soviet army strength, U.S. commitments, Communist aggression.  Army's "forward strategy"--Strategic Army Corps concept.  Need for modernization--new missile programs, Nike-Zeus project.

Gen. Lemnitzer, Army:  Nike-Hercules program, other missile programs.

Discussion of Soviet readiness, adequacy of Army strength, adequacy of airlift, and Red Chinese threat.


--*Part 2:  Financial Statements.*

Testimony by service representatives.


--*Part 3:  Reserve Programs.*

Testimony by service representatives.


--*Part 4:  Operations and Maintenance.*

Testimony by service representatives.

*--Part 5:   Procurement.*

Testimony by service representatives.

*--Part 6:   Research, Development, Test and Evaluations*

Testimony by service representatives.


## ARMED SERVICES COMMITTEE

*Military Construction Authorization* (February, March 1960)

Herbert York, Defense Department:  Changing role of Advanced Research Projects Agency, discussion of role in Office of the Secretary of Defense.
Gen. Curtin, Air Force:  Air Force philosophy in the positioning of hardened silos.
Gen. Seeman, Air Force:  Construction and placement of Nike-Hercules sites.


*Hearings before Special Defense Committee on Utilization of Military Manpower:  Air Force Manuals* (March 1960)

Discussion of Air Force anticommunism indoctrination in Air Force manuals.  Witnesses include Air Force officers.


*Hearings before Special Subcommittee on National Military Airlift* (March, April 1960)

Dep. Sec. Douglas, Defense Department:  General soundness of military airlift capabilities, role of Military Air Transport Service in strategic airlift

and of Tactical Air Command in tactical airlift.
Role of airlift in limited-war situations.

Discussion of C-124, new cargo aircraft.

Sec. Brucker, Army:  Army dependence on Air
Force airlift, need for integration of airlift
capabilities, creation of Strategic Army Corps
strike forces, need to deploy rapidly.

Discussion of capabilities and conditions necessary for rapid deployment.

Sec. Sharp, Air Force:  Need for Military Air
Transport Service modernization, jet cargo aircraft, role of civil air carriers, discussion of
Air Force civil reserve air fleet proposal, need
for civil cargo fleet modernization.

Gen. Lemnitzer, Army:  Discussion of Pine-Big
Slam airlift operation, need for limited-war capabilities, Joint Chiefs' contingency-plan require-
ments--Korea, Middle East, Southeast Asia.
Objection to Air Force civil air fleet proposal;
discussion of world-wide commitments; tactics in a
limited-war situation.

Gen. Wheeless, Air Force:  Airlift experience in
Lebanon, differences between strategic and tactical
airlift, Air Force emphasis on general war operations.

Discussion of Army requirements in Air Force
Military Air Transport Service operation.  Capabilities of C-119, C-130.  Development of new turbine
transport--K-135--"interim aircraft."

Adm. Cooper, Navy:  Testimony classified.

Maj. Gen. Binney, Marine Corps:  Marine doctrine, airlift requirements.

Lt. Gen. Tunner, Military Air Transport Service:
Transport Service history, role and requirements in
general war situation.  Military Air Transport Service aircraft and deployments, discussion of Civil
Reserve Air Force concept, costs; discussion of
Military Air Transport Service role in limited-war
operations.

Col. Oglesby, Air Force:  Discussion of strategic airlift, readiness, contingencies.

Gen. Harrell, Continental Army Council:  Army

requirements for tactical airlift. Types of operation, use of aircraft; discussion of Air Force and Army roles in airlift and Air Force neglect of air support mission.

Maj. Gen. Childre, Tactical Air Command: Tactical Air Command mission, "zone of interior" concept; discussion of Lebanon experience, general war requirements, C-130 deployment capabilities.

Gen. Hester, Air Force: Discussion of Civil Reserve Air Force program, Military Air Transport Service and civil operators—contractual relationship.

Gen. Holloway, Air Force: Development of new cargo plane requirements.

Adm. Cooper, Navy: Navy and Marine airlift requirements, capabilities of R-6D's, relationship with Military Air Transport Service.

Rear Adm. Long, Quick Trans: Navy commercial cargo airlift.

E. R. Quesada, Federal Aviation Administration: Deficiencies in Military Air Transport Service and civil operations; need for new aircraft development.

J. Price, Office of Civil Defense Mobilization: Discussion of military-civilian plans for transport cooperation.

John Allen, Department of Commerce: Difficulty in maintaining civilian reserve cargo fleet.

T. Burwell, Civil Aeronautics Board: Commercial role in air transport.

Witnesses also include major airline executives.


*Special Subcommittee on Procurement Practices of the Department of Defense* (April, May, June 1960)

G. C. Bannerman, Philip Le Boutillier, and James Nash, Defense Department: Defense Department studies of contracts and procurement efficiency, cost principles, price negotiation, cost analysis and auditing.

Courtney Johnson and Brig. Gen. McMorrow, Army:

Army experience in procurement (advertised and negotiated), types of contracts and subcontracting problems.

Fred Bantz and Rear Adm. Stuart, Navy:  Subcontracting competitions, Naval Procurement Objectives System.

Philip Taylor and Maj. Gen. Davis, Air Force: Pricing management, purchasing system, estimating, subcontracting, and procurement training.

Joseph Campbell, General Accounting Office: General Accounting responsibilities, legal basis, types of contracts and General Accounting studies.

Thomas Coggeshall, Renegotiation Board:  Lack of individual contract information possessed by Renegotiation Board studies of contract negotiations.


*Review of the Reserve Program, Hearings before Subcommittee #3* (May 1960)


Stephen Jackson, Defense Department:  Reserve strengths, enlistment rates, requirements and need for reorganization.  Discussion of ROTC programs, reduction of reserve strength, differences with Army.

Richard Jackson, Navy:  Naval reserve progress, Navy ROTC program.

Adm. Brandley, Adm. Smedberg, Gen. Fairbourn, Navy:  Naval and Marine reserve programs.

Dewey Short, Army:  Army Reserve, structure of Army Reserve, ROTC.

Gen. McGowan, Army:  Army Reserve, discussion of Defense Department program of reduction and National Guard.

Gen. Fridge, Air Force:  Air National Guard, ROTC programs.  Discussion of decline in strength.

Gen. Urlson, Air Force:  Air National Guard aircraft, discussion of combat readiness.

Capt. Sands, Coast Guard:  Coast Guard Reserve.

Col. Boyer, Reserve Officers Association:  Need for strong Reserve, more funding.

Howard Markey, Air Force Association:  Need for

modern equipment, airlift improvements.


*Hearings on Development and Procurement of New Combat
and Tactical Vehicles by the Department of the Army*
(June, August, September 1960)

<u>James</u> <u>Campbell</u>, <u>General</u> <u>Accounting</u> <u>Office</u>:
Criticism of Army procurement practices, vehicle
defects; discussion of procurement practices, need
for management control.
Discussion and testimony by Army witnesses on
tactical vehicles' performance and contracting procedures, including tanks, small arms.


FOREIGN AFFAIRS COMMITTEE


*Briefing on Current World Situation* (1960)

<u>Sec</u>. <u>Dulles</u>, <u>State</u> <u>Department</u>:  Importance of
Africa, growing Soviet and Chinese power, Soviet
economic demands, Berlin situation.
Discussion of Soviet economy, Berlin situation,
Soviet tactics.
<u>Under</u> <u>Sec</u>. <u>Dillion</u>, <u>State</u> <u>Department</u>:  Soviet
aid and technical assistance.


*Communist Threat in Latin America* (June 1960)

<u>Asst</u>. <u>Sec</u>. <u>Rubottom</u>, <u>State</u> <u>Department</u>:  Commu-
nist activity in Latin America growing, support for
Cuban revolution.

GOVERNMENT OPERATIONS COMMITTEE

*Organization and Management of Missile Programs,
Part 1* (May 1960)

Dep. Sec. Douglas, Defense Department:  Transfer
of projects to National Aeronautics and Space Administration; Advanced Research Projects Agency's
current status and current missile program--Saturn,
Skybolt, Dynasoar, Nike-Zeus.

*--Part 2*

J. D. Ruina, Defense Department:  Ballistic missile early warning system, Midas, over-the-horizon
radar, Nike-Zeus.
Maj. Gen. Estes, Air Force:  Air Force air defense plans, objectives, interservice cooperation.
Discussion of Nike-Zeus, Bomarc cancellation,
base hardening, completion of Sage.

*--Part 3*

Under Sec. Chauyk, Air Force:  Air Force pro-
grams, Strategic Air Command bombers, Atlas and
Thor deployment, Titan testing.  Report of Air
Force management study committee.
Discussion of Air Force space responsibilities.


JOINT COMMITTEES OF HOUSE AND SENATE


JOINT ATOMIC ENERGY COMMITTEE


*AEC Authorization Legislation FY 61, Subcommittee on
Legislation* (March, April 1960)

John McCone, Atomic Energy Commission:  New construction program, Rover nuclear rocket program,
cooperation with National Aeronautics and Space
Administration.  Discussion of problems with nuclear rocket.

Vice Adm. Rickover, Navy:  Existence of a submarine gap, potential nuclear submarine gap.

Discussion of success of Polaris and Russian
submarine-launched ballistic missile threat.

*Technical Aspects of Selection and Inspection Con-
trols of a Nuclear Weapons Test Ban, Special Subcommittee on Radiation and Subcommittee on R&D* (April
1960)

Dr. Brown, University of Southern California:
Report of Conference of Experts on nuclear test
inspection, high probability of detection in the
atmosphere, in the oceans.

Discussion of seismic detection of underground
tests, "decoupling," physical problems related to
seismic detection.

Wolfgang Panofsky:  Detecting tests in outer
space, relationship with ballistic missile defense,
problems in concealment, problems in negotiating
with the Soviets.

Dr. Romney, Air Force:  Seismic detection, procedures used in detection of underground tests.

Dr. Latter, RAND Corp.:  Decoupling of underground nuclear tests.

Dr. Teller, University of Southern California:
Procedures of decoupling, ease of disguising underground testing, lack of facilities to monitor tests
in space.

Discussion of inspection as only viable means to
insure test ban compliance.

Dr. Bethe, Cornell University:  Possibility of
setting up remote control stations to monitor testing.

Dr. Violt:  Methods of underground testing.

Dr. Foose:  Procedures of on-site inspections.

Dr. Beers:  Detection of cavities resulting from underground testing.

Dr. Leonard:  Space vehicle requirements for detection of space testing.

Dr. Latter:  Need for nuclear explosions for research program to detect nuclear explosions.


--*Part 2* (April 1960)

Appendices:  RAND reports, statements.


*Radiation Protection Criteria and Standards:  Their Basis and Use, Special Subcommittee on Radiation* (May, June 1960)

Extensive hearings with expert witnesses on the application and derivation of radiation standards.


JOINT ECONOMIC COMMITTEE


*Impact of Defense Procurement, Subcommittee on Defense Procurement* (January 1960)

Joseph Campbell, General Accounting Office: Negotiated contracts--90% of total defense contracts, other uneconomical procurement practices, military supply management, concurrent buying and selling, need for overall controls.  Unwarranted new construction, support for McCormack Amendment to use single agencies for procurement.

Discussion of single agency proposal, concentration of procurement.

Franklin Floete, General Services Administration:  General Services' supply program, relations with Defense Department.

C. D. Bear, General Services Administration: Discussion of Eisenhower decision, limiting General

Services' control over service practices.

Ray Ward, General Services Administration: Need
for strengthened General Services; service supply
abuse.

Rep. Whitten: Need for strong domestic economy,
excess service requests, threat to economy, inflation, government intrusion in private industry.

Elmer Staats, Bureau of the Budget: Military
budget estimates, magnitude of government purchases, need for greater General Services responsibility.

Discussion of Bureau of the Budget authority,
supply studies, surplus properties.

Asst. Sec. McGuire, Defense Department: Defense
Department supply management and inventory management, defense material management programs, need
for flexible relations with General Services Administration.

Discussion of procurement policies--competitive
and negotiated bidding.

Perry Shoemaker, Hoover Commission: Size of defense supply activities, integration of common supply activities, improvements in General Services
Administration.


SENATE COMMITTEES


APPROPRIATIONS COMMITTEE


*DOD Appropriation for FY 61* (1960)

Sec. Gates, Defense Department: Adequacy of
budget, moderate Soviet missile superiority, superiority of Strategic Air Command, U.S. naval superiority, continued Polaris construction, B-70
slowdown, Strategic Air Command airborne alert,
dispersal and hardening of Atlas and Titan.
Approval of conventional attack carrier,

Nike-Zeus research and development.

Discussion of U.S. retaliatory capability, carrier program, ballistic missile defense, role of the Bureau of the Budget in budget formulation, B-70 development.

Summary of major military forces, procurement programs.

Sec. Brucker, Army:  Status of Army, Red Chinese threat, situation in Laos, Strategic Army Corps, modern army role, National Guard and Reserve strength.

Gen. Lemnitzer, Army:  Soviet reductions in force, custody of nuclear weapons, Army research and development.

Sec. Franke, Navy:  Submarine program, changes in appropriation structure, major procurement, need for new carrier.

Adm. Burke, Navy:  Budget consideration, Polaris effectiveness.

Discussion of strategic mission differences with Air Force, new carrier (*Enterprise*), FRAM II program, shipbuilding and conversion.

Gen. Shoup, Marine Corps:  Marine strength, changes in military concepts, limited-war capability.

Sec. Sharp, Air Force:  Total request, missile programs, Titan tests, Minuteman progress, ballistic missile early warning system, Midas and Samos satellites, airborne alert.

Gen. White, Air Force:  Air defense, missile programs, bomber strength, B-70 and Dynasoar.

Asst. Sec. Lincoln, Defense Department:  Total request FY 1961.

Discussion of 1958 reorganization of Defense Department, service rivalry, budget breakdown.

Gen. Bradley, Air Force:  Index of aircraft and missile characteristics.

Herbert York, Defense Department:  Defense Department research and development activities, missile program--Nike-Zeus, ballistic missile defense. Discussion of B-70, Skybolt decisions.

Adm. Raborn, Navy:  Polaris program, successful launching.

Gen. Rilaid, Air Force:  Atlas, Titan, and Minuteman programs.

Brig. Gen. Bells, Advanced Research Projects
Agency:  Satellite programs, Nike-Zeus.

Gen. White, Air Force:  Air Force air defense
program--Bomarc, Sage, and ballistic missile early
warning system.

Discussion of B-70, need for manned bomber, Skybolt.

Sec. Franke, Navy:  Need for Forrestal class
carrier, carrier performance characteristics.

Sen. Goldwater:  Limitations of missiles, need
for B-70.


ARMED SERVICES COMMITTEE


*Missiles, Space, and Other Major Defense Matters*
(February, March 1960)

Gen. Power and Gen. Schriever, Air Force:  Strategic Air Command's 15-minute ground alert, importance of worst-case analysis, need for better
intelligence data.  Need for B-70 to replace B-52.
Airborne alert discussed; role of intercontinental
ballistic missiles in Strategic Air Command; next
four or five years dangerous until Minuteman deployed.

Discussion of when B-52 will be obsolete.  Discussion of military uses in space and Soviet intercontinental ballistic missile levels.  Suggestion
that economy could bear increased budget spending.

Dr. Smith, Strategic Air Command:  Strategic Air
Command study of Soviet missile threat and what Soviet capability would be required to knock out air
bases.

Gen. Power and Gen. Schriever, Air Force:  Discussion of Soviet missile study, Soviet submarine-
launched ballistic missile threat, Atlas and Titan
programs.  Necessity of airborne alert.

Maj. Gen. Walsh, Air Force: Discussion of intelligence estimate of numbers of Soviet missiles
and what that figure was based upon.

Discussion of differences in Air Force and Central Intelligence Agency figures.

Gen. White, Air Force: Need for airborne alert,
prevented by budgetary limitation.

Discussion of F-108 cancellation and B-70 cutback, advantages of bombers over missiles. Speed
of B-70 a major aeronautical breakthrough.

Vice Adm. Rickover, Navy: Soviet defense management, technical training superior to U.S.; problems in U.S. education. Soviets' program of world
domination; Soviets have less fear of nuclear war.
U.S. educational standards must be raised, defense
system produces bureaucratic hacks. Executive
branch responsible for U.S. shortcomings. Need for
congressional intercession in defense, better
schools, more discipline. American home must
stress education, triumph over Communist totalitar-
ianism.

Gen. Taylor, Army: Long-term defense strategies
more crucial than short-term emergency measures,
need for new decision-making machinery; never de-
termined how much is enough, never balanced commitments against capabilities; need to revise plans
for limited-war. Problem of frozen service per-
centages and Joint Chiefs of Staff disagreements.

Discussion of Jupiter programs, changes in the
Joint Chiefs of Staff, limited-war and airlift requirements.

Gen. Lemnitzer, Army: Need to fight limited
war, importance of Nike-Zeus and determination of
budget in functional categories.

Discussion of airlift capability, interservice
rivalry, problems of service unification.

Adm. Burke, Navy: Soviet naval strength, submarine superiority. United States vulnerability to
submarine-launched missiles; and Navy problems of
block obsolescence. Navy dissatisfaction with
Polaris program, need for additional submarines.

Discussion of fleet modernization, Polaris

tests, naval aviation capability.  Missiles seen as superior to B-70 capability and Soviet limited-war capability seen as limited.

Gen. Twining, Joint Chiefs of Staff:  Discussion of Strategic Air Command's request for airborne alert, role of manned bomber, delay of B-70.

Discussion of Joint Chiefs' disagreements and decision-making processes, intelligence estimates and estimation of danger during the next five years, variance in Central Intelligence Agency and service estimates.

Sec. Gates, Defense Department:  U.S. strength adequate, including intercontinental ballistic missiles and air defense.  Soviets not engaged in crash intercontinental ballistic missile program, U.S. programs going forward.

Discussion of missile cost overruns and lack of emphasis on limited-war capability.  Discussion of B-70 being considered with other strategic weapons.  Discussion of Soviet-American intercontinental ballistic missile ratio.  Rationale for air alert decision and discussion of Midas system.

*Military Construction Authorization, FY 61* (April 1960)

Asst. Sec. Bryant, Defense Department:  1% of authorization in support of nuclear retaliatory forces, dispersed bomber leases, forward deployed intermediate-range ballistic missile bases and new construction for intercontinental ballistic missile bases, 17% directed toward support of air defense.

*Assistance to Civil Defense by Reserves* (July 1960)

Sen. Curtis:  Need to reorganize Reserves to meet needs of civil defense, importance of civil defense in atomic warfare.  Reserve authority would not change and would remain locally administered.

Discussion of how Reserves would be utilized.

Leo Hoegh, Office of Civil Defense Mobilization:
The operation of civil defense, need for civilian
and military cooperation.  Outline of Reserve
proposal--making Reserve forces temporarily available to civil defense authorities.

Asst. Sec. Finucane, Defense Department:  Military assistance to local authorities a long-
standing U.S. tradition.

Col. Carlton, Reserve Officers Association:  Retired Reserve personnel better suited for civil
defense activities.

Dr. Kennard:  Support for proposal; discussion
of whether it is wise to interrupt combat training
for civil defense role.

## FOREIGN RELATIONS COMMITTEE

*Technical Problems and the Geneva Test Ban Negotia-
tions, Subcommittee on Disarmament* (February 1960)

Dr. Fisk, U.S. Geneva Delegation:  Major areas
of U.S.-Soviet disagreement over test inspection.

Dr. Panofsky, Geneva Group, State Department:
Problems in detecting underground tests.

Phillip Farley, State Department:  Problems
raised by Big Hole theory.

Dr. Tukey, Geneva Group, State Department:  Detection possible, arms agreement primarily a political problem.

*Mutual Security Act of 1960* (March, April 1960)

Sec. Herter, State Department:  Increase in assistance primarily military, program cannot be
abandoned, Communist goals unchanged.

Asst. Sec. Irwin, State Department:  NATO situation, FY 1961 program.

Asst. Sec. Kohler, State Department:  Level of

military aid for Europe viewed as satisfactory.

   Asst. Sec. Gores, State Department:  Middle East
and South Asia situation, increased stability.

   Asst. Sec. Steeves, State Department:  Far
East--Red China growing in power, FY 1961 Military
Assistance Program.


*Event Incident to the Summit Conference, Subcommittee*
(May, June 1960)

   Sec. Gates, Defense Department:  U-2 responsibilities, U-2 produced vital information.


GOVERNMENT OPERATIONS COMMITTEE


*Organizing for National Security, Subcommittee on
National Policy Machinery, Part 1* (February 1960)

   Sen. Jackson:  Purpose of hearing.
   Robert Lovett:  Executive department overlap and
clash of organizational interests.  Department of
Defense, need for national security policy, need to
restore Executive authority.  Problems of civilian
turnover, split Joint Chiefs of Staff, close cooperation with Department of State.
   Discussion of turnover, management, one-year
budget system.
   Robert Sprague:  Need for greater presidential
flexibility in assigning service roles and missions, size of defense budget, Strategic Air Command vulnerability, role of Congress in policy
making.
   Discussion of Soviet spending and U.S. power.
   James Baxter, III, Williams College:  Policy
making in a democracy, U.S. diplomatic history,
effect of arms race, United States can support
larger defense effort.
   Discussion of whether threat increasing or decreasing.

Thomas Watson, I.B.M. Corp.: Soviet industry, threat in underdeveloped world, need for military superiority.

Appendix: "The Nature and Feasibility of War and Deterrence" by Herman Kahn.

*--Part 2*

James Perkins, Carnegie Corp.: Science and national security, need for greater expertise in the military.

Discussion of university research in national security problems, civilian advice, structure of the Office of the Secretary of Defense, reform of Department of Defense and National Security Council.

Appendix: "Delicate Balance of Terror" by Albert Wohlstetter.

James Fisk, Bell Laboratories: Importance of science and technology to national security, functions of the Presidential Science Advisory Committee, possibilities of arms control.

Discussion of research and development spending, interservice rivalry, function of the director of Defense Research and Engineering.

William Pickering, Jet Propulsion Laboratory: Need to define national goals, need for strong government support, more expertise among military and civilian leadership.

Discussion of military uses of space, nuclear rocket engine, scientific expertise in the Defense and State departments.

Dr. Mettler, Space Technology Laboratory: Problems associated with long-range programs, need to define major missions of importance.

Discussion of whether development cycle can be compressed. Comments on government organization.

Eugene Wigner, Princeton University: U.S. and Soviet theoretical advance, Soviet strength in applied sciences, need for balanced science program.

Discussion of research fellowships.

Edward Purcell, Harvard University:  Need to commit government to basic research and to long-range planning.

Herbert York, Defense Department:  Budget cycle, role of Bureau of the Budget, need for better personnel in government, history of RAND.

## --Part 3 (May 1960)

Harold Boschenstein, Owens-Corning Co.:  Problem of attracting talent to government, individuals with business experience.

Roger Jones, Civil Service:  Removing partisan politics from Defense Department, lessons from World War II, changes in Civil Service procedures, discussion of turnover.

Marion Folsom, Eastman Kodak Co.:  Difficulties of businessmen in government, recruiting, promotion.

## --Part 4

Sidney Soers, National Security Council:  Council's operations, relations with State and Defense departments, role of Bureau of the Budget.

Gen. Cuiller, National Security Council:  Council's mission, make-up and operations.

Dillon Anderson, National Security Council:  Discussion of National Security Council operations, relationship of the Council and budgetary process.

## --Part 5

Ambassador Harriman, State Department:  U-2 incident, the White House staff, the Secretary of State, State Department organizational problems.

Adm. Radford, Joint Chiefs of Staff:  White House, National Security Council and Joint Chiefs interaction, role of the Council in formulating defense policies.

Sec. Herter, State Department:  Role of Secretary of State, relations with President and Defense Department.

Discussion of "Super-Secretary" suggestion.

Sec. Gates, Defense Department:  Defense Department organization, sound streamlining command, reforms during the 1960s, the effectiveness of the National Security Council.

Discussion of Defense Department organization, role of Joint Chiefs, meshing of foreign and defense policy.

Gen. Taylor (Ret.), Army:  Problems with national budget, no fixed responsibility, interservice rivalry, predominance of fiscal consideration in budget; present system creates loss of control of the military.  List of suggestions for improvements --functional budgets, better staff guidance, more clearly defined policy.

--*Part 6* (May, June 1960)

George Herman, State Department:  Policy Planning Staff, role of State Department in national security policy, problems of using experts, and problems of State Department overstaffing.

Paul Nitze, State Department:  Department of State organization.

Robert Bowie, State Department:  National Security Council and State Department administration.

# 1961 CONGRESSIONAL HEARINGS

## 87th Congress, First Session

APPROPRIATIONS COMMITTEE

*DOD Appropriations for FY 1962, Part 1* (February, March 1961)

Statement of service representatives on overall military personnel costs.

*--Part 2*

Statement of service representatives on overall operation and maintenance costs.

*--Part 3*

Sec. <u>McNamara</u>, <u>Defense</u> <u>Department</u>: Reappraisal of defense posture, cost changes, major strategic missile programs--speed-up of Polaris and Minuteman programs. Role of strategic aircraft, Skybolt, B-70, Dynasoar slowdowns.

Strengthening of limited-war capability, development of triservice tactical fighter, increase in Army strengths.

Discussion of role of Joint Chiefs of Staff in decision making.

241

Gen. Lemnitzer, Joint Chiefs of Staff: Discussion of military-civilian relationships in the Pentagon, differences of opinion in Joint Chiefs.

Discussion of Nike-Zeus decision, B-70 decision.

Sec. McNamara, Defense Department: Discussion of "deterrent gap," preparedness for limited war.

Sec. Stahr, Army: Army Special Forces, Soviet military capability, airlift capability, new missile programs.

Gen. Decker, Army: Communist threat, Army strength, Strategic Army Corps capability, air defense research.

Discussion of low-level wars, Army modernization, M-14 rifle, M-60 tank, Soviet vs. U.S. equipment, Nike-Zeus development.

Sec. Connally, Navy: Navy budget, Polaris program, limited-war capability, antisubmarine warfare, major procurement.

Adm. Burke, Navy: Polaris program, costs. Major antisubmarine warfare programs, the future of aircraft carriers.

Discussion of F4 Phantom program, manpower, Communist naval strength.

Gen. Shoup, Marine Corps: Fleet Marine forces, personnel strength, new role of amphibious power.

Sec. Zuckert, Air Force: Air Force missions, Strategic Air Command operations, need for manned systems, B-70, and for space capability.

Gen. White, Air Force: Soviet space achievements, Air Force deployment, manned bomber systems, need for B-70.

Discussion of comparative force strengths, Strategic Air Command readiness, mobile Minuteman program.


--Part 4


Testimony of service representatives on research, development, test and evaluation.

*--Part 5*

Testimony of service representatives on procurement.

*--Part 6*

Testimony of service representatives on nuclear propulsion. Includes Rear Admiral Rickover on Navy's nuclear propulsion program.

*Military Posture Briefings* (February, March 1961)

Sec. McNamara, Defense Department, and Gen. Lemnitzer, Joint Chiefs of Staff: Presentation deleted. (See hearings before Senate Armed Services Committee, April 1961.)

Sec. Stahr and Gen. Decker, Army: Army needs, new concept of mobility, strategic forces--Army missiles, counterinsurgency, tactical nuclear weapons.

Sec. Korth and Adm. Burke, Navy: Naval forces, Polaris program, Regulus program, need for new aircraft, problem of block obsolescence.

Adm. Raborn, Navy: Polaris program progress, functioning of program evaluation review technique.

Sec. Zuckert and Gen. White, Air Force: Strategic Air Command force levels, B-70 development, Skybolt, Minuteman and Titan.

Sec. McNamara, Defense Department: Discussion of B-70 bomber research and development cutback.

Presentation of service research and development requests.

*Sole Source Procurement, Special Subcommittee for Investigations* (May, June, July 1961)

Extensive hearings on military procurement practices; testifying are Assistant Secretary of the

Services for Logistics, General Accounting Office and Defense Department officials, and industry spokesmen.

*Authorization for Additional Appropriations and for Ordering Ready Reserves to Active Duty* (July 1961)

Sec. <u>McNamara</u>, <u>Defense Department</u>, and <u>Gen. Lemnitzer, Joint Chiefs of Staff</u>: Increasing ready status of B-52's, increased appropriations for aircraft, radar sites, Strategic Army Corps divisions; strengthening forces in Europe and improving airlift and sealift.

## FOREIGN AFFAIRS COMMITTEE

*Hearings on Bay of Pigs Invasion* (1961)

Closed session.

*Foreign Economic Assistance* (June, July 1961)

For McNamara testimony, see hearings before Senate Foreign Relations Committee (May, June 1961).

## SENATE COMMITTEES

## APPROPRIATIONS COMMITTEE

*DOD Appropriations for FY 1962* (1961)

Sec. <u>McNamara</u>, <u>Defense Department</u>:

Strengthening strategic deterrent, acceleration of Minuteman and Polaris programs, phase-out of Snark, reexamination of B-70 program.

Discussion of space research, NATO study, requirement to fight brush-fire wars.

Sec. Stahr, Army: Major military objectives, attempt to achieve "balanced forces," NATO cooperation.

Gen. Decker, Army: Communist threat, Army structure, forces in Asia and Europe, role of Strategic Army Corps.

Discussion of Nike-Zeus development, military assistance program.

Sec. Connally, Navy: Polaris program, antisubmarine warfare effort, role of Marine Corps, major Navy procurement.

Discussion of ship construction, retention of skilled personnel.

Adm. Burke, Navy: Technical changes, allied naval programs.

Gen. Shoup, Marine Corps: Fleet Marine forces, breakdown of budget request.

Charles Hitch, Defense Department: Major budget revisions, adequacy of funds.

Sec. Zuckert, Air Force: B-70 program, Strategic Air Command operations.

Discussion of B-70 effectiveness, role of Air Force in space, missile programs.

Gen. White, Air Force: Soviet space efforts, need to maintain missile-bomber mix.

Dep. Sec. Gilpatric, Defense Department: Appeals for House action, restorations required.

Discussion of B-70 program, Air Force manned aircraft threat.


*DOD Procurement and R&D Authorization* (April 1961)

Sec. McNamara, Defense Department: Reappraisal of defense posture, strategic missiles emphasized, ground alert ordered, increased research and development, Skybolt cancelled and new appraisal of conventional strategies.

Sec. Stahr and Gen. Decker, Army: Military threats, major conventional increase, airlift, counterinsurgency, and Nike-Zeus emphasized.

Sec. Connally and Adm. Burke, Navy: Polaris program, antisubmarine warfare research, sealift development.

Sec. Zuckert and Gen. White, Air Force: Need for B-70, military uses of space, airlift; need for TFX; discussion of ground alert, Skybolt decision, Minuteman, reduction of B-47's.

Presentation of service research and development requests.


FOREIGN RELATIONS COMMITTEE


*Foreign Economic Assistance* (May, June 1961)

Sec. McNamara, Defense Department: Military and economic aid complementary, deterrence of guerrilla wars, no hope for terminating military aid in the future.


*Hearings to Establish an Arms Control and Disarmament Agency* (August 1961)

Sec. Rusk, State Department: Berlin crisis, urgency of arms control.

John McCloy, Arms Control and Disarmament Agency: Need for disarmament.

Gen. Lemnitzer, Joint Chiefs of Staff: Need for military strength in disarmament progress.

Dep. Sec. Gilpatric, Defense Department, Leland Haworth, Robert Lovett: Support establishment of agency.

Gen. Gruenther, NATO: Need for agency to convince world of "unwarlike" nature.

<u>Trevor Gardner</u>:   Spread of nuclear weapons, Chinese capability.

# 1962 CONGRESSIONAL HEARINGS

## 87th Congress, Second Session

HOUSE COMMITTEES

APPROPRIATIONS COMMITTEE

*DOD Appropriations for FY 1963, Part 1* (1962)

Testimony of service representatives on military personnel.

*--Part 2*

Sec. McNamara, Defense Department:  Description of programmed budget, 5-year defense program, major defense problem areas--NATO, airlift and balanced forces.  B-52 build-up, Minuteman and Polaris programs, B-70 unnecessary; U.S. capability for destroying Soviet target system.

Discussion of Reserve reductions, accuracy of cost estimates, B-70 decision, nuclear powered carrier, antiballistic missile research, civil defense program.

Charles Hitch, Defense Department:  Summary of budget, new appropriations titles.

Discussion of spending in each program area.

Sec. Stahr, Army:  Soviet army capabilities, current build-up.

Gen. Decker, Army:  Missions of the Army, air

and sealift, reorganization of Reserves.

Discussion of Special Forces, adequacy of equipment, situation in Laos and Vietnam.

Sec. Korth, Navy:  Summary of Navy budget, spending trends.

Adm. Anderson, Navy:  Polaris operations, personnel problems, limited-war capability, Soviet submarine-launched missile threat.

Discussion of nuclear vs. conventional strategy, naval strategy.

Gen. Shoup, Marine Corps:  Marine readiness, summary of budget.

Sec. Korth and Adm. Anderson, Navy:  Antisubmarine warfare activities, torpedo programs, amphibious capabilities.

Discussion of carrier vulnerability, Polaris patrols.

Sec. Zuckert, Air Force:  Organizational changes, space programs, strategic forces, B-70 test development.

Gen. Smith, Air Force:  Soviet strategic threat, intercontinental ballistic missile readiness, Soviet space threat.

Sec. Zuckert, Air Force:  Discussion of nuclear strategies, Titan, Minuteman programs, B-70 decision, airlift capability.


*--Part 3*

Testimony by service representatives on operation and maintenance.


*--Part 4*

Testimony by service representatives on procurement.

*--Part 5*

Testimony of service representatives on research, development, test and evaluation.


*--Part 6*

Testimony by service representatives on Reserves, biological and chemical warfare programs.


ARMED SERVICES COMMITTEE


*Authorization for DOD Procurement and R&D* (January,
February 1962)

Sec. McNamara, Defense Department: Strategic
forces, Polaris and Minuteman presentations; discussion of problems with B-70, NATO force levels,
conventional capabilities. Tactical air power,
TFX, SEATO obligations and Reserve force levels.
Sec. Stahr and Gen. Decker, Army: Army
strength, Reserve build-up, Nike-Zeus presentation.
Sec. Korth and Adm. Anderson, Navy, Gen. Shoup,
Marine Corps: Polaris progress, Phantom II, TFX,
antisubmarine warfare study, problems of block obsolescence.
Sec. Zuckert and Gen. Smith, Air Force: Military Air Transport Service capability, strategic
forces, Soviet missile and bomber capability, Reserves.
Gen. LeMay, Air Force: Need for long-range
bomber, urged expansion of RS-70 program, defined
new mission.
Presentations of service research and development requests and justifications.

*Hearings on Block Obsolescence, Special Subcommittee on Block Obsolescence* (August 1962)

Sec. Korth, Navy:  Necessity for modern Navy.
Adm. Ricketts, Navy:  Expansion of Soviet fleet.
Adm. Griffen, Navy:  Outline of present Navy shipbuilding program.
Adm. Moorer, Navy:  Soviet and American naval capabilities, progress in antisubmarine warfare.
Rear Adm. Brocket, Navy:  Navy shipbuilding problems.

## FOREIGN AFFAIRS

*Foreign Economic Assistance* (March, April 1962)

Sec. McNamara, Defense Department:  Breakdown of military assistance expenditures, discussion of tighter controls.
Gen. Lemnitzer, Joint Chiefs of Staff:  Steadily increasing strength of Communist bloc and insurgency situations.
Bonners Tellers:  Need for drastically reduced military aid; need for overwhelming aerospace striking power.

## GOVERNMENT OPERATIONS COMMITTEE

*Government Civil Defense Plans, Military Operations Subcommittee* (February 1962)

Steuart Pittman, Office of Civil Defense Mobilization:  Proposed programs could save millions of lives, would be established on a community basis; discussed cost of program as small and stated that greater protection would be prohibitively more expensive.

Walter Strope, Office of Civil Defense Mobilization: Need for shelter research and post-attack
research. Noted progress in warning system.

James Roembike, Office of Civil Defense Mobilization: Presentation of new shelter designs.

Paul Visher, Office of Civil Defense Mobilization: Presentation of plans to protect population
not sheltered.


## SENATE COMMITTEES


## APPROPRIATIONS COMMITTEE


*DOD Appropriations for FY 1963* (January, February
1962)

Sec. McNamara, Defense Department: Defense Department approach to budget, major policy areas,
impact of defense on economy, programming and budgeting procedure, NATO situation, Berlin crisis.

Gen. Lemnitzer, Joint Chiefs of Staff: Possibility of all-out nuclear war, adequacy of army
size.

Asst. Sec. Hitch, Defense Department: New appropriation titles, major budget titles.

Sec. Zuckert, Air Force: Air Force organization, accuracy of cost estimates, space programs.

Gen. LeMay, Air Force: Need to initiate moon
program, Soviet threat, need to maintain manned
bomber program.

Discussion of B-70.

Sec. Korth, Navy: Program package system, attack carrier program, antisubmarine warfare. Increasing obsolescence of fleet.

Discussion of obsolescence, nuclear powered
carrier, TFX.

Adm. Anderson, Navy: Polaris program, need for
nuclear propulsion.

Gen. Shoup, Marine Corps:  Overall budget request.

Sec. Stahr, Army:  Berlin build-up, improving
Army posture, Nike-Zeus program, Reserve call-up,
problems encountered during build-up.

Gen. Decker, Army:  Importance of Army mission,
lessons learned by build-up.

Discussion of NATO cooperation, Laos situation.

Sec. McNamara, Defense Department:  Reorganization of Reserve and National Guard forces, House
action, reprogramming request.

Discussion of manpower reductions, NATO effectiveness.

## ARMED SERVICES COMMITTEE

*DOD Authorization for Procurement and R&D for FY
1963, Joint Hearings* . . . (January, February 1962)

Sec. McNamara, Defense Department:  Introduction
of five-year defense plan; discussion of Office of
the Secretary of Defense role, Berlin crisis and
NATO troop strength, strategic forces--Polaris,
Minuteman, B-70.  Presentation of general purpose
forces.

Gen. Lemnitzer, Joint Chiefs of Staff:  Concept
of Army flexibility and tactical mobility.

Sec. Stahr and Gen. Decker, Army:  Army reorganization, tactical mobility, Strike Command concept.

Sec. Korth and Adm. Anderson, Navy, Gen. Shoup,
Marine Corps:  Polaris program, vertical/short
take-off and landing craft, antisubmarine warfare
research.

Sec. Zuckert and Gen. Smith, Air Force:  Atlas,
Titan, Minuteman forces, need for manned bomber,
discussion of nuclear testing.

Presentation of service research and development
requests and justification.

FOREIGN RELATIONS COMMITTEE

*Review of Operations of the Arms Control and Disarmament Agency* (March 1962)

William Foster, Arms Control and Disarmament Agency:  Disarmament negotiations, difficulties, personnel; discussion of Soviet attitudes toward testing.

*Foreign Economic Assistance* (April 1962)

Sec. Rusk, State Department:  Necessity of military aid for security.

Sec. McNamara, Defense Department:  Defended use of funds in Latin America and training of officers in U.S. schools.

# 1963 CONGRESSIONAL HEARINGS

## 88th Congress, First Session

HOUSE COMMITTEES

APPROPRIATIONS COMMITTEE

*DOD Appropriations for FY 1964, Part 1* (January, February 1963)

Sec. <u>McNamara</u>, <u>Defense</u> <u>Department</u>: Offensive weapons in Cuba, scenario of Cuban missile crisis.

Discussion of Soviet intentions, U.S. reconnaissance, early reports on missiles, discussion of Bay of Pigs invasion.

Sec. <u>McNamara</u>, <u>Defense</u> <u>Department</u>: 1964-68 five-year defense plan, threat of wars of national liberation, region-by-region internal threats, NATO effectiveness. Soviet and Chinese threats, impact of defense spending on economy, need for arms control. Present U.S. strategic capability, future of manned bombers, Skybolt decision. Air defense program, general purpose forces.

Discussion of conventional build-up, "flexible response" doctrine, cost reduction program.

Gen. <u>Taylor</u>, <u>Joint</u> <u>Chiefs</u> <u>of</u> <u>Staff</u>: Importance of planning.

*--Part 2*

Gen. Taylor, Joint Chiefs of Staff:  Organization for national security, influence of military policy, necessity for foreign aid.

Discussion of missile crisis, Red Chinese threat.

Charles Hitch, Defense Department:  Financial summary of budget.

Sec. Vance, Army:  Army organization, budget plan, Reserve organization.

Gen. Wheeler, Army:  Missions, counterinsurgency operations.

Discussion of Soviet army strength, NATO strength, withdrawal of forces in Europe.

Sec. Korth, Navy:  Management, Navy strength, shipbuilding program, budget programs.

Adm. Anderson, Navy:  Nature of Navy, Cuban experience, Soviet naval strength.

Gen. Shoup, Marine Corps:  Marine budget.

Sec. Korth, Navy:  Naval districts, sealift capability, Polaris program.

Adm. Anderson, Navy:  Naval strategy, Polaris invulnerability, Navy role in limited war.

Sec. Zuckert, Air Force:  Status of Air Force.

Gen. LeMay, Air Force:  Major programs, strategic forces, management.

Discussion of Soviet threat, viability of "mutual deterrence," superior strength vs. parity, targeting policy, options in nuclear strikes.

Discussion of RS-70 system, other manned bomber alternatives.


*--Part 3*

Testimony of service representatives on military personnel.

--*Part 4*

Testimony of service representatives on operation and maintenance.

--*Part 5*

Testimony of service representatives on procurement.

--*Part 6*

Testimony by service representatives on research, development, test and evaluation.

--*Part 7*

Vice Adm. Rickover, Navy:  Criticism of government contracting procedures.


ARMED SERVICES COMMITTEE


*DOD Authorization for Procurement and R&D* (1963)

Sec. McNamara, Defense Department:  Soviet increase of hardened sites and missile-launching submarines--"assured destruction" level reached.

Discussion of damage-limitation strategy--withholding cities.  Maintenance of B-52 and B-58 force levels, no procurement of B-70 and RS-70. Skybolt discontinued ("disadvantages of bomber and missile"), downgrading of Nike-Zeus and development of Nike-X.

Conventional forces seen as adequate, except in Europe where tactical nuclear weapons would augment force.  New concepts of Army aviation--air assault division.

Sec. Vance, Army:  Improvement of Army personnel; Army aviation program not viewed as infringement upon Air Force--emphasis on special warfare, air mobility, and ballistic missile defense.  Need for global combat capability stressed.

Gen. Wheeler, Army:  Cuban missile crisis demonstrated value of maintaining Army at high state of alert.

Sec. Korth, Navy:  Ship obsolescence by late 1960s; missile crisis created scheduling difficulties at Navy yards.  Significant increase of antisubmarine warfare and naval study of the oceans.

Adm. Griffin, Navy:  Soviet naval build-up--large submarine force and merchant marine.

Sec. Zuckert, Air Force:  High state of Air Force readiness, ability to meet Army combat requirements, space capabilities and effectiveness of strategic forces.

Air Force studying feasibility of low altitude bomber aircraft if antiballistic missile effectiveness downgrades intercontinental ballistic missile.

Gen. LeMay, Air Force:  Requirements for strategic retaliatory forces--more options necessary for response, Defense Department must explore every feasible weapons system approach.


*Authorization for Civil Defense Fall-Out Shelter Construction* (May, June, July 1963)

Steuart Pittman, Defense Department:  Possibilities of an effective shelter program and significant survival in post-attack world.  Sees no adverse effects of shelter program, argues that failure of an adequate shelter program would undermine value of nuclear deterrent.

Gen. Wheeler, Army:  Importance of civil defense, especially for effectiveness of planned antiballistic missile system.

Numerous witnesses--labor, business, religious, scientific and medical groups--arguing pro and con.

## FOREIGN AFFAIRS COMMITTEE

*Foreign Economic Assistance* (April, May, June 1963)

Sec. Rusk, State Department:  United States winning the Cold War, but military and economic assistance vital.

Sec. McNamara, Defense Department:  Absolute
importance of military assistance.

Gen. Taylor, Army:  United States getting its
money's worth with military assistance; discussion
of prohibitive cost of replacing supported troops
with U.S. troops.

Gen. Clay, Army:  Points out areas where foreign
aid cuts should be made.

## GOVERNMENT OPERATIONS COMMITTEE

*Use of Military Satellites* (1963)

## SENATE COMMITTEES

## AERONATICAL AND SPACE SCIENCES COMMITTEE

*NASA Authorization for FY 1964* (June 1963)

Lloyd Berkner, National Aeronautics and Space
Administration:  Military implications and applications of the space race.

APPROPRIATIONS COMMITTEE

*DOD Appropriations for FY 1964* (1963)

Sec. McNamara, Defense Department:  Cuban missile crisis, possibility of limited war, strength of strategic forces, role of manned bombers, need for Army and Navy modernization.

Discussion of contracting procedure, effectiveness of antiballistic missiles, military assistance, TFX program, B-70 systems.

Charles Hitch, Defense Department:  New appropriation titles, explanation of budget, prior year funds, reprogramming.

Sec. Zuckert, Air Force:  Need for trained personnel, F-111 program, B-70 slowdown, program and budget development.

Discussion of future of manned bombers, Skybolt cancellation decision.

Gen. LeMay, Air Force:  Need for manned bombers, anticipated life of current bomber force, Hound Dog development.

Sec. Vance, Army:  Combat conditions, Army strength, reduction in Army budget request.

Discussion of modernization, reenlistment rate, concept of air assault, M-14 rifle effectiveness.

Gen. Wheeler, Army:  Strategic Army Corps forces, NATO situation and European contributions.

Discussion of airlift, deterioration of equipment.

Sec. Korth, Navy:  Military posture, major procurement, personnel strength, loss of *Thresher* submarine, Soviet overflights at sea.

Adm. Anderson, Navy:  Polaris program progress, Subroc missile torpedo, growing Soviet naval threat.

ARMED SERVICES COMMITTEE


*DOD Authorization--Procurement and R&D for FY 1964*
(1963)

   See hearings before House Armed Services Committee (1963)


*Test-Ban Treaty--Military Implications; Closed Hear-
ings before Preparedness Investigating Subcommittee*
(August 1963)

   Gen. Taylor, Army; Gen. LeMay, Air Force; Adm.
McDonald, Navy; Gen. Wheeler, Army; Gen. Shoup, Marine Corps; Edward Teller, University of Southern
California: United States unable to match Soviet
high-yield technology; need for atmospheric tests
for proposed antiballistic missile; discussion of
penetrability of warheads.



FOREIGN RELATIONS COMMITTEE


*Foreign Economic Assistance* (June, July 1963)

   Sec. Rusk, State Department: Discussion of aid
to India, Pakistan, and Indonesia.


*Test-Ban Treaty* (August 1963)

   Sec. Rusk, State Department: Treaty does not
affect use of weapons in war, no side arrangements.
   Sec. McNamara, Defense Department: Unqualified
support for treaty, discussion of U.S. experience
in underground testing and current superiority of
U.S. forces. Treaty would not affect accuracy of
U.S. weapons; clandestine tests could be detected;

present information in missile site vulnerability
sufficient and antiballistic missile could be de-
veloped without atmospheric testing.

Glenn Seaborg, Atomic Energy Commission:  Expresses hope that peaceful, above-ground tests
could be permitted.

Gen. Taylor, Joint Chiefs of Staff:  Calls for
four safeguards--continued underground testing, retaining labs and scientists, improvement of detection technology, and prompt resumption of testing
if necessary.

Gen. LeMay, Air Force; Gen. Wheeler, Army; Adm.
McDonald, Navy:  Urge adoption of safeguards discussed by Taylor.

Edward Teller, University of Southern California:  Soviet "cheating," retardation of antiballistic missile research and development, unable to
test high-yield weapons, unable to study radar
"black-out," unable to verify missile site hardness.  Stated that treaty would increase arms race
due to uncertainty.

Sec. Brown, Air Force, and John Foster, Defense
Department:  Brown favors treaty; Foster opposes
it.

Willard Libby:  U.S. failure to test high-yield
weapons serious.

Herbert York, University of Southern California:
Counters Teller's argument concerning antiballistic
missile, successful antiballistic missile highly
doubtful.

Arthur Dean, State Department:  Supports treaty.

George Kistiakowsky, Harvard University:  Supports treaty.

GOVERNMENT OPERATIONS COMMITTEE

*Hearings on TFX* (1963)*

--*Part 1* (February, March 1963)

   John Stack, Republic Aviation:  Discussion of
requirements for TFX, Navy and Air Force requirements in 1959, multi-mission problems.
   Robert Duane, Defense Department:  Boeing opti-
mism in proposal, problems of redesign.
   Col. Roy Jaynes and Col. Charles Gayle, Air
Force:  Source selection procedures, decision mak-
ing, Secretary of Defense role in process.
   David McGiffert, Defense Department:  Informa-
tion concerning TFX case, Defense Department cover-
up discussed.
   Thomas Nunnally, General Accounting Office:
Boeing and General Dynamics proposals, cost of air-
craft, contract procedures.
   E. A. Niccolini, Air Force:  Discussion of
Source Selection Board's pointing system.
   Benjamin Gilleas, Government Operations, Commit-
tee staff:  Discussion of commonality principle.

--*Part 2* (March 1963)

   Arthur Sylvester, Defense Department:  Defense
of Defense Department criticism of hearings on TFX.
   George Spangenberg, Navy:  Navy's evaluation of

---

*TFX hearings extended from 26 February 1963 through
20 November 1963--over 2800 pages of testimony.
Only highlights of testimony will be listed.  See
*Index to TFX Investigation*, Permanent Subcommittee
on Investigations, 1964--Interim Index to Parts
1-10.

TFX, carrier requirements.  General Dynamics preferred option.

Rear Adm. Ashworth, Navy; Maj. Gen. Ruegg and
Maj. Gen. Moore, Air Force:  Evaluation techniques,
source selection, Navy and Air Force perspectives.

Sec. McNamara, Defense Department:  History of
TFX decision.

--*Part 3* (April, May 1963)

Rear Adm. Ashworth, Navy; Maj. Gen. Bennett,
Maj. Gen. Moore, and Maj. Gen. Ruegg, Air Force:
Continued discussion of selection procedure and
requirements--service requirements.

Gen. Sweeney and Gen. LeMay, Air Force:  Discussion of Boeing preference, reasons for Air Force
preference.

Louis Koepnick, Defense Department:  Discussion
of civilian influence in decision.

Donald Jordan, Pratt and Whitney Co.:  Engine
development, General Dynamics contract.

Hassell Bell, Joseph Campbell, Robert Keller,
Paul Newell, William Newman, Controller General and
staff:  TFX contract, cost-monitoring.

--*Part 4* (May 1963)

William Allen, Roy Anderson, Charles Keeton,
William Lancaster, Edward Wells, and H. W. Withing-
ton, Boeing:  Boeing experience, cost estimates,
government decision, competitive bid and technical
problems.

Frank Davis, Roger Lewis and Corwin Meyes, General Dynamics:  Aircraft experience, TFX contract,
design approach--basic design and mission.

Roger Harris, Government Operations Committee
investigator:  Discussion of Roswell Gilpatric's
connection with General Dynamics.

Robert Dunne, Government Operations Committee
investigator:  Deleted.

Thomas Nunnally, General Accounting Office:
Management approaches to TFX.
Clinton Towl, Grumman Co.:  Discussion of TFX
wing design and commonality.

--*Part* 5 (May, June 1963)

Albert Blackburn, Defense Department:  Discussion of Air Force-Navy interface, McNamara involvement with decision.
Seth Kantor:  Discussion of General Dynamics
decision--leak of government contract to press.
John Rubel, Defense Department:  Defense Department decision making, role of R. Gilpatric, methods
of source selection.
Andy Eshman, George Gerard, Walter Hyler, Ward
Minkler, Roy Quadt, Arnold Rustay, Arne Sorensen
and Robert Watson, Boeing:  Discussion of Boeing
design problems, possibilities of solutions.

--*Part* 6 (June, July 1963)

Sec. Korth and James Wakelin, Navy:  Navy
requirements--in both contract proposals--problems
of compromise, difficulties of commonality-carrier
compatibility.
H. B. Henderson, General Dynamics:  Discussion
of Navy TFX capabilities.

--*Part* 7

Sec. Korth and James Wakelin, Navy:  Problems
with carriers, evaluation procedures, Navy-Air
Force differences.
Robert Dunne, Government Operations Committee
investigator:  Discussion of pro-Boeing Air Force
bias.
Col. Rogers, Air Force:  Discussion of wording
in Source Selection Reports to give false impressions.

*--Part 8*

Aaron Racusin and Sec. Zuckert, Air Force:  Air
Force TFX mission, McNamara views, Air Force evalu-
ation techniques, Boeing preference.
Col. Gayle and Col. Gregory, Air Force:  Air
Force decisions, guidelines and requirements pre-
sented to bidders.
R. E. Koepp, Air Force:  Discussion of Air Force
requirements.

*--Part 9* (August 1963)

Joseph Charyk, Air Force:  Technical evaluation
of competing systems, inlet design, swing-wing,
developmental problems.
Sec. Zuckert and Aaron Racusin, Air Force:  Cost
estimates, discussion of realism in both estimates.

*--Part 10* (November 1963)

Asst. Sec. Gilpatric, Defense Department:  Discussion of TFX contract, expected sales, involvement in contract award.
Jerome Adlerman, Government Operations Committee
staff:  Possibilities of conflict-of-interest in
TFX case.
Robert Dunne, Government Operations Committee
staff:  Relationship of Gilpatric's former law firm
to General Dynamics.

# 1964 CONGRESSIONAL HEARINGS

## 88th Congress, Second Session

HOUSE COMMITTEES

APPROPRIATIONS COMMITTEE

*DOD Appropriations for FY 65, Part 1* (January, February 1964)

Testimony of service representatives on personnel.

*--Part 2*

Testimony of service representatives on operation and maintenance.

*--Part 3*

Testimony of service representatives on procurement.

*--Part 4*

Sec. McNamara, Defense Department: Defense funds, national security, assessment of international situation. Region-by-region analysis of security problem.

Importance of NATO, effect of budget on economy, defense program changes, future of strategic forces, dependability.

New strategic systems, changes in general purpose forces.

Discussion of NATO strength vs. Soviet strength, new manned bomber, modernization of Polaris, TFX development.

Discussion of Vietnam situation, foreign aid, Soviet foreign aid, dependability of U.S. missiles, concept of "damage-limiting" nuclear strategy.

Charles Hitch, Defense Department: General spending trends, summary of budget programs.

Asst. Sec. Zuckert, Air Force: Weapons reliability, F-111 program, manned orbiting laboratory, airlift capability.

Gen. LeMay, Air Force: Strategic Air Command readiness, megatonnage of Soviet weapons, desirability of larger weapons, need for follow-on manned system.

Discussion of advanced bomber, vertical/short take-off and landing aircraft, role of Office of the Secretary of Defense in budget process.

Sec. Ailes, Army: New Army programs, organization.

Gen. Wheeler, Army: Missile, tank programs.

Discussion of "tight" funds, Reserve readiness, helicopter development.

Sec. Nitze, Navy: U.S. naval power, Soviet capabilities growing.

Discussion of budget limitations, carrier forces, antisubmarine warfare program.

Adm. McDonald, Navy: Need for new ships and new aircraft.

Discussion of Polaris effectiveness, power of Joint Chiefs of Staff, Navy disappointment over budget.


--Part 5

Testimony of service representatives on research, development, test and evaluation.

ARMED SERVICES COMMITTEE

*DOD Procurement and R&D Authorization for FY 1965*
(January, February 1964)

Sec. McNamara, Defense Department: Impossibility of either a counterforce nuclear force or a minimum deterrent—damage-limitation strategy
described will assure destruction on second strike.
Missile favored over bomber force for emphasis in
strategic force, but mixed force maintained through
1969. Need for civil defense, antiballistic missile defense, and adequacy of air defenses. Need
for flexible counterinsurgency force and ability to
meet conventional Soviet threat in Europe.
Sec. Ailes, Army: Army force request, new
housing and need for tactical mobility.
Sec. Nitze, Navy: Long-range nuclear conversion
for Navy, need for second nuclear carrier and new
light attack airplane.
Asst. Sec. Zuckert, Air Force: Discussion of
cost analysis, need to balance technological improvements with cost. Air Force research and development programs—new missiles and F-111.
Gen. LeMay, Air Force: U.S. strategic superiority narrowing, need for bombers and importance of
Soviet 100 megaton bomb.
Service chiefs and research and development di-
rectors present specific requests and justification.

*Hearings on V/STOL, Special Subcommittee on Research
and Development* (May 1964)

Sec. Brown, Air Force: Research and development
efforts for vertical/short take-off and landing
craft, deployment; analyzes three research programs
with services and discusses European efforts.
Gen. Dick, Air Force; Lt. Col. Favoute, Army;
Rear Adm. Fawkes, Navy: Services' vertical/short

take-off and landing craft programs.

Spokesmen from industry--United, Curtiss-Wright, Sikorsky, General Dynamics, General Electric.


# FOREIGN AFFAIRS COMMITTEE


*Foreign Economic Assistance for FY 1965* (March, April, May 1964)

Sec. Rusk, State Department:  Threat of Communist imperialism, need for long-term aid commitment.

David Bell, Agency for International Development:  Possible need for additional aid funds for Vietnam.

Sec. McNamara, Defense Department:  Need for at least $1 billion in military aid; Congress must be willing to appropriate more.

Gen. Taylor, Joint Chiefs of Staff:  Serious consequences of the FY 1964 cut in military assistance; description of poor state of allied combat readiness.

Gen. O'Meara, Army:  Need for military assistance in Latin America.

Adm. Felt, Navy:  Asian fear of American abandonment.

Gen. Lemnitzer, NATO:  Military assistance vital to cohesiveness of European alliance structure.


# JOINT COMMITTEES OF HOUSE AND SENATE


# JOINT ATOMIC ENERGY COMMITTEE


*AEC Authorization for FY 1965* (January, February 1964)

Sec. McNamara, Defense Department:  Cost of
CVAN-67 nuclear carrier prohibitive; discussion of
cost figures.

Discussion of President Johnson's nuclear pile
cutback and Soviet nuclear threat.

# SENATE COMMITTEES

## APPROPRIATIONS COMMITTEE

*DOD Appropriations for FY 1965* (1964)

Sec. McNamara, Defense Department:  Joint committee procedures, reduction of budget request,
appraisal of Soviet bloc, situation in Southeast
Asia, NATO difficulties, studies of strategic
forces, capability of missiles vs. bombers, Nike-X
development.

Discussion of missile phase-out, Soviet troops
in Cuba, missile dependability, future of manned
bombers, status of antiballistic missile program,
new contracting procedures.

Harold Brown, Defense Department:  Major research and development programs, missile capabilities, adequacy of budget for bomber studies,
satellite surveillance program.

Gen. Wheeler, Army:  Tactical mobility, Special
Forces Group in Vietnam, Reserve forces.

Discussion of European build-up.

Sec. Nitze, Navy:  Polaris and attack carrier
forces, Typhon missile system, antisubmarine warfare capability, obsolescence problems.

Adm. McDonald, Navy:  Naval transition to nuclear propulsion, major ship construction.

Gen. Green, Marine Corps:  Marine role in armed
forces.

Sec. Nitze, Navy:  Discussion of *Thresher* disaster, effects of House cut, ship obsolescence.

Sec. Zuckert, Air Force:  Cost reduction program, missile development.

Gen. LeMay, Air Force:  Air Force missions, summary of programs.

Discussion of TFX, bomber development, military safeguards relating to Test Ban Treaty.


## ARMED SERVICES COMMITTEE


*DOD Authorization for Procurement and R&D for FY 1965* (1964)

See joint hearings before Senate Appropriations Committee (1964).


## FOREIGN RELATIONS COMMITTEE


*Foreign Economic Assistance* (March, April 1964)

Sec. McNamara, Defense Department:  Foreign aid has become one of most critical elements of national security policy; discussion of need for collective defense.

# 1965 CONGRESSIONAL HEARINGS

## 89th Congress, First Session

HOUSE COMMITTEES

APPROPRIATIONS COMMITTEE

*DOD Appropriations for FY 1966, Part 1* (February, March, April 1965)

Testimony of service representatives on military personnel.

*--Part 2*

Testimony of service representatives on operation and maintenance.

*--Part 3*

Sec. McNamara, Defense Department: Chinese explosion of A-bomb, Chinese military strength, Vietnam situation, nuclear control in NATO, strategy of damage-limitation, Nike-X program and discussion of no change in active force levels. Strengths and weaknesses of Communist bloc, review of international situation. Nature of nuclear war problem-- use of manned bombers, ballistic missile defense. Discussion of damage-limiting strategies,

missile modernization, Vietnam strategy and U.S.
capability to fight conventional wars.

Gen. Wheeler, Joint Chiefs of Staff: Responsibilities of Joint Chiefs, decision to introduce
U.S. forces into Vietnam.

Discussion of freedom of Joint Chiefs to present
personal views, merits of ballistic missile defense, history of M-16 rifle.

Asst. Sec. Hitch, Defense Department: Breakdown
of budget.

Discussion of contract procedures, budgeting
system, effect of cost-reduction program.

Sec. Ailes, Army: Army readiness, deployment of
weapons in Vietnam, training and manpower problems,
ROTC program.

Discussion of Army instruction, manpower problems.

Gen. Abrams, Army: STEP program, need for instruction program.

Discussion of alternative training methods,
standards for Army enlistment. Current Army deployment in Vietnam, new procurement programs, new
helicopter and missile programs.

Sec. Nitze, Navy: Personnel situation, Polaris,
antisubmarine warfare programs. Summary of appropriation requests.

Adm. McDonald, Navy: Strategic threat of general war, role of seapower, role of attack carrier--
necessity for nuclear power.

Gen. Green, Marine Corps: Marine deployment in
Vietnam.

Sec. Nitze, Navy: Discussion of personnel
costs, ship obsolescence, aircraft programs.

Sec. Zuckert, Air Force: Air Force evolution,
management, strategic offensive force.

Gen. McConnell, Air Force: Challenges to Air
Force, missile and bomber forces, advanced manned
strategic aircraft. Close air support mission,
airlift capability.

Discussion of interceptor program, F-111 cost,
delays, the future of manned aircraft.

Asst. Sec. Zuckert, Air Force: Discussion of

advanced manned strategic aircraft funding, extent of vertical/short take-off and landing craft research.

## --Part 4

Testimony of service representatives on procurement.

## --Part 5

Testimony of service representatives on research, development, test and evaluation.

## --Part 6

Testimony of Vice Admiral Rickover on nuclear propulsion.

## ARMED SERVICES COMMITTEE

*DOD Authorization for Procurement and R&D: Military Posture Hearings* (February, March 1965)

Sec. McNamara, Defense Department: Strategic offensive and defensive forces, proposed research and development, capability of assured destruction.
Sec. Brown, Air Force: Airborne warning and control system, antisubmarine warfare, F-111, Phoenix missile, Shrike missile, and Dynasoar program.
Sec. Ailes and Gen. Johnson, Army: Airlift capabilities, deployment in Vietnam, Army missile development. Readiness and personnel problems discussed.
Sec. Nitze and Adm. McDonald, Navy: Naval administration, Polaris program, nuclear ships and

submarines needed, Soviet expenditures discussed
and need for antisubmarine warfare research and
attack carrier.

Robert Moise, Navy: Naval research and development requests--antisubmarine warfare, Fleet Ballistic Missile system and Polaris.

Asst. Sec. Zuckert and Gen. McConnell, Air
Force: Relations with National Aeronautics and
Space Administration, need for RS-70, status of
TFX, vertical/short take-off and landing craft,
Manned Orbiting Lab and Air Force airlift capabili-
ties.

Lt. Gen. Ferguson, Air Force: Air Force research and development requests--C-5A, Over-the-
horizon radar, advanced intercontinental ballistic
missile, F-111 and vertical/short take-off and
landing craft.

FOREIGN AFFAIRS COMMITTEE

*Arms Control and Disarmament Agency Authorization for
FY 1966* (January 1965)

William Foster, Defense Department: Chinese
A-bomb detonation, threat of nuclear proliferation,
need for research in arms control.

*Foreign Economic Assistance* (February, March, April
1965)

David Bell, Agency for International Development: Unstable less-developed countries viewed as
security threats; discussion of funds for Vietnam,
Laos, Korea, and Jordan.

Asst. Sec. Williams, State Department: Africa
vulnerable to Communist subversion.

Sec. McNamara, Defense Department: Economic aid
transferred to military aid, discussion of military
assistance program to Latin America.

## SCIENCE AND ASTRONAUTICS COMMITTEE

*Authorization for NASA for FY 1966* (March 1965)

Rep. Roudibush and Rep. Rumsfield:  Concern over
low priority given to the development of military
capabilities in space.
Rep. Aylder:  Military control of space should
be placed on a "crash" basis.


## JOINT COMMITTEES OF HOUSE AND SENATE

## JOINT ATOMIC ENERGY COMMITTEE

*AEC FY 1966 Authorization* (January, February, March
1965)

Glenn Seaborg, Atomic Energy Commission:  Reduction in operating costs, particularly in weapons
production.  Discussion of reduction of stockpile
and increase of investment in peaceful atomic uses.


## SENATE COMMITTEES

## APPROPRIATIONS COMMITTEE

*DOD Appropriations for FY 1966* (February, March 1965)

See joint hearings before the Senate Appropriations Committee (1965).
Sec. McNamara, Defense Department:  Strategic
forces, damage limitation, and assured destruction,
bomber-missile mix, manned bomber phase-out,

effectiveness of Nike-X, North Vietnamese military capability.

Discussion of bomber capability, Soviet missile threat, civil defense effectiveness, B-52 modifications.

Gen. Wheeler, Joint Chiefs of Staff:  Adequacy of budget.

Sec. McNamara, Defense Department:  Army readiness, naval strength.

Discussion of nuclear power for Navy, adequacy of military pay, Vietnam war costs.

Harold Brown, Defense Department:  Research and development programs, advanced manned strategic aircraft, Poseidon.  Vietnam security research, manned bomber requirement.

Sec. Ailes, Army:  Deployment of Army forces, Vietnam deployment, West Point expansion.

Gen. Johnson, Army:  Preparation for different kinds of war, Vietnam strength, military pay, STEP program, air mobility.

Sec. Ailes, Army:  Discussion of STEP program, military assistance programs, helicopter development.

Sec. Nitze, Navy:  Navy management, Polaris, antisubmarine warfare, attack carrier capability.

Adm. McDonald, Navy:  Red China's navy capability, deep submergence research, personnel requirements.

Discussion of Soviet naval strength, F-111B weight problem, Indian Ocean capability, multilateral naval forces.

Asst. Sec. Zuckert, Air Force:  New Air Force programs, F-12 interceptor, SR-71 development, SRAM development.

Gen. McConnell, Air Force:  Bomber forces, progress on advanced manned strategic aircraft, pay problems.

Discussion of SRAM, Air Force morale, advanced manned strategic aircraft decision.

*Vietnam Supplemental Appropriations* (August 1965)

    Sec. McNamara, Defense Department: Presentation
of Communist build-up in South Vietnam, infiltration from North. Discussion of Project Camelot
affair.


ARMED SERVICES COMMITTEE


*DOD Procurement and R&D Authorization for FY 1966*
(February, March 1965)

    See joint hearings before the Senate Appropria-
tions Committee (1965).


*Merger of National Guard and Army Reserve, Prepared-
ness Investigating Subcommittee* (March, April, May
1965)

    Sec. McNamara, Defense Department: Supports
proposed merger; discussion of cost savings and
contribution to readiness.
    Gen. Wilson, Army: Proposed merger would lead
to the elimination of certain units.
    Maj. Gen. Cantwell, National Guard: Endorses
McNamara concept but does not want merger to lead
to weakened strength.
    John Carlton, Army Reserve: Charges Defense De-
partment with deception.


FOREIGN RELATIONS COMMITTEE


*Foreign Economic Assistance for FY 1966* (March, April
1965)

Sec. Rusk, State Department: Anti-Americanism in the Third World.

Sec. McNamara, Defense Department: Security threats in the Third World.

*Authorization for Arms Control and Disarmament Agency, FY 1966* (April 1965)

William Foster, Arms Control and Disarmament Agency: Need for arms control, Soviet and U.S. nuclear balance.

Stanley Andrews: Arms Control and Disarmament Agency is against American traditions and its activities are nebulous.

Amitai Etzioni, Columbia University: Need for research in arms control, particularly in small-scale confrontations.

Robert Morris: Charges Arms Control and Disarmament Agency with holding unrealistic attitude about Soviets.

# 1966 CONGRESSIONAL HEARINGS

## 89th Congress, Second Session

HOUSE COMMITTEES

APPROPRIATIONS COMMITTEE

*DOD Appropriations for FY 1967, Part 1* (February, March, April 1966)

Sec. McNamara, Defense Department: Shift of defense to the Far East, Vietnam, policy toward wars of national liberation, Nike-X project, discussion of advanced manned strategic aircraft. Assessment of international situation, South Vietnam military strength, general nuclear war threat, role of manned bomber force, cost of damage-limiting measures.

Discussion of multiple independently targeted re-entry vehicle programs, SRAM missile design, major procurement programs.

*--Part 2*

Sec. Resor, Army: Army build-up, training base, aircraft, ammunition.

Gen. Johnson, Army: South Vietnam situation, North Vietnam.

Discussion of Reserves, confrontation with China, experience with airmobile division, Nike-X program.

Sec. Brown, Air Force:  Support of Southeast
Asia operations, strategic modernization.

Discussion of adequacy of Air Force budget, Air
Force missions in Vietnam, future of F-12 interceptor.

Gen. McConnell, Air Force:  Need for advanced
manned strategic aircraft, Southeast Asia operations.

Discussion of advanced manned strategic aircraft, C-5A.

Sec. Nitze, Navy:  Navy deployment in Southeast
Asia, Marine deployment in Vietnam, Polaris program, antisubmarine warfare in Southeast Asia.

Adm. McDonald, Navy:  Navy deployment in Vietnam, rotational procedures.

Discussion of ship overhaul experience.


*--Part 3*

Testimony of service representatives on operation and maintenance.


*--Part 4*

Testimony of service representatives on procurement.


*--Part 5*

Testimony of service representatives on research, development, test, and evaluation.


*--Part 6*

Testimony of service representatives on crash of
XB-70, recovery of lost nuclear weapons in Spain.

Testimony of Vice Admiral Rickover on nuclear
propulsion.

## ARMED SERVICES COMMITTEE

*DOD Decision to Reduce Numbers and Types of Manned Bombers in SAC* (January, February 1966)

Sec. McNamara, Defense Department: General nuclear war problem, damage-limitation strategy, adequacy of forces for assured destruction.

Sec. Brown, Air Force: Air Force policies and plans for strategic forces.

Lt. Gen. Ferguson, Air Force: Mixed force concept, role of FB-111, B-52 and advanced manned strategic aircraft development.

John Foster, Defense Department: Advanced manned strategic aircraft, contract definition and performance characteristics.

Gen. LeMay, Air Force: Need for mixed forces, discussion of uncertain value of bombers. Characteristics of B-52, B-70 and advanced manned strategic aircraft.

Gen. McConnell, Air Force: Importance of Triad concept, Soviet antiballistic missile capability.

Gen. Ryan, Air Force: SRAM system explained, need for strategic aircraft in 1970s.

*DOD Authorization for Procurement and R&D: Hearings on Military Posture* (February, March, April 1966)

Sec. McNamara, Defense Department: Manpower needs, Vietnam, management changes within Defense Department, Navy carriers and antisubmarine warfare, discussion of SRAM and Nike-X, Poseidon, F-111, expected threats and discussion of role of manned bomber.

John Foster, Defense Department: Need for defensive strategic forces, Nike-X, research and development effort directed toward Vietnam, SRAM, M-16 rifle.

Sec. Resor and Gen. Johnson, Army: Shortages in Vietnam, civilian defense, Reserves, Shillelagh missile, M-16 and helicopter development.

Lt. Gen. Dick, Army:  Army research and development request.

Sec. Brown and Gen. McConnell, Air Force:  Airlift capability, strategic posture, B-52 follow-on.

Lt. Gen. Ferguson, Air Force:  Air Force research and development request--avionics, XB-70 and vertical/short take-off and landing.

Sec. Nitze, Navy:  Navy worldwide commitments, antisubmarine warfare, attack carrier program, fast deployment launches (FDL).

Vice Adm. Colwell, Navy:  Navy research and development--CVAN (carrier), DDGN and DLGN (destroyers), F-111B and Poseidon.

Vice Adm. Rickover, Navy:  Need for nuclear frigates.

*Hearings on Airlift, Special Subcommittee on Airlift* (March, April 1966)

Asst. Sec. Vance, Defense Department:  Airlift capability, Military Air Transport Service and Tactical Air Command, Fleet Logistical Support squadrons.

Gen. Wheeler, Joint Chiefs of Staff:  U.S. commitments that could call for airlift capability.

Gen. Adams, Army:  Army Strike Command--coordination of airlift capabilities.

Other witnesses include Harold Brown, Air Force, industrial spokesmen, and airlift and logistical commanders testifying on airlift capability.

*Administration and Operation of Draft System* (June 1966)

Witnesses and testimony include Lt. Gen. Hershey, Selective Service, and many others on operation of draft.

*Nature and Extent of U.S. Military Commitments*
(August 1966)

Sec. <u>Rusk</u>, <u>State</u> <u>Department</u>:  Nature of military
treaties, SEATO and CENTO, need for military commitments and military assistance.  Discussion of
Central Intelligence Agency influence and "no win"
policy in Vietnam.


FOREIGN AFFAIRS COMMITTEE


*U.S. Policy toward China, Subcommittee on the Far*
*East and China* (January, February, March 1966)

Ralph <u>Powell</u>:  Chinese nuclear capabilities,
missiles.
Samuel <u>Griffith</u>, <u>M.I.T.</u>:  Chinese use of guerrilla war techniques.
<u>Doak</u> <u>Barnett</u>:  Chinese military intentions.
John <u>Lindbeck</u>:  Chinese technological and military capabilities.
Hans <u>Morgenthau</u>, <u>University</u> <u>of</u> <u>Chicago</u>:  Chinese
influence seen as "psychological" not military;
mistake of containment policy.
Roger <u>Hilsman</u>, <u>Columbia</u> <u>University</u>:  China and
United States on collision course.
Sec. <u>Rusk</u>, <u>State</u> <u>Department</u>:  Discussion of containment policy.


*Foreign Economic Assistance* (February, March 1966)

David <u>Bell</u>, <u>Agency</u> <u>for</u> <u>International</u> <u>Develop-</u>
<u>ment</u>:  Vietnam largest recipient.
Asst. Sec. <u>Williams</u>, <u>State</u> <u>Department</u>:  Discus-
sion of military takeovers in Africa.
Sec. <u>McNamara</u>, <u>Defense</u> <u>Department</u>:  Shift of
Vietnam aid into defense budget; discussion of how
much aid goes to what countries.

## JOINT COMMITTEES OF HOUSE AND SENATE

### JOINT ATOMIC ENERGY COMMITTEE

*The Spread of Nuclear Weapons* (February, March 1966)

    Sec. <u>Rusk</u>, <u>State</u> <u>Department</u>:  No conflict between nonproliferation treaty and NATO.
    William <u>Foster</u>, <u>Defense</u> <u>Department</u>:  Need for security assurances to non-nuclear allies.
    Glenn <u>Seaborg</u>, <u>Atomic</u> <u>Energy</u> <u>Commission</u>:  Need for system of international safeguards.
    Sec. <u>McNamara</u>, <u>Defense</u> <u>Department</u>:  Chinese nuclear capability, need for security assurances.

## SENATE COMMITTEES

### APPROPRIATIONS COMMITTEE

*DOD Appropriations for FY 1967* (February, March 1966)

    See joint hearings before Senate Armed Services Committee (February, March 1966).

### ARMED SERVICES COMMITTEE

*Authorization for DOD Procurement and R&D* (February, March 1966)

    Sec. <u>McNamara</u>, <u>Defense</u> <u>Department</u>:  Defensive strategic posture, manpower requirements, procurement problems, threats in the Third World, importance of research and development.

John Foster, Defense Department: Equipment in Vietnam, MOL, Polaris A-3, Poseidon, SRAM, Nike-X, antisubmarine warfare, streamlined research and development procedures.

Gen. Johnson, Army: Situation in Vietnam, sufficiency of materials, Army in Europe, operation of Strike Command and Nike-X.

Gen. Dick, Army: Army research and development --Lance, Chaparrel, Vulcan cannon, Sprint, and TOW.

Sec. Nitze and Adm. McDonald, Navy: Naval posture, importance of carrier, and status of amphibious forces.

Sec. Brown and Gen. McConnell, Air Force: Airlift, Minuteman II and III, space program, C-5A and advanced manned strategic aircraft.

Discussion of pilot shortage, advanced manned strategic aircraft, Soviet strategic capabilities.

Lt. Gen. Ferguson, Air Force: Assault aircraft development, systems development, Hound Dog missile, C-5A and advanced manned strategic aircraft.

*U.S. Army Combat Readiness, Preparedness Investigating Subcommittee* (May 1966)

Gen. Freeman, Army: Functions of Strike Command, U.S. Strategic Army Force (STRAF), Reserve component readiness and Vietnam situation.

Gen. Johnson, Army: Vietnam and NATO commitments, capability of units in Vietnam.

*Administration of Reserve Components, Preparedness Investigating Subcommittee* (August 1966)

Sec. Resor, Army: Opposed to minimum force levels, supports proposal for National Guard-Reserves merger.

Maj. Gen. Cantwell, National Guard: Approval of the proposed merger.

Col. Carllion, Reserve Officers Association: Opposed to proposed merger.

FOREIGN RELATIONS COMMITTEE

*Supplemental Foreign Assistance* (1966)

Sec. Rusk, State Department, and Sec. McNamara, Defense Department: Status of military assistance in Vietnam, need for increase, discussion of problems in Thailand.

*Administration Policies in Southeast Asia* (January, February 1966)

Sec. Rusk, State Department: Gulf of Tonkin Resolution and its military implications.
Gen. Gavin (Ret.), Army: Discussion of "enclave strategy" in Vietnam.
George Kennan, Princeton University: Supports withdrawal.
Gen. Taylor (Ret.), Army: Supports escalation of war.
Sec. Rusk, State Department: Implications of SEATO treaty.
Sec. McNamara, Defense Department: North Vietnamese aggression.

*U.S. Policy toward China* (March 1966)

John Fairbank, Harvard University: Containment policy a mistake.
Morton Halperin, Harvard University: Chinese nuclear capability and missile strategy.
Harold Hinton, Harvard University: Unlikely that Chinese could challenge the United States in strategic military power.
George Taylor: Threat of Chinese militancy and rationality.

*Foreign Economic Assistance* (April, May 1966)

David Bell, Agency for International Development: Breakdown of aid package.

Sec. Rusk, State Department: Aid given to countries where U.S. security interests greatest.

Sec. McNamara, Defense Department: "Fortress America" concept, defends aid program to Latin America; importance of military aid emphasized.

John K. Galbraith, Harvard University: Aid to counter communism foolish; one of the causes of the India-Pakistan war.


*U.S. Policy toward NATO* (June 1966)

Asst. Sec. Bundy, Defense Department: Nuclear proliferation, East-West relations; discussion of multilateral nuclear force.

Gen. Norstad, NATO: Opposition to troop withdrawal from Europe; discussion of French withdrawal from NATO.

Henry Kissinger, Harvard University: Basis of French policy; discussion of U.S. pressure on West Germany.

Norman Cousins, *Saturday Review*: Need for conventional and nuclear agreements in Europe; discussed European nuclear consultation.


GOVERNMENT OPERATIONS COMMITTEE


*National Security Policy and the Atlantic Alliance, Subcommittee on National Security and International Operations* (April, May, June 1966)

Dean Acheson: The necessity of NATO, need for U.S. presence, and the problem of French withdrawal.

Christian Herter: Plans for reconstruction of NATO.

Gen. <u>Norstad</u> (<u>Ret</u>.), <u>Air</u> <u>Force</u>:  Discussion of nuclear weapon control in NATO.

Thomas <u>Schelling</u>, <u>Harvard</u> <u>University</u>:  Highest priority--keeping troops in Europe, advisability of nuclear sharing.

John <u>McCloy</u>:  Need to continue NATO, opposition to Mansfield's "token force" concept.

Sec. <u>Rusk</u>, <u>State</u> <u>Department</u>:  Discussion of French policy, opposition to unilateral force reduction.

Sec. <u>McNamara</u>, <u>Defense</u> <u>Department</u>:  NATO essential, French withdrawal not viewed as disastrous, and discussion of possibility of reciprocal force reductions.

# 1967 CONGRESSIONAL HEARINGS

## 90th Congress, First Session

HOUSE COMMITTEES

APPROPRIATIONS COMMITTEE

*DOD Appropriations for FY 1968, Part 1* (1967)

Testimony of service representatives on personnel.

*--Part 2*

Sec. McNamara, Defense Department: Funds for Vietnam, policy objectives, military tasks in Vietnam, South Vietnam's armed forces, U.S. deployment in Vietnam.

Discussion of target limitation, North Vietnam's involvement, role of South Vietnamese forces, role of B-52's, decision making in war.

Sec. McNamara, Defense Department: General defense budget statement, spectrum of military threats, strategic forces, damage-limiting capabilities, Nike-X system, strategic bomber forces.

Discussion of adequacy of budget, advanced manned strategic aircraft, antiballistic missile, bombing of North Vietnam, SEATO treaty obligations.

Requirements for general purpose forces, new research and development programs.

*--Part 3*

 Sec. Resor, Army:   Operations in Vietnam, overall build-up, Reserve training.
 Gen. Johnson, Army:   Vietnam, Special Forces,
posture elsewhere.
 Discussion of pacification programs, adequacy of
budget, production of M-16, quality of soldiers.
 Discussion of antiballistic missile system, Soviet missile threat.
 Sec. Brown, Air Force:   Strategic forces, FB-
111's, role of B-52's in Vietnam.   Air operations
in Vietnam and role of Tactical Air Command.
 Gen. McConnell, Air Force:   Soviet threat, readiness of strategic forces, future of manned bomber,
need for advanced manned strategic aircraft.   Operations against North Vietnam, destruction inflict-
ed.
 Discussion of C-5A, future of advanced manned
strategic aircraft, B-52 phase-out, Air Force space
program, training of pilots.
 Sec. Nitze, Navy:   Navy forces, naval air force
in Vietnam, size of fleet, operations in Vietnam.
New ship procurement.
 Adm. McDonald, Navy:   Combat role in Vietnam,
new missile programs.


*--Part 4*

 Testimony of service representatives on procurement.


*--Part 5*

 Testimony of service representatives on operation and maintenance.

*--Part 6*

Testimony of Admiral Rickover on nuclear propulsion.


ARMED SERVICES COMMITTEE


*DOD Authorization for Procurement and R&D* (1967)

Sec. McNamara, Defense Department: See hearings of the Senate Armed Services Committee (January 1967).

Sec. Brown and Gen. McConnell, Air Force: Air Force posture and procurement--advanced manned strategic aircraft, antiballistic missile; discussion of air actions in Southeast Asia and Soviet threat.

Lt. Gen. Holzapple, Air Force: Air Force research and development request.

Sec. Resor and Gen. Johnson, Army: Nike-X, strategic capabilities; discussion of Army in Vietnam and M-16 rifle.

Asst. Sec. Nitze, Defense Department, and Adm. McDonald, Navy: Poseidon, posture and procurement requests, ship research--DLBN (destroyer) and antisubmarine warfare.

John Foster, Defense Department: Soviet antiballistic missile defense, Soviet research and development, problems with FB-111, development of vertical/short take-off and landing aircraft, Nike-X; discussion of contracting practices.

Vice Adm. Rickover, Navy: Need for nuclear DLGN (destroyer); discussion of nuclear versus conventional costs; need for nuclear carriers.


*Hearings on Draft Extension* (May 1967)

T. Morris, Defense Department: Concept of all-volunteer Army.

*Examination of DOD Cost Reduction Program, Subcommittee for Special Investigations* (July 1967)

Morton Seward, Defense Department: Procurement of Navy's F-4, discussion of Defense Department procurement policy.

Asst. Sec. Ignatius and Robert Anthony, Defense Department: Defense Department policy audit program, discussion of savings.

Statements by Army, Navy and Air Force logistics officers on programs of cost reduction.


BANKING AND CURRENCY COMMITTEE


*Hearings on Import-Export Bank Arms Credit* (July, August, September 1967)

Asst. Sec. Rostow, State Department: Lending viewed as fundamental to security, Communist lending practices and economic effects.


FOREIGN AFFAIRS COMMITTEE


*Military Assistance Hearings* (April 1967)

Sec. McNamara, Defense Department: Need for military aid to protect security interests. Aid to Greece, Turkey, Nationalist China, South Korea, and Middle East explained.

Gen. Wheeler, Joint Chiefs of Staff: Obsolescence of equipment, improvement of Soviet and Chinese military equipment.

Discussion of aid to Latin America.

JOINT COMMITTEES OF HOUSE AND SENATE


JOINT ATOMIC ENERGY COMMITTEE


*AEC Authorization for FY 1968* (January, February, March 1967)

James Ramey and Harold Fuger, Atomic Energy Commission: Nuclear rocket and weapons development.


*Hearings on ABM Defense, Subcommittee on Military Applications* (November 1967)

Asst. Sec. Nitze, Defense Department: New computer capability, use of area defense against Chinese intercontinental ballistic missile threat.

John Foster, Defense Department: Soviet fractional orbital bombardment system threat; discussion of new radar technology.

Phillip Mosely: Military balance changing, new technologies and Soviet aggressiveness.

Thomas Wolfe, RAND Corp.: Soviets would consider antiballistic missile aimed at them and this would create new round of arms race.

Alice Hsieh, RAND Corp.: Chinese possess defense-oriented strategic system and have highly rational military policies.


SENATE COMMITTEES


APPROPRIATIONS COMMITTEE


*DOD Appropriations for FY 1968* (1967)

See hearings before Senate Armed Services Committee (January 1967).

ARMED SERVICES COMMITTEE

*DOD Authorization for Procurement and R&D, FY 1968, Defense Appropriations Subcommittee, Joint Hearings . . .* (January 1967)

Sec. McNamara, Defense Department:  Arguments for installing antiballistic missile, damage-limitation strategy, Soviet strategic forces and Chinese capabilities.  Situation in Vietnam and NATO strength.

John Foster, Defense Department:  SRAM development and FB-111, Minuteman II, development of Poseidon, antiballistic missile, advanced manned strategic aircraft, and Nike-X.

Sec. Resor and Gen. Johnson, Army:  U.S. strength in Vietnam, M-16 rifle problems; and discussion of bombing of North Vietnam.

Asst. Sec. Nitze, Defense Department, Adm. McDonald, Navy, Gen. Green, Marine Corps:  Soviet naval development, Phoenix missile, F-111 for Navy, need for fast deployment ships.

Sec. Brown and Gen. McConnell, Air Force:  Air Force strategic forces, Soviet strategic deployments, need for advanced manned strategic aircraft, electronic warfare, F-111; discussion of Minuteman follow-on and discussion of C-5A and operations against Vietnam.

*Vietnam Supplemental Funds* (January 1967)

Sec. McNamara, Defense Department:  Costs of Vietnam war, effectiveness of bombing.

Gen. Wheeler, Joint Chiefs of Staff:  Discussion of enclave strategy, effectiveness of bombings, disagreement with McNamara.

*World Wide Military Commitments, Preparedness Investigating Subcommittee* (February, March 1967)

Sec. Rusk, State Department:  Vietnam strategy, SEATO commitment, treaty commitments worldwide, De Gaulle's strategy, role of Central Intelligence Agency, threat to NATO, developments in nuclear strategy.

Adm. McDonald, Navy:  Problem of naval obsolescence.

Gen. Johnson, Army:  NATO commitments, Chinese troop strengths, force levels in Vietnam.

Gen. McConnell, Air Force:  Air Force conventional needs, need for antiballistic missile, airlift capabilities.

Gen. Green, Marine Corps:  Marine helicopter forces, transport capabilities, Vietnam requirements.

*U.S. Troops in Europe, Combined Subcommittee of Foreign Relations and Armed Services Committees on Troop Reduction* (April, May 1967)

See hearings of the Senate Foreign Relations Committee (April, May 1967).

*Air and Sea War in Vietnam, Preparedness Investigating Subcommittee* (August 1967)

Gen. Wheeler, Joint Chiefs of Staff:  Necessity of intensifying war, need for more bombing and new targets.

Gen. McConnell, Air Force:  Need for more bombing.

Sec. McNamara, Defense Department:  Success of bombing in North Vietnam.

Gen. Johnson, Army:  Need for wider bombing and more important targets--Haiphong.

*Hearings on Reserve Merger* (October 1967)

Sec. Resor, Army:  Opposed to concept of

permanent minimum force strengths and to an Assistant Secretary for Reserve Affairs.

Number of spokesmen for National Guard and Reserves in favor of minimum force levels.


## BANKING AND CURRENCY COMMITTEE

*Hearings for Export-Import Arms Credit* (July 1967)

Asst. Sec. Nitze, Defense Department, and Asst.
Sec. Rostow, State Department:  Use of Bank vital
for security to offset Soviet aid.

Sen. Ellender:  Quoted Defense Department's
opposite position of 1964.


## GOVERNMENT OPERATIONS COMMITTEE

*Programming and Budgeting Systems in Government (PPBS
Hearings), Subcommittee on National Security and International Operations* (March, April, May, June, July
1967)

Charles Schultze, Bureau of the Budget:  Uses of
planning, programming, budgeting system, its nature
and uses in different agencies.

Discussion of risks with use and possible bias,
discussion of Budget Bureau responsibility in budgeting process.

Asst. Sec. Enthoven, Defense Department:  Planning, programming, budgeting system in Defense
Department, its functional uses--Skybolt, TFX, Navy
F-111B, B-70 and Nike-X decisions.  Criticism of
prior Defense Department management.  Use for determining level of forces for Europe and role of
computers in decision making.

Discussion of "cost" as a defense factor.

Elmer Staats, General Accounting Office:  Comptroller General's use of planning, programming,
budgeting, role in budget review process, application to M-16 rifle.

William Gaud, Agency for International Development:  Benefits and risks of planning, programming,
budgeting use in foreign affairs.


FOREIGN RELATIONS COMMITTEE


*Hearings on Responsibilities of U.S. as a Great Power*
(January 1967)

George Kennan, Princeton University:  Changes in
nature of the Communist bloc.

Edwin O. Reischauer, Harvard University:  Over-
estimation of Chinese military threat.

Harrison Salisbury, *New York Times*:  U.S. bombing of North Vietnam discussed.

Henry Commager, Amherst College:  Discussion of
resources that enable the United States to be a
great power.

Lt. Gen. Gavin (Ret.), Army:  Reduction of U.S.
troop strength in Europe advised.


*Treaty on Outer Space* (March, April 1967)

Sec. McNamara, Defense Department:  Implications
of treaty for weapons development programs; national security enhanced with treaty.

Gen. Wheeler, Joint Chiefs of Staff:  Joint
Chiefs concerned with verification capability.
Need for detection capabilities.

Cyrus Vance, Defense Department:  Capability of
surveillance systems, impossibility of large deployment of space weapons without detection.

*U.S. Troops in Europe, Combined Subcommittee of Foreign Relations and Armed Services Committees on Troop Reductions* (April, May 1967)

Asst. Sec. Rostow, State Department:  Importance of U.S. troops to allied defense, size necessary to guarantee confidence.

Discussion of NATO without France.

Sec. McNamara, Defense Department:  Troop reduction impossible, costs of troops and discussion of defense burden-sharing.

Sec. Rusk, State Department:  Importance of conventional capability, Soviet threat, nature of tactical nuclear force and Middle East situation.


*Hearings on Foreign Commitments Abroad and Legislative Approval* (August 1967)

Ruhl Bartlett, Fletcher School of Law and Diplomacy:  Need for congressional role in making foreign military commitments.

Asst. Sec. Katzenbach, Justice Department:  Distinctions between presidential and congressional roles in foreign policy.

# 1968 CONGRESSIONAL HEARINGS

## 90th Congress, Second Session

HOUSE COMMITTEES

APPROPRIATIONS COMMITTEE

*DOD Appropriations for FY 1969, Part 1* (1968)

Sec. <u>McNamara</u>, <u>Defense</u> <u>Department</u>: Pueblo seizure, Khesanh stand, pacification program, strate-
gic balance, budget preparation, NATO decision
making, Soviet cruise missile threat, proposed
antiballistic missile system.

Sec. <u>Resor</u>, <u>Army</u>: Army forces in Vietnam, performance of new weapons.

Gen. <u>Johnson</u>, <u>Army</u>: Vietnam situation, new procurement programs, risks in budget.

Discussion of troops in Europe, Communist tactics in Vietnam, rotation program.

*--Part 2*

Sec. <u>Brown</u>, <u>Air</u> <u>Force</u>: Offensive missile and
bomber improvements, aircraft improvements, air-
lift, operations in Vietnam.

Gen. <u>McConnell</u>, <u>Air</u> <u>Force</u>: Increased Soviet
strategic threat, B-52 contribution in Vietnam,
improvement of airlift capability.

Discussion of advanced manned strategic aircraft

development, Soviet air defense, Soviet intercontinental ballistic missile build-up.

Sec. Ignatius, Navy: Navy deployment in Southeast Asia.

Adm. Moorer, Navy: Antisubmarine warfare capability, growing Soviet navy.

*--Part 3*

Testimony of service representatives on procurement.

*--Part 4*

Testimony of service representatives on operation and maintenance.

*--Part 5*

Testimony of service representatives on military personnel.

*--Part 6*

Testimony of Admiral Rickover on nuclear propulsion.

Hearing on F-111 aircraft programs.

ARMED SERVICES COMMITTEE

*DOD Authorization, Procurement and R&D for FY 1969* (February, March, April, May, June 1968)

Sec. McNamara, Defense Department: Major military threats, antiballistic missile research and

development and deployment, Vietnam progress, discussion of strategic capability, F-111 and fast
deployment launches (FDL).

Gen. Wheeler, Joint Chiefs of Staff:  Full-scale
development of advanced manned strategic aircraft,
development of Poseidon, hardened silos for Minuteman and preliminary development of a ballistic missile ship.

Sec. Clifford, Defense Department:  Pueblo affair, F-111B, DLGN (destroyer) program.

John Foster, Defense Department:  Military research and development austerity, Chinese intercontinental ballistic missile, Sentinel antiballistic
missile, Russian fractional orbital bombardment
system and advanced manned strategic aircraft.

Gen. McConnell, Air Force:  Airlift forces, general purpose forces.

Alexander Flax, Air Force:  Air Force research
and development request, Vietnam barrier, FB-111,
vertical/short take-off and landing aircraft and
Russian antiballistic missile capabilities.

Gen. Johnson, Army:  Army force levels, rapid
deployment.

Lt. Gen. Betts, Army:  Army research and development request--Cobra helicopter, Lance missile,
night vision, SAM-D and antiballistic missile.

Sec. Resor, Army:  Army overall budget request.

Lt. Gen. Starbird, Navy:  Antiballistic missile
request and justification.

Sec. Ignatius, Navy:  Navy overall request--
fleet defense, F-111B, sealift forces, strategic
forces.

Vice Adm. Caldwell, Navy:  Antisubmarine warfare
program.

Adm. Moorer, Navy:  Aircraft, amphibious forces,
sea-based offensive and defensive forces.

Gen. Chapman, Marine Corps:  Marine request,
commitment of forces and mission description.

*Military Construction Authorization, FY 1969* (April 1968)

Hearings include discussion of procurement of land for antiballistic missile sites.


## BANKING AND CURRENCY COMMITTEE


*Extension of 1950 Defense Procurement Act* (May 1968)

Witnesses and testimony by Defense Department and General Accounting Office officials on problems of military procurement under Defense Production Act. Vice Admiral Rickover, Navy analyzes Defense Department as "fourth branch of government."


## FOREIGN AFFAIRS COMMITTEE


*Foreign Military Assistance, FY 1969* (February 1968)

Asst. Sec. Warnke, Defense Department: Necessity of military aid for collective security.
William Bundy, Defense Department: U.S. military policy in East Asia and Pacific.
Sec. Rusk, State Department: Purposes of military assistance.


## SCIENCE AND ASTRONAUTICS COMMITTEE


*NASA Authorization for FY 1969* (March 1968)

Witnesses and testimony include Werner von Braun and others on effect of cut of Nerva nuclear rocket program.

JOINT COMMITTEES OF HOUSE AND SENATE

JOINT ATOMIC ENERGY COMMITTEE

*Naval Nuclear Propulsion* (March 1968)

Witnesses and testimony include Vice Admiral
Rickover, Navy, discussing difficulty in contracting nuclear work, need for nuclear guided missile
frigates, and need for nuclear escort ships.

*AEC Authorization* (April 1969)

Witnesses and testimony include testimony of
Vice Admiral Rickover, Navy, and discussion of Soviet nuclear submarine build-up.

JOINT ECONOMIC COMMITTEE

*DOD Spending Policies and Efficiency, Military Pro-
curement Policies* (November 1968 through 1969)

Elmer Staats, General Accounting Office:  No information on defense profits, per cent of contracts
awarded competitively and otherwise.
John Malloy, Defense Department:  Defense profits not viewed as too high.
William Petty, Defense Department:  Discussion
of post-award audit studies.
A. E. Fitzgerald, Air Force:  C-5A contract
twice as expensive as planned.
A. W. Buesking, University of Southern California:  Aerospace contracts 50% higher than planned.
Irving Fisher, RAND Corp.:  Problems with incentive contracts.
Robert Charles, Air Force:  C-5A called

outstanding program, effects of inflation on costs,
no retaliation against Fitzgerald for his testimony.

Elmer Staats, General Accounting Office:  Ways
of analyzing defense spending, problems with use of
planning, programming, budgeting system.

Jack Carlson, Bureau of the Budget:  Problems of
measuring and comparing defense and non-defense
items.

John K. Galbraith, Harvard University:  Proposal
for congressional military audit commission, discussion of military-industrial complex, need to
reduce defense expenditures.

Charles Schultze, Brookings Institution:  Vietnam savings disappearing; the tendency to plan
every defense contingency and the desire to modern-
ize cited as responsible for high budgets, urged
examination of attack carrier, F-14, military
transport and support troops.

Leonard Lecht:  Effect of reduced defense spending on economy.

Kenneth Boulding, University of Colorado:  War
industry's increased share of the economy, use of
Japanese analogy.

Malcolm Hoag, RAND Corp.:  Need for cost effi-
ciencies and arms control agreement.

William Kaufman, M.I.T.:  Possibility of budget
ceiling and $60 billion budget.

Carl Kaysen, Princeton University:  Possibility
of $50 billion budget with arms control agreement.

Stewart Udall:  Inability of Congress to deal
effectively with military requests.

Robert Moot, Defense Department:  Vietnam savings would not automatically cut Defense Department
budget, discussion of efficiency of Defense Department.

Walter Reuther, United Auto Workers:  Critical
of military-industrial ties, advocated cuts in defense spending.

SENATE COMMITTEES

## AERONAUTICAL AND SPACE SCIENCES COMMITTEE

*NASA Authorization for FY 1969* (1968)

Testimony includes discussion of nuclear rocket program.

## APPROPRIATIONS COMMITTEE

*DOD Appropriations for FY 1969* (1968)

See hearings of the Senate Armed Services Committee.

## ARMED SERVICES COMMITTEE

*Hearings on M-16 Rifle, Special Investigating Committee of Preparedness Investigating Subcommittee* (1968)

Sen. Muskie and Sen. McGovern: Discussion of Army mismanagement.
Berge Thonasian, Maremont Corp.: Strength of Army business ties.

*DOD Authorization for Procurement and R&D FY 1969, Joint Hearings* . . . (February, March, April, May, June 1968)

Sec. McNamara, Defense Department: Soviet strength capabilities, gains in Vietnam, Soviet antiballistic missile system, Sentinel antiballistic missile, Chinese intercontinental ballistic missile capabilities, FB-111 and advanced manned strategic aircraft; discussion of nuclear carrier fleet.

Gen. Wheeler, Joint Chiefs of Staff: Strategic forces and capability, status of general purpose forces, strategy of assured destruction.

John Foster, Defense Department: Over-the-horizon radar, Condor and Maverick missile development, Minuteman III; discussion of Soviet research and development.

Sec. Resor and Gen. Johnson, Army: Army deployments and research and development--antiballistic missile and SAM-D.

Sec. Ignatius, Navy: Fleet ballistic missile force, need for new fighter, multiple independently targeted re-entry vehicle for submarine-launched ballistic missiles, Phoenix missile and nuclear frigates.

Adm. Moorer, Navy: Russian naval and submarine threat.

Sec. Brown and Gen. McConnell, Air Force: Minuteman III, Soviet fractional orbital bombardment system, threat of Soviet antiballistic missile, and need for advanced manned strategic aircraft.

Asst. Sec. O'Neal and Lt. Gen. Betts, Army: Army research and development program.

Asst. Sec. Frosch, Navy: Navy research and development program.

Lt. Gen. Holzapple, Air Force: Air Force research and development program.

Rear Adm. Clancy, Vice Adm. Connolly, Asst. Sec. Frosch, Navy: Navy F-111 program, cost and performance problems.


*Hearings on U.S. Submarine Program, Preparedness Investigating Subcommittee* (March 1968)

Capt. Bradley, Navy: Threat of Soviet submarine force.

John Foster, Defense Department: Discussion of

Navy nuclear attack submarine.

Sec. Ignatius and Adm. Moorer, Navy:  Navy antisubmarine warfare strategy, mission of attack submarines.

Vice Adm. Rickover, Navy:  Defense Department
management, number of attack submarines needed.


*Status of U.S. Strategic Power, Preparedness Investi-
gating Subcommittee* (April 1968)


Gen. Wheeler, Joint Chiefs of Staff:  General
status of overall strategic forces, future projections.

John Foster, Defense Department:  Need for increased research and development to protect strategic power.

Asst. Sec. Enthoven, Defense Department:
Decision-making procedures for strategic forces.


*--Part 2* (April, May 1968)

Testimony from Harold Brown, James Ferguson, and
Gen. Nazzaro, Air Force, on need for manned bomber,
advanced manned strategic aircraft, for secure deterrent.


*Military Construction Authorization, FY 1969* (April,
May 1968)


Thomas Morris, Defense Department:  Discussion
of Sentinel program.


*U.S. Tactical Air Power Program, Preparedness Inves-
tigating Subcommittee* (May, June 1968)


Adm. Moorer, Navy, Gen. Chapman, Marine Corps,
Vice Adm. Connolly, Navy:  Soviet capability, U.S.
carrier strength, numbers of Navy fighter aircraft,

chronology of aircraft development.

Gen. Disoway, Air Force:  Air Force tactical
fighter program, F-X concept, A-X, F-111 role.
Discussion of NATO fighter doctrine.

Asst. Sec. Enthoven, Defense Department:  McNamara tactical fighter strategy, methods of judging
aircraft.

Discussion of civilians' ability to judge military requirements.


## FOREIGN RELATIONS COMMITTEE


*Hearings on Foreign Revolutions* (February 1968)

Crane Brinton, James Thompson, Louis Harz, and
John McAlister:  Nature of guerrilla wars and military responses.


*Hearings on Tonkin Gulf Incident* (February 1968)

Sec. McNamara, Defense Department, and Gen.
Wheeler, Joint Chiefs of Staff:  Closed session--
statement of incident and policy reaction.


*Military Assistance Program* (March, April, May 1968)

Sec. Rusk, State Department:  U.S. involvement
in Vietnam, security implications of aid-treaty
commitments.

Sec. Clifford, Defense Department:  Curtailment
of military assistance would lead to isolationism.
Need for allied confidence and credit plan for arms
assistance.


*Non-Proliferation Treaty* (July 1968)

Sec. Rusk, State Department:  Cost of developing advanced weapons systems.

William Foster, Arms Control and Disarmament Agency:  Amount of nuclear materials throughout the world.

Paul Nitze, Defense Department:  Support for treaty, United States not favoring unilateral disarmament.  List of nations capable of producing nuclear weapons.

Edward Teller, University of Southern California:  Need for nuclear guarantees to defend non-nuclear allies.

Rep. Findley:  Treaty would weaken western alliance.

# 1969 CONGRESSIONAL HEARINGS

## 91st Congress, First Session

HOUSE COMMITTEES

APPROPRIATIONS COMMITTEE

*DOD Appropriations for FY 70, Part 1* (1969)

Testimony of service representatives on military personnel.

*--Part 2*

Testimony of service representatives on operation and maintenance.

*--Part 3*

Testimony of service representatives on research, development, test, and evaluation--Air Force, Navy.

*--Part 4*

Testimony of service representatives on research, development, test, and evaluation--Army.

*--Part 5*

Testimony of service representatives on procurement.

*--Part 6*

Testimony of Admiral Rickover on nuclear propulsion.

*--Part 7*

Sec. <u>Seamans</u>, <u>Air</u> <u>Force</u>:  Soviet intercontinental ballistic missile build-up, need to improve procurement.

Gen. <u>Ryan</u>, <u>Air</u> <u>Force</u>:  Soviet strategic threat increasing, need for B-1 and advanced intercontinental ballistic missile technology.

Discussion of effects of budget reductions on Vietnam forces, cost of F-111, B-52 modifications, C-5A problems, multiple independently targeted reentry vehicle capabilities.

Sec. <u>Resor</u>, <u>Army</u>:  Army actions in Vietnam, training of South Vietnamese army, new procurement programs.

Discussion of Cheyenne procurement, new missile systems, present strategy in Vietnam.

Gen. <u>Westmoreland</u>, <u>Army</u>:  Vietnam strategy, Army requirements.

Sec. <u>Chafee</u>, <u>Navy</u>:  Navy procurement, need for new destroyers and frigates, F-14 program.

Adm. <u>Moorer</u>, <u>Navy</u>:  Soviet maritime expansion, value of sea basing, need for F-14, long-range shipbuilding program.

Discussion of Vietnam activities, shipbuilding problems, cost of carrier task force.

Sec. <u>Laird</u>, <u>Defense</u> <u>Department</u>:  Federal budget situation, retention of B-52's, megatonnage study, new bomber development.

Gen. <u>Wheeler</u>, <u>Joint</u> <u>Chiefs</u> <u>of</u> <u>Staff</u>:  Joint

Chiefs' participation in budget making, effect of reductions, cost of Vietnam war.

Discussion of all-volunteer armed forces, Vietnamization, Vietnam troop withdrawals.

## ARMED SERVICES COMMITTEE

*Hearings on Army Tank Program, Investigating Subcommittee* (March, April 1969)

Elmer Staats, General Accounting Office: Technical problems and cost of Sheridan tank program, optimism of Army.

Lt. Gen. Betts, Army: Tank working efficiently, technical problems being overcome, role of Shillelagh missile.

*Pueblo Investigation, Special Subcommittee* (March, April 1969)

Witnesses include Admiral Moorer, Navy, Lieutenant General McKee, Air Force, and General Wheeler, Joint Chiefs of Staff, discussing the importance of intelligence gathering.

*DOD Authorization, Procurement and R&D for FY 1970* (March, April, May, July, August 1969)

Sec. Laird, Defense Department: Vietnam policy, challenges to U.S. forces, growing threat of Soviet strategic forces, need to deploy antiballistic missile.

John Foster, Defense Department: Need to deploy antiballistic missile, improving U.S. weapons system acquisition process.

Sec. Laird, Defense Department: Safeguard antiballistic missile program, President Nixon's plans

for peace. South Vietnam's capability for defense,
Soviet strategic threat.

Discussion of Pentagon decision making, bomber
funding, Soviet navy program, Navy antisubmarine
warfare program, Pueblo incident.

Gen. Wheeler, Joint Chiefs of Staff: Pueblo
incident, new procurement programs.

Dep. Sec. Packard, Defense Department: Necessity of antiballistic missile system, description of
Safeguard program.

Discussion of Soviet strategic threat, antiballistic missile alternatives, threat to Minuteman
missile.

John Foster, Defense Department: Description of
Safeguard system.

Marvin Kalkstein, University of New York: Soviets do not possess first-strike capability.

John Wheeler, Princeton University: Need for
antiballistic missile to enhance defense credibili-
ty.

George Rathjens, M.I.T.: Technical and strategic problems of Safeguard.

Frank Collins, Brooklyn Polytechnic Institute:
Money for antiballistic missile should go for social expenses.

Donald Brennan, Hudson Institute: Ballistic
missile defense makes sense, can be successful.

Lawrence O'Neill: Need for hard-site defense
of Minuteman.

Gen. McConnell, Air Force: Soviet strategic
threat, need for B-1, airborne warning and control
system.

Discussion of B-1, space program.

Sec. Seamans, Air Force: Discussion of procurement practices, Fitzgerald scandal.

Sec. Chafee, Navy: Poseidon program, new shipbuilding program.

Adm. Moorer, Navy: Operations in Southeast
Asia, underwater long-range missile system program.

Antiballistic missile discussion includes:
George Rathjens, Jerome Wiesner, and Frank Collins
opposed to antiballistic missile deployment and

Lawrence O'Neill and Donald G. Brennan supporting
its deployment.

*Hearings on C-5A Controversy* (May 1969)

Maj. Gen. Jeffrey, Air Force:  Estimates of
Lockheed's losses; discussion of possibility that
Lockheed purposely underestimated bid to get con-
tract.
Lt. Gen. Crow, Air Force:  Boeing's preferred
design discussed.
A. Ernest Fitzgerald, Air Force:  Explanation of
higher cost.

*Military Construction Authorization* (July 1969)

Hearings include discussion of test facilities
for Kwajalein Island test for antiballistic missile.

*Hearings on Draft Law to Establish Lottery System,
Special Subcommittee on the Draft* (September, October
1969)

Testimony includes statements and discussion by
Roger Kelley, Defense Department, Lieutenant General Hershey, Selective Service, and many others.

*Air Defense of Southeastern United States, Special
Subcommittee on Air Defense of Southeastern United
States* (November, December 1969)
Y4.Ar5/2a:969-70/39

Rep. Roger:  Facts surrounding Cuban Mig-17 penetration of U.S. air space, problem of detecting
low altitude targets.
Col. De Bruter, Air Force:  Types of planes or
missiles used against United States from Cuba,

possibility of clandestine missiles in Cuba, capabilities of Cuban air force.

E. E. Rodenburg, Navy:  Threat of Soviet naval weapons to East Coast.

Col. Ballou, Air Force:  Briefing of Continental Air Defense Command mission and organization.

Col. Graves, Air Force:  Principles of current and advanced radar systems.

Adm. Morrison, Navy:  Naval surveillance of Soviet navy in Gulf of Mexico and defense against aircraft and missiles.

Gen. McKee, Air Force:  North American Air Defense Command's capabilities for air defense.


FOREIGN AFFAIRS COMMITTEE


*Effects of Space and Weapons Development on U.S. Alliance Policies, Subcommittee on National Security Policy and Scientific Developments* (1969)

Jerome Wiesner, M.I.T., and Charles Herzfeld: Opposition to thick antiballistic missile deployment, question of problems surrounding thin deployment.

Discussion of possible Chinese reaction and effect of arms control.

Harold Linstone, Lockheed Aircraft:  Prediction of development in next three decades; discussion of less dependency on overseas bases.

Eugene Rostow, Yale University:  Need for stability in arms race and closer nuclear cooperation with allies.

George Kistakowsky, M.I.T.:  Suspension of multiple independently targeted re-entry vehicle (MIRV) testing, challenged conception of SS-9 as a first-strike weapon.

Donald G. Brennan, Hudson Institute:  U.S. antiballistic missile deployment would not necessitate MIRV program.

Thomas Wolfe, RAND Corp.: Soviet MIRV capability, effect of MIRV on disarmament attempts.

J. I. Coffey, University of Pittsburgh: MIRV suspension possible with other weapon advances.

Rep. Hosmer: Moratorium of MIRV would weaken bargaining position at Strategic Arms Limitation Talks.

Rep. Anderson: MIRV will escalate arms race.

John Foster, Defense Department: Need for MIRV --survival ability and penetration; discussion of Soviet Galosh antiballistic missile. MIRVs not seen as threatening arms race stability.


*Foreign Military Assistance* (June, July, August 1969)

Sec. Laird, Defense Department, and Gen. Wheeler, Joint Chiefs of Staff: Soviet threats in Europe, Asia, and Latin America.

Sec. Rogers, State Department: Military sales to Latin America and to Turkey discussed.


*Chemical-Biological Warfare: U.S. Policies and International Effects, Subcommittee on National Security Policy and Scientific Developments* (November, December 1969)
Y4.F76/1:W19/6

Rep. McCarthy: Effects of toxins, herbicides and incapacitating agents and Soviet chemical and biological weapon capability.

Dr. Bennett, New York University: Proliferation of chemical and biological weapons.

Arthur Galston, Yale University: Use of herbicides as military weapons.

Thomas Pickering, State Department: National Security Council review of Geneva protocol and its implications.

Rear Adm. Lemos, Defense Department: Use of riot control agents.

GOVERNMENT OPERATIONS COMMITTEE

*Hearings to Establish a Commission on Government Procurement, Subcommittee on Military Operations* (March, April, May 1969)

John Malloy, Defense Department:  Defense of Defense Department against charges of waste, complexity of procurement process.

Robert Moat, Defense Department:  Extent of examination and supervision of Defense Department program.

Phillip Hughes, Bureau of the Budget:  Small amount of attention given Defense Department programs.

Heinz Abersfeller, General Services Administration:  Efforts at cost reduction in contract-letting.

Brig. Gen. Lee, Air Force, and Rear Adm. Howard, Navy:  Need for public confidence in government-industry relationships.

John Foster, Defense Department:  New management procedures to reduce costs.

Aaron Racusin, Air Force:  C-5A overrun, nature of information concerning costs that was kept secret.

Capt. Freeman, Navy:  Navy cost problems--antisubmarine destroyer escorts.

Gordon Rule, Navy:  Navy techniques for reducing F-111B costs.


*Military Supply Systems, Military Operations Subcommittee* (November, December 1969)

Hearings focus on management, communications, transportation, and data processing.

JOINT COMMITTEES OF HOUSE AND SENATE

JOINT ATOMIC ENERGY COMMITTEE

*AEC Authorization FY 1970* (April 1969)

Glenn Seaborg, Atomic Energy Commission:  Highest priorities of Atomic Energy Commission civilian
cutback in weapons production.  Antiballistic missile and multiple independently targeted re-entry
vehicle testing.
Vice Adm. Rickover, Navy:  Naval nuclear needs
and Soviet submarine production.

JOINT ECONOMIC COMMITTEE

*Hearings on Soviet Economy, Subcommittee on Economy
in Government* (June 1969)

Merle Fainsod, Harvard University:  Increase of
Soviet defense budget, skeptical of arms agreement.
Alex Inkeles, Harvard University:  Views Soviet
military strength as not global in nature.
Thomas Wolfe, RAND Corp.:  Reasons for increased
Soviet defense; feelings of Soviet vulnerability,
Soviet fear of massive antiballistic missile.
Abram Bergson, Harvard University:  Amount of
Soviet military spending.
David Mark, State Department:  "Keeping up with
U.S." as reason for Soviet defense build-up.

*Economic Analysis and Efficiency of Government*
(August 1969)
Y4.Ec7:Ec7/23

Robert Anthony, Harvard University:  Evaluation

of systems analysis, suggestions for improving weapons systems analysis and acquisition.

Thomas Nelson: Need for long-term planning in weapons acquisition.


*Dismissal of A. Ernest Fitzgerald by the DOD* (November 1969)
Y4.Ec7:F57

Arthur Fitzgerald, Air Force: Procurement and policy procedures for C-5A.

Sec. Seamans, Air Force: Cost overruns of C-5A.


*Hearings into Waste and Inefficiency in Defense Spending, Economic Subcommittee* (December 1969)

Robert Keller, General Accounting Office: Reasons for cost increases, no central monitoring system in Defense Department, discussion of Navy's Deep Submerging Rescue Vehicle and Army's Gama Goat program.


## SENATE COMMITTEES


## APPROPRIATIONS COMMITTEE


*DOD Appropriations for FY 1970* (1969)

See also joint hearings before Senate Armed Services Committee (March, April, May, June 1969).


*--Part 1*

Testimony of service representatives on military personnel.

*--Part 2*

   Testimony of service representatives of the Department of the Army.

*--Part 3*

   Testimony of service representatives of the Department of the Navy.

*--Part 4*

   Testimony of service representatives of the Department of the Air Force.

*--Part 5*

   Testimony on the F-111 program, including testimony of Air Force General John O'Neill on F-111 status report.
   Sec. Laird, Defense Department:  Appeals for budget restoration--helicopter, pilot training, F-14 aircraft, SRAM missile.
   Discussion of B-52 durability, adequacy of air defenses.


ARMED SERVICES COMMITTEE


*Hearings on Nuclear Non-Proliferation Treaty* (February 1969)

   Glenn Seaborg, Atomic Energy Commission:  Treaty would neither jeopardize U.S. security nor impose additional restrictions on U.S. nuclear programs.

*DOD Procurement and R&D Authorization for FY 1970*
(March, April, May, June 1969) [Joint hearings of the
Senate Appropriations and Armed Services Committees]

Sec. Laird, Defense Department: Modernization
of Vietnamese armed forces, challenges to U.S. security, modification of Sentinel antiballistic missile system to protect Minuteman, reduction of
FB-111 acquisition, need for Poseidon development,
satellite early warning system.  Administration's
rationale for antiballistic missile deployment.
Growing threat of Soviet strategic power.

Dep. Sec. Packard, Defense Department:  Soviet
deployment of SS-9's and Soviet fractional orbital
bombardment system.  Discussion of the ability of
U.S. forces to meet Soviet challenges in the 1970s.

Paul Nitze, Defense Department:  Support for
antiballistic missile deployment.

Herbert York, University of Southern California:
Antiballistic missile deployment "technically ques-
tionable."

William McMillan, U.C.L.A.:  Deployment of
SS-9's creates doubt about land-based deterrent
without antiballistic missile.

Wolfgang Panofsky, Stanford University:  U.S.
forces not challenged by SS-9, not a first-strike
weapon.

Albert Wohlstetter, University of Chicago:  U.S.
missile force could be 95% destroyed by 1976 without antiballistic missile.

George Rathjens, M.I.T.:  SS-9's could over-
whelm Safeguard—need for an arms control agreement.

Frederick Seitz:  Danger of another Pearl Har-
bor.

Abram Chayes, Harvard University:  Need to preserve present strategic balance, antiballistic
missile would create instability.

Sec. Seamans, Air Force:  Modification of C-5A
contract to prevent excessive Lockheed profits.
Mission of C-5A defended.

Thomas May, Lockheed Aircraft:  Hopes of

reducing contract loss by future sales.

Discussion of Army, Navy, and Air Force procurement—cut funds for A-7D tactical fighter, funds for F-14, nuclear submarines, and fast deployment logistic ships.


FOREIGN RELATIONS COMMITTEE


*U.S. Security Agreements and Commitments Abroad, Part 2: Philippines* (1969)

Lt. Gen. Gideon, Army, Rear Adm. Kaufman, Navy, and Col. Pale, Air Force: Nature of security agreements and Military Assistance Program, discussion of treaty expansion by the Executive.


*—Part 3: Thailand*

Ambassador Unger, State Department: Commitments to Thailand, U.S. assistance, role of Army Special Forces and purpose and effect of U.S. military construction and air operations.


*—Part 4: Republic of China*

Ambassador McConaughy, State Department: Security interests, Military Assistance Program, U.S. forces and use of airfields by B-52's.


*Hearings on Nuclear Proliferation Treaty* (February 1969)

Sec. Rogers, State Department: Nixon Administration in "complete agreement" with treaty, discussion of effect of antiballistic missile on treaty.

Glenn Seaborg, Atomic Energy Commission:  Safeguards and inspection procedures under treaty.

Sec. Laird, Defense Department:  Treaty would
not disadvantage military position, discussion of
antiballistic missile deployment with future negotiations planned.


*U.S.-Soviet Strategic Limitations, ABM and MIRV, In-
ternational Organization and Disarmament Affairs Subcommittee* (March, April, May, June, July 1969)

Garard Smith, Arms Control and Disarmament Agency:  Antiballistic missile would not prejudice
disarmament talks.

Daniel Fink:  Detailed history of Sentinel, support for continuation.

Hans Bethe, Cornell University:  Intercontinental ballistic missile's easy penetrability of thin
antiballistic missile, destabilizing effect of
thick deployment.

George Kistiakowsky, Harvard University, Herbert
York, University of Southern California, James
Killian, M.I.T.:  Sentinel system would accelerate
arms race, antiballistic missile could provoke nuclear war.

Sec. Laird, Defense Department:  Advantages of
antiballistic missile system, discussion of antiballistic missile's ability to offer protection.

Dep. Sec. Packard, Defense Department:  Shift of
antiballistic missile from city defense from Chinese attack to Minuteman defense.

Discussion of Soviet missile build-up.

Wolfgang Panofsky, Stanford University, and
George Rathjens, M.I.T.:  Opposed to deployment,
concern for arms race, Soviet first-strike capability seen as distant.  Technical difficulties of
antiballistic missile.

Donald Brennan, Hudson Institute:  Defense of
antiballistic missile, it would make arms limitation possible.

Jerome Wiesner, M.I.T.:  Antiballistic missile

would not work and would reduce U.S. security.
U.S. possession of adequate retaliatory capacity
and inadequacy of Sprint against large number of
SS-9's.  Difficulty of Sentinel's computer system.

Edward Teller, University of Southern California:  Need for defensive capabilities and ability
of scientists to work out technical problems.
Stated fear of Soviet technical lead.

Eugene Wigner, M.I.T.:  Vulnerability of antiballistic missile radar, but need to continue antiballistic missile research and development.

Gordon McDonald, University of California:
Antiballistic missile should be continued, U.S.
should deny Soviets invulnerability.

Donald Hornig:  Antiballistic missile sites
should be built for limited research and development purposes, Sentinel system too big and ineffec-
tual.

J. P. Ruina, M.I.T., Herbert York, University of
Southern California, Gordon McDonald, University of
California:  Suspension of multiple independently
targeted re-entry vehicle because of adverse effect
on arms race.  Obsolescence of Minuteman discussed.


*Military Aid to Latin America, Subcommittee on West-
ern Hemisphere Affairs* (June, July 1969)

Ralph Duncan:  U.S. military assistance as imperialism.

Charles Myers, State Department:  Aid program in
Latin America decreasing.

G. Warren Nutter, Defense Department:  Phase-out
of aid to Latin America.


*Foreign Military Assistance* (July, August 1969)

Sec. Rogers, State Department:  Aid to Spain,
discussion of airbases renewal and aid to Thailand.

Sec. Laird, Defense Department:  New sales policy and discussion of aid to Vietnam.

# 1970 CONGRESSIONAL HEARINGS

## 91st Congress, Second Session

HOUSE COMMITTEES

APPROPRIATIONS COMMITTEE

*DOD Appropriations for FY 1971, Subcommittee on Defense, Part 1* (February, March 1970)
Y4.Ap6/1:D36/5/971

Sec. <u>Resor</u> and <u>Gen</u>. <u>Westmoreland</u>, <u>Army</u>: Security in Western Europe and Southeast Asia, "strategic mobility," major research and development programs; discussion of inflation, tank and antitank weapons.

Sec. <u>Laird</u>, <u>Defense</u> <u>Department</u>, and <u>Gen</u>. <u>Wheeler</u>, <u>Joint</u> <u>Chiefs</u> <u>of</u> <u>Staff</u>: Overall budget presentation, spectrum of threats, problems created by divergency between Joint Chiefs' recommendations and actual budget, Phase 2 of Safeguard.

Discussion of antiballistic missile, Strategic Arms Limitation Talks, Vietnamization, and status of "peace dividend."

Sec. <u>Seamans</u> and <u>Gen</u>. <u>Ryan</u>, <u>Air</u> <u>Force</u>: Air Force budget requests—C-5A transport, F-111, Minuteman III, B-1 bomber, F-15, advanced vertical/short take-off and landing, and radar detection systems. Discussion of air defense, adequacy of retaliatory forces and status of strategic forces. Cost problems of SRAM, comparative satellite intercept capabilities of United States and Soviet Union.

Sec. Chafee and Adm. Moorer, Navy, and Gen.
Chapman, Marine Corps:  Naval budget requests, increasing importance of sea-basing forces, expansion
of Soviet navy, upgrading sea-based strategic force
and antisubmarine warfare programs.

Discussion of Soviet cruise missile threat, comparative U.S.-U.S.S.R. force levels, rationale for
sea-based missiles in context of antiballistic missile.

--*Part 2* (February, March 1970)

Budget requests for personnel.  Includes discussion of volunteer army, role of Reserves and
National Guard.

--*Part 3* (March 1970)

Vice Adm. Mustin, Defense Department:  Need for
research on high altitude effects of nuclear blasts
used for communication blackouts.

--*Part 4* (April 1970)

John Foster, Lt. Gen. Starbird, Dep. Sec. Packard, Defense Department:  Status of Phase 2 of
Safeguard, revised evaluation of Chinese and Soviet
threats, description of Spartan and Sprint missiles, deployment of radar systems.

Discussion of Strategic Arms Limitation Talks,
authenticity of Chinese threat.

--*Part 5* (February, March 1970)

Asst. Sec. Fox, Army:  Major changes in equipment and weapons procurement.

Brig. Gen. Kornet, Army:  Army budget request
for equipment and missiles--Cheyenne helicopter,

status of Chaparral, Hawk missiles, phase-out of
Nike-Hercules, comparisons of Shillelagh and TOW,
Lance and Pershing missiles, experimental radar,
xenon searchlight, electronic binoculars.

Vice Adm. Connolly, Navy: Navy request for aircraft and missiles, "1 1/2 war" strategy and budget
planning, F-14, early warning aircraft proposal;
progress on Poseidon, Sparrow, and Sidewinder programs; justification for Phoenix and Shrike missiles.

Vice Adm. Cousins, Navy: Shipbuilding budget,
status of smaller, "quality" Navy, nuclear attack
submarine, progress of CVAN nuclear carrier, nuclear guided missile frigates, applications of ocean-
ographic research.

Vice Adm. Shiffley, Navy: Navy progress in
long-range sonar development.

Gen. Ferguson, Air Force: Air Force requests
for aircraft and missiles, techniques of Air Force
procurement, description of Minuteman III, F-111,
and C-5A programs, development of F-15 and A-7D
aircraft. Dissatisfaction with F-111 discussed.

Lt. Gen. Glasser, Air Force: Air Force missiles, justification for Titan and Minuteman II and
III, the Shrike, Maverick, SRAM, and Sparrow.

Sec. Chafee, Navy: Problems with "fly before
buy" doctrine, nature of recent cost overruns.


--*Part 6* (April, May, June 1970)


John Foster, Defense Department: Defense research and development, long-range defense needs,
Soviet research and development, electronic warfare, early warning aircraft, practicality of a
space-based defense system. Comparison of Poseidon
and ULMS, trade-offs between manned bombers and
sea-based missiles. Policy changes due to increasing service alienation from Pentagon.

Asst. Sec. Johnson and Lt. Gen. Betts, Army:
Army research, development, testing and evaluation,
the antiballistic missile system, hardening costs

for Minuteman, MBT-70 program, Project Mallard--
tactical communication and chemical warfare.  Priorities for aircraft development discussed and
electronic battlefield described.

Asst. Sec. Frosch, Navy:  Navy research, development, testing, and evaluation request; description of Soviet threat; and discussion of U.S.
capability against Soviet cruise missile.  Funding
for antisubmarine warfare, justification for Phoenix and ULMS.

Asst. Sec. Hanson and Lt. Gen. Glasser, Air
Force:  Air Force research, development, testing,
and evaluation request, comparison of Soviet and
U.S. Air Force development of F-15, planning advanced tanker, potential utility of B-1, justification for SRAM, Minuteman III, and Maverick.

Eberhardt Rechtin, Defense Department:  Research
results in material sciences, behavioral science;
advanced monitoring and surface effects vehicles.
Quiet aircraft and mid-ocean floating platforms
discussed.

George Rathjens, M.I.T., and Sidney Drell, Stanford University:  Review of antiballistic missile,
of deployment of multiple independently targeted
re-entry vehicle and of Strategic Arms Limitation
Talks.  Assertions concerning Soviet missile
strength, technical problems of antiballistic missile radar.

Discussion of "numbers game" and Soviet first-
strike capacity.

Frederick Kieomanoff:  Comparison of defense
spending and domestic funding; urges new priorities.

*--Part 7* (May 1970)

Vice Adm. Rickover, Navy:  Naval nuclear ship
program; Soviet submarine program discussed.  Need
for development of silent electric submarines and
nuclear-powered surface ships.

*Foreign Assistance Appropriations for FY 1971, Sub-committee on Foreign Operations Appropriations, Part 1* (February, March 1970)
Y4.Ap6/1:F76/3/971

Sec. <u>Laird</u>, <u>Defense Department</u>, and <u>Gen</u>. <u>Wheeler</u>, <u>Joint Chiefs of Staff</u>: Military Assistance and Foreign Military Sales programs; discussion of military sales and overseas commitments.

*Military Construction Appropriations for FY 1971* (March 1970)
Y4.Ap6/1:M59/6/971

Lt. <u>Gen</u>. <u>Starbird</u>, <u>Army</u>: Safeguard program, requirements for research and development.
<u>Maj</u>. <u>Gen</u>. <u>Dalrymple</u>, <u>Army</u>: Cost sharing in NATO.

ARMED SERVICES COMMITTEE

*Military Airlift, Subcommittee on Military Airlift* (January, February 1970)
Y4.Ar5/2a:969-70/51

Lt. <u>Gen</u>. <u>Boylan</u>, <u>Air Force</u>: Air Force briefings on aspects of MAC C-5 cargo airlift, capability to respond to emergencies, potential of global strategic airlift system.
<u>Col</u>. <u>Richardson</u>, <u>Air Force</u>: Worldwide tactical airlift.
Lt. <u>Gen</u>. <u>Sitwell</u>, <u>Army</u>: Airlift components of Army, integration with Fast Deployment Ships, C-5A, short and vertical take-off and landing aircraft; discussion of civil air carriers' capabilities for military airlift.

*Independent Research and Development, R&D Investi-*
*gating Subcommittee* (February, March 1970) -
Y4.Ar5/a:R31/6

   Karl Harr:  Importance of private research and
development, particularly in aerospace industry.


*DOD Procurement and R&D Authorization, Part 1* (March,
April 1970)
Y4.Ar5/2a:969-70/53

   Sec. Laird, Defense Department, and Gen.
Wheeler, Joint Chiefs of Staff:  Major threats, assessment of Soviet and Chinese capabilities--
general purpose, strategic, guerrilla forces.  Key
programs affected by budget reductions; discussion
of role of National Security Council.
   Dep. Sec. Packard and John Foster, Defense Department:  C-5A and Lockheed fiasco, continuation
of Safeguard, assessment of Soviet and Chinese
threats against missile sites.
   Discussion of program alternatives with possible
failure of Strategic Arms Limitation Talks and
capability of warning system to alert President of
nuclear attack.
   Sec. Chafee and Adm. Moorer, Navy, and Gen.
Chapman, Marine Corps:  Importance of sea-basing
for rapid deployment.
   Vice Adm. Connolly, Navy:  Navy's aircraft and
missile procurement program, cost tables for electronic warfare; discussion of vertical/short take-
off and landing, early warning, and Poseidon,
Shrike and Phoenix.
   Vice Adm. Cousins, Navy:  Details for attack
submarines, nuclear guided missile frigates, Posei-
don and nuclear carriers.
   Sec. Seamans and Gen. Ryan, Air Force:  Air
Force authorization, Soviet capabilities, C-5A situation, alternate procurement policies, F-15, B-1,
A-X aircraft.
   Lt. Gen. Glasser, Air Force:  Specific Air Force

procurement requests; discussion of compatibility
of Minuteman and Safeguard system.

Sec. Resor and Gen. Westmoreland, Army: Pacification and Vietnamization programs, posture in
Europe, discussion of aircraft losses in Vietnam,
joint German-U.S. effort to build MBT-70.

Asst. Sec. Fox and Brig. Gen. Kornet, Army:
Army aircraft, missile, and vehicle requests. Data
on helicopters (Cobra, Chinook), Safeguard, Chaparrel, Shillelagh, TOW and tanks.

Gen. Palmer, Army: TOW-Shillelagh controversy,
Army reasons for choosing TOW.

--*Part 2* (February, March, April 1970)

John Foster, Defense Department: National technological manpower comparison with Soviet Union,
new management technique, discussion of Defense Department mismanagement and relation of technology
to the arms race.

Asst. Sec. Frosch, Navy: Navy research and development program--propellants, oceanography, radar
and sensors, carriers and underseas cargo vessels.

Asst. Sec. Jones, Air Force: Air Force research
and development budget requests, Minuteman, SRAM,
F-15 and A-7D fighters, strategic bombers and decoys.

Asst. Sec. Johnson, Army: Army research and development budget requests, helicopters, Safeguard,
SAM-D air defense, military position on enemy
"capability," vs. civilian position on "intent."

Vice Adm. Mustin, Defense Department: Discussion of Spartan and Sprint firings on civilian
populations.

Eberhardt Rechtin, Defense Department: Major
accomplishments of Advanced Research Projects Agency.

*Military Construction Authorization FY 1971, Joint Senate-House Armed Services Subcommittee* (April 1970)
Y4.Ar5/2a:969-70/55

    See hearings before Senate Armed Services Committee.


FOREIGN AFFAIRS COMMITTEE


*Arms Control and Disarmament Act Amendments, 1970* (February 1970)

    Gerard Smith, Arms Control and Disarmament Agency:  Discussion of research budget cut, progress of Strategic Arms Limitation Talks.


*U.S. Relations with Europe in the Decade of the 1970's, Subcommittee on Europe* (February, March, April 1970)
Y4.F76/1:Eu7/13

    Gen. Goodpaster, NATO:  Adverse effects of U.S. troop withdrawal, slow progress of convincing allies to share NATO burden.
    Martin Hillenbrand, State Department:  NATO role in defense stability of Europe, strategic considerations, discussion of defense expenditures of European countries and cost of maintaining troops in Europe.
    Gen. Lemnitzer, NATO:  Threat posed by Warsaw Pact, discussion of Mutual Balanced Force Reduction, Soviet intentions and use of tactical nuclear weapons.
    Marshall Shulman, Columbia University:  Soviet policy toward Europe, Soviet proposals for a security conference, advantage of conventional forces over nuclear forces.
    Timothy Stanley, School of Advanced International

Studies: "Balance of deterrence," discussion of number of U.S. troops necessary for NATO, evaluation of nuclear deterrent.

David Shoenbrum, Columbia University: Support for two-thirds reduction of troops in Europe, discussion of France's role in European defense and effects of possible troop withdrawal on Strategic Arms Limitation Talks.

Zbigniew Brzezinski, Columbia University: Economic and technical decline of Russia, possible European security through Strategic Arms Limitation Talks.

James King, Institute for Defense Analysis: Need for reorganization of NATO, European assumption of defense responsibilities, continuation of U.S. nuclear deterrent.

Rep. Reuss: Proposals for reducing costs by streamlining defense structure in Europe.

Paul Wohl, *Christian Science Monitor*: Future status of Soviet strength, benefits of Soviet-proposed European security conference.

*United States-China Relations: A Strategy for the Future, Subcommittee on Asian and Pacific Affairs* (September, October 1970)
Y4.F76/1:C44/9

Harold Hinton and Wayne Wilcox, Columbia University: Chinese military capabilities, discussion of Chinese infiltration.

Morton Halperin, Brookings Institution, and William Whitson, RAND Corp.: Basis of Chinese nuclear strategy, nature of military threat, discussion of Chinese attitudes toward antiballistic missile and Strategic Arms Limitation Talks.

*Military Assistance Training, Subcommittee on National Security Policy and Scientific Development* (October, December 1970)
Y4.F76/1:M59/4

Ernest Lefever, Brookings Institution:  Military
Assistance Program as a foreign policy instrument.

Paul Hammond, RAND Corp.:  Characteristics of
Military Assistance Advisory Group, organizational
oppositions for military assistance.

Amelia Leiss, M.I.T., and Geoffrey Kemp, M.I.T.
and Fletcher:  The use of military assistance to
control conflicts.

Col. Jordan, West Point:  Effects of Military
Assistance Program training in Korea, Vietnam,
Taiwan, and Thailand.

Alfred Stepan, Yale University, and Ross Baker,
Rutgers University:  Military Assistance Program
training in Latin America and Africa.

Asst. Sec. Nutter, Defense Department:  Accomp-
plishments and plans for Military Assistance Program.

*To Amend the Foreign Assistance Act of 1961:  Supple-
mental Authorization for Assistance to Cambodia*
(November, December 1970)
Y4.F76/1:F76/46

Sec. Laird, Defense Department:  Need for Military Sales Bill for military assistance to Cambodia.

Bernard Gordon:  Need for only a modest military
assistance program.

GOVERNMENT OPERATIONS COMMITTEE

*Policy Changes in Weapons System Procurement, Mili-
tary Operations Subcommittee* (September 1970)
Y4.G74/7:W37/2

Dep. Sec. Packard, Defense Department:  Difficulty of procurement, incentive system, use of
parallel development and need for improved research
and development.

Vice Adm. DePoux, Defense Department: Defense Department organization and responsibilities for procurement, need for competition and encouragement for simplification of weapons systems.

Asst. Sec. Sanders, Navy: Navy use of Milestone concept, use of "should cost" studies.

Asst. Sec. Fox, Army: Defining weapons systems requirements, problems of using "warm" production base concept and techniques of risk evaluation.

Asst. Sec. Whittaker, Air Force: Air Force procurement techniques, improvement of F-15 and B-1 management, use of increased trade-off flexibility.


SCIENCE AND ASTRONAUTICS COMMITTEE


*National Science Policy* (July, August 1970)
Y4.Sc2/9:91-2/23

Don Price, M.I.T.: Need for shifting science funding away from Defense Department.

Sec. Seamans, Air Force: Description of Air Force scientific programs, impact of new relevancy standards to research.

James Killian and Jerome Wiesner, M.I.T.: Consequences of relevancy standards on research and national security.

John Foster, Defense Department: Importance of science to national security.


JOINT COMMITTEES OF HOUSE AND SENATE


JOINT ATOMIC ENERGY COMMITTEE


*AEC Authorization for FY 1971, Part 1* (February 1970)
Y4.At7/2:L52/971

Glenn Seaborg, Atomic Energy Commission:  Nuclear activities, including weapons and space nuclear research.

Milton Klein, Atomic Energy Commission:  Nuclear rocket program--Nerva technology.


*Naval Nuclear Propulsion Program* (March 1970)
Y4.At7/2:N88/4/970

Adm. Rickover, Navy:  Size of nuclear fleet, complexity of weapons systems, Soviet submarine threat, need for nuclear carriers, discussion of overall carrier force levels, status of nuclear frigate program.


JOINT ECONOMIC COMMITTEE


*The Acquisition of Weapons Systems, Subcommittee on Economy in Government, Part 2* (May 1970)
Y4.Ec7:W37/4

Towbridge von Baur:  Waste in Defense Department management, civil-military responsibilities in procurement.

Elmer Staats, General Accounting Office:  General Accounting Office study on defense industry profits, identification of basic causes of cost overruns.

Asst. Sec. Fox, Army:  Army plans for procurement improvements, use of "should cost" studies for Hawk missile and Cheyenne helicopter.

Phillip Wittaker, Air Force:  Causes for procurement overruns, cost breakdown for SRAM and C-5A.

Frank Sanders, Navy:  Navy actions to reduce overruns--F-14, Poseidon, Mark 48 Torpedo program.

SENATE COMMITTEES

AERONAUTICAL AND SPACE SCIENCES COMMITTEE

*NASA Authorization for FY 1971* (February, March 1970)
Y4.Ae8:N21a/971

Thomas Paine, National Aeronautics and Space Administration: Review of aerospace accomplishments, discussion of Defense Department space program cancellation.

Dale Myers, National Aeronautics and Space Administration: Status of Air Force—National Aeronautics and Space Administration space shuttle program, nature of cooperation.

Oran Nicks, National Aeronautics and Space Administration: Research in nuclear rockets, short take-off and landing, space shuttle.

APPROPRIATIONS COMMITTEE

*DOD Appropriations for FY 1971, Part 1*

See Senate Armed Services Committee (February, March 1970), Y4.Ar5/3:D94/6/971.

*—Part 2* (April, May 1970)
Y4.Ap6/2:D36/4/971

Sec. Resor and Gen. Westmoreland, Army: Army budget explanation—manpower status, procurement, strategic mobility and research and development.

Discussion of Vietnam and European troop reductions, Soviet capabilities in Europe, European contributions to NATO, tank and antitank development, deployment of Safeguard.

Lt. Gen. Starbird, Army:  Program and schedules
of Safeguard, deployment, reliability, radar, research on advance antiballistic missile components.

Maj. Gen. Taylor, Army:  Army operations, strategic forces, intelligence and communications, airlift and sealift, reserve forces.

Asst. Sec. Fox, Army:  New budget management
developments.

Asst. Sec. Johnson, Army:  Army's research, development, testing and evaluation program, missiles, communication, non-nuclear weapons,
herbicides and surveillance.


--*Part 3* (April, May 1970)

Sec. Chafee and Adm. Moorer, Navy, and Gen.
Chapman, Marine Corps:  Navy budget explanation,
modernization, growth of Soviet navy, discussion of
carrier costs, status of E-2C early warning aircraft.

Vice Adm. Duncan, Navy:  Budget request for Reserve personnel.

Vice Adm. Shiffley, Navy:  Naval operations
under general and strategic purpose missions, intelligence and communications; discussion of development of fleet ballistic missile system.

Vice Adm. Connolly, Navy:  Budget request for
aircraft and missiles, status of missile defense.

Vice Adm. Cousins, Navy:  Shipbuilding request,
nuclear carriers, attack submarines and guided missile frigates.

Asst. Sec. Frosch, Navy:  Navy research, development, testing and evaluation request.


--*Part 4* (May 1970)

Sec. Seamans and Gen. Ryan, Air Force:  Effect
of budget cuts on procurement, status of C-5A,
F-111 and Minuteman III, nature of Soviet and Chinese threats.

Maj. Gen. Pitts, Air Force:  Air Force operations, strategic forces, air defense, intelligence
and communications, airlift.
Gen. Ferguson, Air Force:  Air Force procurement, B-1 bomber development and Minuteman III.
Grant Hanson and Lt. Gen. Glasser, Air Force:
Priorities in Air Force research, effect of budget
reductions.

--*Part 5* (November 1970)

Sec. Laird, Defense Department:  Defense Department request for restoration of cuts, threats to
national security.
Adm. Moorer, Joint Chiefs of Staff:  Comparison
of U.S. and Soviet navies, need for restoration of
cuts for air support, carrier force, and nuclear
submarine program.

--*Parts 6 and 7* (February, April, May 1971)

Asst. Sec. Moot, Defense Department:  Changing
national priorities reflected in budget.
John Foster, Defense Department:  Defense Department research and development request, review
of major programs, discussion of Chinese intercontinental ballistic missile threat, Strategic Arms
Limitation Talks, status of Soviet missile development.
Eberhardt Rechtin, Defense Department:  Advanced
sensors, information systems and behavioral research.
Robert Froehlke, Defense Department:  Reorganization of Defense Department intelligence.
Vice Adm. Mustin, Defense Department:  Storage
of nuclear weapons, vulnerability of strategic
weapons, hardening sites.
Mathew Meselson, Harvard University:  Security
implications of U.S. policy toward chemical weapons.

*Foreign Assistance Appropriations* (August, September 1970)
Y4.Ap6/2:F76/8/971

   Lt. Gen. Warren, Defense Department: Budget explanation for military assistance, elimination of aid to other countries in order to finance Cambodia, Korea, and Indonesia.
   Sec. Rogers, State Department: Military assistance to East Asia, shift of assistance from grants to credit sales.


ARMED SERVICES COMMITTEE


*DOD Authorization, Procurement and R&D* (February, March 1970)
Y4.Ar5/3:D94/6/971

   Sec. Laird, Defense Department: U.S. strategic forces and Soviet and Chinese threats, U.S. general purpose forces and hostile forces; need for research and development and Defense Department management improvements; discussion of eliminating independent budget recommendations by Joint Chiefs; Joint Chiefs' disagreements with Defense Department.
   Gen. Wheeler, Joint Chiefs of Staff: Joint Chiefs' view of budget as "borderline of acceptable risk."
   Discussion of Vietnamization, effect of budget cuts on research and development, adequacy of Joint Chiefs' input into budget determination.
   Sec. Laird, John Foster, and Dep. Sec. Packard, Defense Department, and Sec. Resor, Army: Presentation of Phase II Safeguard, additional sites and Sprint missiles and further research. Estimated Soviet and Chinese missile capabilities and effect of Strategic Arms Limitation Talks. Applicability of Safeguard to Chinese threat.

John Foster, Defense Department:  Need for defense research, major research programs and Soviet
technical capabilities.

Sec. Resor and Gen. Westmoreland, Army:  Army
budget, forces, weapons systems and significant research and development.

Asst. Sec. Fox, Army:  New management procedures
for procurement of helicopters, missile systems and
combat vehicles.


--*Part 2* (March 1970)

Dep. Sec. Packard, Defense Department:  Cost
overruns, reorientation of MBT-70 development.

Sec. Seamans and Gen. Ryan, Air Force:  Air
Force budget, aircraft and missile procurement, research and development, Soviet and Chinese capabilities.

Discussion of costs of various systems.

Asst. Sec. Hanson and Lt. Gen. Glasser, Air
Force:  Description of Air Force research and development.

Sec. Chafee and Adm. Moorer, Navy:  Importance
of sea-based forces, Navy objectives, growing Soviet threat.

Vice Adm. Connolly, Navy:  Naval aircraft and
missile procurement.

Col. Bates, Army:  Strategy of U.S. tank force
in Europe, Soviet capabilities, and need for MBT-70
tank.


--*Part 3, Ad Hoc Research and Development Subcommittee* (March, May 1970)

Sen. Proxmire:  Advisability of abolishing
uncontrollable research, difficulty in assessing
cost of defense procurements.

Sen. Cranston:  Importance of research, small
relative costs.

Sec. Laird, Defense Department:  Conduct of

Strategic Arms Limitation Talks, need to consider alternatives if Talks fail.

Wolfgang Panofsky, Stanford University: Opposition to antiballistic missile, misrepresentation of Soviet and Chinese threat.

Albert Wohlstetter, University of Chicago: Efficacy of Safeguard, inadequacy of alternatives.

Donald Horniz, University of Rochester: Political advisability of infallible defense, technical capabilities of Safeguard, incompatibility of city defense versus hard point missile defense.


*CVAN-70 Aircraft Carrier, Joint Senate-House Armed Services Committees* (April 1970)
Y4.Ar5/3:Ai7/12

Sec. Chafee, Navy: Consequences on breaking carrier production line.

Adm. Moorer and Rear Adm. Holloway, Navy: Navy cases for carrier production, capabilities and effectiveness, comparison with Soviet navy.

Discussion of comparative costs of land-basing and sea-basing aircraft.

Sen. Mondale: Carriers wasteful, Soviet lack of carriers, duplication of Air Force capability.

Rep. Moorhead: Recommends 12 carriers, discussion of costs and vulnerability.

Adm. Moorer, Navy: Rebuttal of Mondale and Moorhead.

Gen. Wheeler, Joint Chiefs of Staff: Supports CVAN-70, role of carriers.

Vice Adm. Rickover, Navy: Expansion of Soviet power, necessity for continual modernization, superiority of nuclear ships, necessity for maintaining lead-time.

William Kaufman, M.I.T.: Relation of carriers to tactical air power, reasons for favoring 12-carrier forces.

FOREIGN RELATIONS COMMITTEE

*U.S. Security Commitments and Agreements Abroad,*
*Part 5:   Japan and Okinawa* (1970)

Hearings to consider security commitments with
the above.  Discussion of the Japanese defense effort.

*--Part 6:   Republic of Korea*

Ambassador Porter, State Department:  Nature of
treaty with South Korea, relative military
strengths.

*--Part 7:   Greece and Turkey*

Robert Pranger, Defense Department:  U.S. assistance to Greece, Greek role in NATO, U.S. facilities and personnel in Turkey.

*--Part 8:   Ethiopia*

Discussion of U.S. grant of military assistance
and training, use of U.S. weapons, importance of
U.S. Strategic Communications Station.

*--Part 9:   Morocco and Libya*

Hearings to discuss naval communications complex
in Morocco and U.S. assistance to Libyan Air Force.

*--Part 10:   U.S. Forces in Europe*

Gen. Burchinal, Army:  Status and costs of assistance programs in Europe.

Gen. Goodpaster, NATO: U.S. NATO commitment, security implications of U.S. reductions.

*Foreign Military Sales Act Administration* (March, May 1970)

Dep. Sec. Packard, Defense Department: Nixon doctrine, discussion of sales program, details of program to Greece, Nationalist China, and Latin America.

Thomas Pickering, State Department: Explanation of excess sales program, policy determination sales.

*ABM, MIRV, SALT and the Nuclear Arms Race, Subcommittee on International Organization and Disarmament Affairs* (March, May, June 1970)
Y4.F76/2:An8/3

Sen. Brooke: No need for multiple independently targeted re-entry vehicle, effect on Strategic Arms Limitation Talks.

Marshall Shulman, Columbia University: Soviet attitudes toward multiple independently targeted re-entry vehicle and Strategic Arms Limitation Talks.

Herbert York, University of Southern California: Arms spiral, suspension of U.S. arms deployment, discussion of antiballistic missile capability.

Doak Barnett, Institute for Policy Analysis: China's nuclear strategy, effect of antiballistic missile on Chinese missile deployment.

Wolfgang Panofsky, Stanford University: Opposes Safeguard expansion; need for "dedicated" Safeguard defense.

Herbert Scoville, University of Southern California: Effect of SS-9 deployment on antiballistic missile and Minuteman, advises postponement of multiple independently targeted re-entry vehicle and Phase II Safeguard.

Sec. Laird, Defense Department:  Questions advisability of postponing multiple independently
targeted re-entry vehicle and Phase II Safeguard.
    Joseph Clark, SANE:  Antiballistic missile un-
suitable for defending Minuteman.
    Donald Hornig, George Kistiakowsky, Jerome Wies-
ner, M.I.T.:  Vulnerability of Safeguard.
    John Foster, Defense Department:  Concern for
vulnerability of U.S. forces with existing Soviet
arms momentum, confidence in antiballistic missile,
effect of multiple independently targeted re-entry
vehicle on Strategic Arms Limitation Talks.


*U.S. Security Agreements  and Commitments:  Broader
Aspects* (November 1970)
Y4.F75/2:Se2/3

    Carl Kaysen, Princeton University:  Goals of
U.S. military policy, purpose and nature of U.S.
forces, defense force sizes and budget projections.


GOVERNMENT OPERATIONS COMMITTEE


*TFX Contract Investigation (Second Series), Permanent
Subcommittee on Investigations, Part 1* (March 1970)
Y4.G74/6:T11/970

    John Brick, Government Operations Committee in-
vestigator:  1963 investigation, background of procurement, role of TFX as fighter/bomber.
    Charles Cromwell, Government Operations Commit-
tee investigator:  Obstruction of Defense Department in attempting to obtain information.


*--Part 2* (March, April 1970)

    Lt. Gen. O'Neill, Air Force:  Changes in F-111

program, reduction in production, production costs, losses of aircraft.

Keith Dental, Navy:  Weight problems in development of Navy F-111.

Sen. Tower:  Support of F-111, its contribution to defense.

George Spangenberg, Navy:  Opposition to bi-service plane, review of problems.

--*Part 3* (April 1970)

Leonard Sullivan, Navy:  Results of recommendations of the 1964 Ad Hoc Study Group on development of TFX.

Thomas Cheatham, Grumman Aircraft Corp.:  Chronological Defense Department decisions on TFX.

Thomas Nunnally, General Accounting Office:  Cost of F-111 program, profits by contractors.

Elmer Staats, General Accounting Office:  Relates TFX problems to other weapons systems.

# 1971 CONGRESSIONAL HEARINGS

## 92nd Congress, First Session

HOUSE COMMITTEES

APPROPRIATIONS COMMITTEE

*The Federal Budget for 1972* (February 24-25, 1971)
Y4.Ap6/1:B85/972

    Discussion by John Connally, Treasury Depart-
ment, and Paul McCracken, Council of Economic Ad-
visors, of government spending of "peace dividend."

*HUD, Space and Science Appropriations for 1972, Sub-
committee on HUD, Space and Science FY 72 Budget*
(March 1971)

    Includes testimony by representatives from the
Office of Science and Technology and National Aeronautics and Space Administration.  Discussion of
space platform, jet short take-off and landing,
aircraft program development and nuclear power propulsion program.

*DOD Appropriations for FY 72, Subcommittee on DOD
Appropriations, Part 1* (March 1971)
Y4.Ap6/1:D36/5/972

Sec. Laird, Defense Department, and Adm. Moorer,
Joint Chiefs of Staff:  Overall strategic issues,
"realistic deterrence" and Vietnamization, Defense
Department organization and management, defense
spending and the economy.  Projected military posture, relative U.S.-U.S.S.R. strategic, general
purpose, and naval forces.  Discussion of budget
cuts, U.S. interests in Indian Ocean.  Procedures
for formulating budget.

Sec. Resor and Gen. Westmoreland, Army:  Army FY
1972 request, summary of Army posture and deployments, discussion of NATO capabilities, strategy in
Vietnam, and capabilities of Safeguard.

Sec. Seamans and Gen. Ryan, Air Force:  Overall
Air Force requests, Sino-Soviet strategic threat,
discussion of U.S.-U.S.S.R. strategic forces, capabilities of F-14 and F-15 aircraft, F-111 program.
Description of Soviet bomber force, Air Force cost
reduction program.

Sec. Chafee and Adm. Zumwalt, Navy:  FY 1972
program, comparison of U.S.-U.S.S.R. naval power in
Mediterranean Sea.

Gen. Chapman, Marine Corps:  Marine FY 1972 requests, Marine status.

Asst. Sec. Moret, Defense Department:  Budget
explanation, impact of inflation described, role of
fiscal guidance, programming and budgeting programs.


--*Part 2* (February, March, April 1971)

Dep. Sec. Packard, Defense Department:  Defense
Department improvements in research and development
programs, discussion of C-5A and F-14 programs and
Safeguard hardsite defense.

Lt. Gen. Starbird, Army:  Status of Safeguard.

Gen. Holloway, Air Force:  Growth of Soviet
strategic forces, Strategic Air Command capabilities, importance of bombers--B-1.

Discussion of situations calling for use of nuclear weapons.

Rear Adm. Smith, Navy:  Poseidon projects and discussion of ULMS.

Maj. Gen. Taylor, Army, Rear Adm. Moore, Navy, Lt. Gen. Glasser, Air Force:  Reprogramming changes.


--*Part 3* (March, April 1971)

Asst. Sec. Kelley, Defense Department:  Budget explanation for all-volunteer Army.

Other testimony concerns pay, promotions, and Reserves and National Guard.


--*Part 4* (April, May 1971)

Requests for service operation and maintenance activities.


--*Part 5*

Asst. Sec. Fox, Army:  Army procurement, discussion of MBT-70 tank costs.

Vice Adm. Connolly, Navy:  Navy aircraft and missile procurement, discussion of Harrier and F-14 aircraft.

Vice Adm. Simmes, Navy:  Naval shipbuilding, capability of DD-963 destroyer.

Lt. Gen. Glasser, Air Force:  Status of F-111, discussion of C-5A performance and contract.

David Packard, Defense Department:  Lockheed contractual disagreements over C-5A, discussion of procurement practices.


--*Part 6*

John Foster, Defense Department:  Review of Defense Department research and development programs, discussion of technical developments and service programs.

Asst. Sec. Hanson, Air Force:  B-1 and F-15 development, A-X program and sensor technology developments.

Asst. Sec. Johnson, Army:  Priority of land-combat programs--Cheyenne helicopter, sensor systems and ballistic missile defense.

Asst. Sec. Frosch, Navy:  Antisubmarine warfare research, pollution abatement, F-14 aircraft.

--*Part 7*

Requests of defense agencies.
Stephen Lukasik, Advanced Research Projects Agency:  Environmental impact of military research and development, providing "tailored" equipment to small armies.

--*Part 8*

Vice Adm. Rickover, Navy:  Executive assumption of congressional power, capabilities of Soviet naval forces.  Need for more nuclear carriers and reduction of Defense Department bureaucracy.  Criticism of defense procurement policies.

--*Part 9*

Gen. Burchinal, Army:  U.S. force posture in Europe, discussion of U.S. withdrawal and Mutual Balanced Force Reductions.

James Wilson, American Legion:  Need for B-1 bomber, antiballistic missile to maintain strategic superiority.

Morton Halperin, American Federation of Scientists:  Methods to reduce size of defense budget.

Holland Hunter, Friends Committee:  Exaggeration of Soviet threat.

Rosalie Reichman, Women's International League for Peace and Freedom:  Recommendation to reduce defense budget.

Edward King, Coalition on National Priorities
and Military Policy:  Misuse of manpower in current
support concepts.


ARMED SERVICES COMMITTEE


*Extension of the Draft and Bills Related to the Vol-
untary Force Concept* (February, March 1971)
Y4.Ar5/2a:971-72/2

Sec. Laird, Defense Department:  Volunteer army
concept.
Asst. Sec. Kelley, Defense Department:  Military
manpower requirements for the 1970s.
Other witnesses include spokesmen for American
Legion and Reserves opposed to volunteer concept.
Appendix:  Defense Department report, "Defense
Military Manpower Requirements for FY 72."


*Authorization for Military Procurement, R&D and Ac-
tive and Reserve Forces. Parts 1 and 2* (March,
April, May 1971)
Y4.Ar5/2a:971-72/9

Sec. Laird, Defense Department:  Five-year defense program, antiballistic missile program,
Strategic Arms Limitation Talks, comparison of
U.S.-U.S.S.R. defense expenditures and Soviet naval
activities.
Adm. Moorer, Joint Chiefs of Staff:  Major pro-
jected military threats, Chinese missile capabili-
ty, Navy nuclear carrier programs.
Gen. Chapman, Gen. Ryan, Gen. Westmoreland, Adm.
Zumwalt, Joint Chiefs of Staff:  Carrier program,
allied contributions to SEATO, CENTO, and NATO,
manpower requirements.
Jeremy Stone, Federation of American Scientists:
Opposition to antiballistic missile, multiple

independently targeted re-entry vehicle, and B-1
programs, technical evaluation of weapons systems
effectiveness.

Discussion of services' use of classified information.

John Foster, Defense Department:  Justification
of research and development programs--multiple
independently targeted re-entry vehicle, Minuteman
III, Poseidon, F-14 and F-15, role of B-1 bomber,
danger of Soviet technical breakthrough.

Joseph Clark, World Federalists:  Budget
restriction to $60 billion.

Sanford Gottlieb, SANE:  Questions U.S. interests.

Charles Shirley, Brookings Institution:  "1 1/2
war strategy."

Leonard Rodberg, Institute for Policy Studies:
Defensive nature of Soviet military strategy.

Gen. Holloway, Air Force:  Continuing need for
manned bomber in Strategic Air Command, need for
B-1.

Maj. Gen. Kornet, Army:  Tactical Army missile
procurement and air defense--antiballistic missile,
TOW, and Shillelagh; Hawk and Lance missiles, MBT-
70 tank, M-16 rifle.

Vice Adm. Simmes, Navy:  FY 1972 Navy authorization for shipbuilding, discussion of naval modernization.

Adm. Zumwalt, Navy:  Growth of Soviet seapower,
CVAN-70 and nuclear frigate.

Vice Adm. Mintner, Navy:  Mark 48 torpedo program.

Maj. Gen. Poggemeyer, Marine Corps:  Marine
Corps authorization, guided missile procurement,
and T-2C aircraft.

Vice Adm. Connolly, Navy:  F-14 and F-15 aircraft, discussion of problems in program.

Sec. Seamans, Air Force:  Air Force authorization request--F-111 and B-1, C-5A contract and
costs.

Lt. Gen. Glasser, Air Force:  Air Force missile
and aircraft procurement--F-111, C-5A, B-1, SRAM
test program.

Asst. Sec. Nutter, Defense Department:  Authorization for military assistance to Vietnam.

Roger Kelley and Theodore Marrs, Defense Department; Vice Adm. Gunn, Navy; Maj. Gen. Fribourg, Marine Corps; and Arthur Allen, Army; Maj. Gen. Wilson and Richard Borda, Air Force; Col. Carellon and Col. Deerin, Reserves; Lt. Cmdr. Carson, National Guard:  Discussion of Reserves and National Guard authorization and policy.

Asst. Sec. Johnson, Army:  Army research and development request, weapons systems development.

Asst. Sec. Frosch, Navy:  Navy research and development request, status of F-14, relations with defense contractors.

Asst. Sec. Hanson, Air Force:  Air Force research and development request, reasons for B-1 development, international fighter program, status of F-111 and C-5A programs, A-X aircraft, SRAM, Maverick and Minuteman III.

Maj. Gen. Deane, Advanced Research Projects Agency:  Defense Special Projects Group authorization request, discussion of electronic battlefield.

Stephen Lukasik, Advanced Research Projects Agency:  Agency request, transfer of projects to National Science Foundation, General Accounting Office criticism of Advanced Research Projects Agency research.

Asst. Sec. Eberhardt, Defense Department:  Defense Department authorization request, comparison of U.S. and Soviet research and development expenditures, weapons systems development.


*Military Construction Authorization, FY 72* (June 1971)
Y4.Ar5/2a:971-72/13

Hearings on construction authorization.  Includes testimony by Maj. Gen. Yates on antiballistic missile construction.

*Review of the Administration and Operation of the Draft Law* (July, August, September, November 1971)
Y4.Ar5/2a:969-70/80

    Hearings to establish the lottery to reduce vul-
nerability from seven years to one year. Witnesses
include Curtis Tarr and Roger Kelley, Defense Department, testifying on the manpower pool, pay
increases, manpower utilization, and size of armed
forces.


FOREIGN AFFAIRS COMMITTEE


*American-Korean Relations* (1971)

    Ambassador Porter, State Department, and Gen.
Michaels, Defense Department:  Impact of possible
troop reductions in South Korea, threat from North
Korea.
    Maj. Gen. Lekson, Defense Department:  Review of
military sales and assistance program in South
Korea.


*Foreign Assistance, Part 1* (April, May 1971)
Y4.F76/1:F76/28/971

    John Irwin, State Department:  Revised manage-
ment of assistance program, new security assistance
goals and policies.
    Dep. Sec. Packard, Defense Department:  Defense
Department management responsibilities for security
assistance--Cambodia, Korea, Greece, Indonesia, and
South America.
    Marshall Green, State Department:  Programs in
Korea, Indochina, and Thailand.

--*Part 2*

Ronald Spiers, State Department:  State Department role in new security programs.

Lt. Gen. Warren, Defense Department:  Explanation of military sales program and military training aid.

Joseph Sisco, State Department:  Explanation of U.S. security assistance in Middle East.

Gen. Mather, Defense Department:  Objectives of of military aid in Latin America, sales program and training.

--*Part 3* (May, June 1971)

Adm. McCain, Navy:  Russian naval threat in the Pacific.

Gen. Throckmorton, Defense Department:  Military sales in Middle East, situation in East Pakistan, Soviet interests in the Indian Ocean, arms sales to Africa.

Gen. Goodpaster, NATO:  Military sales and assistance to Greece, Turkey, Spain, Portugal, and North African countries.  Warsaw Pact threat.

*The Cold War:  Origins and Developments, Subcommittee on Europe* (June 1971)
Y4.F76/1:C67/3

Arthur Schlesinger, Harvard University, Adam Ulam, Princeton University:  Historical causes of Cold War, misunderstandings.

Asst. Sec. Morse, Defense Department:  Need for continued military presence.

Richard Barnet, Institute for Policy Studies:  Future role of NATO, support for European withdrawal.

Robert Bowie, Harvard University:  Development of European unity, need for U.S. military presence.

*Indian Ocean:  Political and Strategic Future, Sub-
committee on National Security Policy and Scientific
Developments* (July 1971)
Y4.F76/1:In2/7

William Bundy, M.I.T.:  Strategic significance
of Indian Ocean, advantages to low U.S. profile,
discussion of role of Japan in the region, Soviet
presence.
Parker Hart, Georgetown University, and Alvin
Cottrell, Columbia University:  Need to maintain
limited U.S. presence, vagueness of Soviet intentions.
Gary Grappert, University of Wisconsin:  Changing trade policies in Africa, minority rule major
threat to region.
Ronald Spiers, State Department:  Support for
reopening of Suez Canal, need for limited U.S.
presence.

## GOVERNMENT OPERATIONS COMMITTEE

*Applications of the Aerospace and Defense Industry
Technology to Environmental Problems, Subcommittee on
Conservation and Natural Resources* (1971)
Y4.G74/7:Ae8

Witnesses and testimony from Departments of
State and Defense, Congress and private business to
ascertain the ability and means of the defense
establishment to move into the environmental area.

*Defense Industry Profit Study of the General Account-
ing Office, Legislative and Military Operations Subcommittee* (March 1971)
Y4.G74/7:G28/2

Rep. Eckhardt:  Questions accuracy of General
Accounting Office study.

Elmer Staats, General Accounting Office:  Defends report; discussion includes Defense Department-contractor relationships.

*U.S. Government Information Policies and Practices: The Pentagon Papers* (June 1971)

Arthur Goldberg:  Recommends framework to reconcile rights and needs of government and public on national security questions.

William Florence, Defense Department:  Defense Department classification practices, difficulty of declassification.

David Cooke, Defense Department:  Defense Department history and description of its classification system, classification problems.

## JOINT COMMITTEES OF HOUSE AND SENATE

### JOINT ATOMIC ENERGY COMMITTEE

*Nuclear Rocket Engine Development Program, Joint Hearings with Senate Aeronautical and Space Sciences Committee* (February 1971)

See hearings of the Senate Aeronautical and Space Sciences Committee (February 1971).

*AEC Authorization FY 1972* (February, March 1971)
Y4.At7/2:152/972

Glenn Seaborg, Atomic Energy Commission:  Overall budget request, production of weapons, surveillance and nuclear propulsion systems.

*Naval Nuclear Propulsion Program, 1971* (March 1971)

Vice Adm. Rickover, Navy:  Status and costs of
nuclear ship programs, including submarines, frigates, and nuclear carrier.  Importance of high
speed nuclear vessels, Soviet threat, Defense Department bureaucratic delays.

JOINT ECONOMIC COMMITTEE

*Economic Issues in Military Assistance, Subcommittee
on Priorities and Economy in Government* (January,
February 1971)

Sen. Fulbright:  Need for better definition and
control of military sales program.
Elmer Staats, General Accounting Office:  Lack
of full accountability by Defense Department for
all types of military assistance.
Townsend Hoopes:  Management and coordination of
Defense and State Departments.  Military assistance
programs, 1965-1967; weakness of Nixon Doctrine.
Need for military assistance.
Nicholas Katzenbach:  Use of Nixon Doctrine in
Southeast Asia.
William Whitson, RAND Corp., Edward Fried and
Morton Halperin, Brookings Institution:  Evolution
of American military assistance, major components
of military assistance and relationship with eco-
nomic assistance.
Discussion of reform opposition from recipient
counters.
Armistead Selden, Defense Department:  Review of
current military assistance and sale programs.
Discussion of congressional accountability; ef-
fect of Nixon Doctrine on military assistance.
Chester Bowles:  History of misuse of military
assistance funds.
Sen. McGovern:  Opposition to using Food for

Peace funds for military assistance programs.
John Irwin, State Department:  Objectives of
Nixon Doctrine, planned improvements in military
assistance.
Charles Wolf, RAND Corp.:  Economic impact of
military assistance.


SENATE COMMITTEES


AERONAUTICAL AND SPACE SCIENCES COMMITTEE


*Nuclear Rocket Engine Development Program, Hearings
with Joint Atomic Energy Committee* (February 1971)

George Low, National Aeronautics and Space Administration, and Glenn Seaborg, Atomic Energy Commission:  Economic impact of nuclear rocket
cutback, nuclear research and development efforts.


*NASA Authorization for FY 1972* (March, April 1971)
Y4.Ae8/N21a/971

Sec. Seamans, Air Force:  Importance of National
Aeronautics and Space Administration to national
security, Air Force–National Aeronautics and Space
Administration cooperation on space shuttle, high
cost of cancelling research and development program.


*--Part 2* (April 1971)

John Foster, Defense Department:  Soviet space
activities, Defense Department space budget and
support for space shuttle.
Discussion of transfer of military research and
development to private industry.

## APPROPRIATIONS COMMITTEE

*DOD Appropriations for FY 1972* (1971)

See hearings before Senate Armed Services Committee (March 1971).

*Military Construction for FY 1972* (1971)

See hearings before Senate Armed Services Committee (June, July 1971).

## ARMED SERVICES COMMITTEE

*Investigation of Electronic Battlefield Program, Preparedness Investigation Subcommittee* (1971)
Y4.Ar5/3:B32

Maj. Gen. Dlan, Army: Description of sensor systems, including conventional barrier, air transport, and ground tactical systems.
Maj. Gen. Williamson, Army: Army combat sensors in Vietnam.
Rear Adm. House, Navy: Naval use of sensors in Vietnam, operation Sealord.
Maj. Gen. Evans, Air Force: Description of Igloo White, Air Force anti-infiltration system in Laos.
Maj. Anderson, Army: Description of integrated night observance in Southeast Asia.
Maj. Gen. Fulton, Army: Description of electronic battlefield, including night vision systems, thermal imaging, radars, air surveillance, and ground sensors.

*Selective Service and Military Compensation* (February 1971)
Y4.Ar5/3:Se4/3

Sec. Laird, Defense Department: All-volunteer army, future status of National Guard and Reserves.
Sen. Kennedy: Opposition to volunteer army.
Sen. Hatfield: Costs of draft versus volunteer force.
Over twenty other witnesses on aspects of present system, the majority opposed to the draft and the Vietnam war.

*Authorization for Military Procurement and R&D* (March 1971) [Joint Hearings]
Y4.Ar5/3:P94/6/972

Sec. Laird, Defense Department, and Adm. Moorer, Joint Chiefs of Staff: Five-year defense program, overall strategic issues and capabilities, and Defense Department management. Projected U.S. posture, U.S.-U.S.S.R. strategic balance and Chinese intercontinental ballistic missile threat.
Discussion of budget cuts and service morale problems.
Sec. Resor and Gen. Westmoreland, Army: Army FY 1972 request, Army mission presently in Vietnam and NATO.
Discussion of NATO capabilities and effect of a troop withdrawal.
Sec. Seamans and Gen. Ryan, Air Force: Air Force strategic and conventional forces, threat of Soviet forces, need for B-1, and discussion of current Air Force research and development.
Sec. Chafee and Adm. Zumwalt, Navy, and Gen. Chapman, Marine Corps: Navy's strategic role, Soviet naval development, importance of Indian Ocean, need for adequate naval bases in the Mediterranean.
John Foster, Defense Department: Soviet and U.S. research and development, need for U.S. increase.

Discussion of multiple independently targeted
re-entry vehicle (MIRV), technology for Minuteman
III and Poseidon, Soviet MIRV capabilities.


--*Part 2*

John Foster, Defense Department:  Review of
antiballistic missile developments, options for
their future use; discussion of Strategic Arms
Limitation Talks and possible antiballistic missile
--limitation and effect on multiple independently
targeted re-entry vehicle deployment.
Lawrence O'Neill, Defense Department:  Need to
protect Minuteman, support for antiballistic missile over Hardsite.
Wolfgang Panofsky:  Support for Hardsite, excess
cost and unreliability of antiballistic missile.
Harold Agnew:  Need for both Hardsite and antiballistic missile options to protect Minuteman.
Herbert York, University of Southern California:
Support for antiballistic missile ban in Strategic
Arms Limitation Talks.
Gen. Holloway, Air Force:  Growth of Soviet
strategic power, possible Soviet nuclear superiority and use to which superiority could be put in
time of crisis.
Joseph Clark, SANE:  Recommendation to reduce
budget to $60 billion, alleged overstatement of
Chinese and Soviet threats.
Herbert Scoville:  Possibility of basing deterrence entirely on submarine strategic forces, recommendation of cutback for intercontinental
ballistic and antiballistic missiles, for multiple
independently targeted re-entry vehicle, and for
B-1.
Leonard Rodberg:  Expensive conventional weapons
questioned due to improbability of major conventional war, questions Navy's charges of block obsolescence.
John Foster, Defense Department:  Discussion of
Soviet first-strike capability in the 1970s,

reemphasizes need for antiballistic missile development.


*--Part 3*

    Adm. Zumwalt, Navy:  Navy requests for surface
effects ships.
    Col. Traynor, Air Force:  Characteristics of
Harrier vertical/short take-off and landing, Marine
use.


*--Part 5A*

    Dep. Sec. Packard, Defense Department:  Grumman
F-14 contract, discussion of costs.
    Adm. Cousins, Navy:  Need for small, fast escort
patrol ship, discussion of shipbuilding practices.
    Sec. Laird, Defense Department:  Opposition to
unilateral U.S. arms limitations, discussion of
Strategic Arms Limitation Talks.


*Authorization for Annual Average Strengths for the
Military Services, Supplemental Manpower Hearings*
(April 1971)
Y4.Ar5/3:M59/12

    Roger Kelley, Defense Department:  Strategy
objectives, manpower requirements, discussion of
U.S. defense spending as compared with European
allies.


*Military Construction Authorization FY 1972* (June,
July 1971)
Y4.Ar5/3:C76/9/972

    Elmer Yates, Army:  Army construction of Safe-
guard.

*Advanced Prototype* (September 1971)
Y.Ar5/3:P94/7

   Dep. Sec. Packard, Defense Department:  Descriptions and cost estimates of services' prototype
programs, advantages of prototype development over
standard procurement practices.


FOREIGN RELATIONS COMMITTEE


*Bombing Operations and the Prisoner of War Rescue
Mission in North Vietnam* (1971)
Y4.F76/2:B63/4

   Sec. Laird, Defense Department:  Review of Defense Department policy and activities regarding
the bombing of targets in North Vietnam.


*U.S. Security Agreements and Commitments Abroad:
Spain and Portugal, Part 11* (1971)

   Asst. Sec. Richardson, State Department:  De-
fense and State Departments' roles in negotiations
concerning commitments.
   Gen. Wheeler, Defense Department:  Value of
Spanish bases.
   Paul Roland and Walter Pincus, Foreign Relations
Committee staff:  Defensive implications of securi-
ty agreements.


*Legislative Proposals Relating to the War in South-
east Asia* (April, May 1971)
Y4.F76/2:A54/13

   Extensive colloquy by committee members on ending the war.  Witnesses include Senators McGovern,
Hartke, Javits, Stevenson, Mondale and other

witnesses including John Kerry, John Gardner,
Averell Harriman, Charles Yost, Richard Falk, Rep.
McCloskey, Joseph Clark.


*Foreign Assistance Authorization for FY 1972* (June
1971)
Y4.F76/2:L52/3

   Sec. Laird, Defense Department:  Importance of
military assistance, military support for Cambodia
and Laos.
   Discussion of NATO and European defense spending.


*Arms Control Implications of Current Defense Budget,
Subcommittee on Arms Control, International Law and
Organizations* (June, July 1971)
Y4.F76/2:Ar5/14

   Adm. Moorer, Joint Chiefs of Staff:  Comparison
of U.S.-U.S.S.R. force levels and trends, strategic
sufficiency and superiority and multiple
independently targeted re-entry vehicle deployment.
   Rear Adm. Healey, Navy:  Soviet submarine threat
and need for Captor mine.
   Rear Adm. Kaufman, Navy:  Development of ULMS,
discussion of characteristics.
   Brig. Gen. Snead, Army:  Army research and development, improvement of technical support.
   Lt. Gen. Starbird, Army:  Hardsite ballistic
missile defense, interface with Safeguard.


*--Part 4*

   Rear Adm. Weeks, Defense Department:  Defense
Computer Agency justification, computer storage and
retrieval systems.
   Maj. Gen. Nelson, Air Force:  Justification of
B-1 program, need for manned bomber, feasibility

of modifications of B-52 fleet.

Col. Coy, Air Force:  Minuteman III program, development of faster targeting devices.

Asst. Sec. Hanson, Air Force:  Air Force research and development request, impact of "fly before buy" policies.

Col. Trapold, Air Force:  SRAM and SCAD programs, discussion of utility of decoys.

Col. Miller, Army:  SAM-D development, potential missions.

Col. Russell, Air Force:  Airborne warning and control system justification, effectiveness of look-down, shoot-down.

Jeremy Stone, Federation of American Scientists, and George Ralkjens, M.I.T.:  Criticize claims of Soviet technological superiority and techniques for estimating Soviet research and development efforts.


--*Part 5*

Maj. Gen. Belser, Air Force:  Organization and mission of Continental Air Defense Command and North American Air Defense Command, Air Force defensive capabilities.

Col. Ahern, Air Force:  Airborne warning and control system, F-15, and SAM-D systems, need for new defensive systems.

Jeremy Stone, Federation of American Scientists: Air Force failure to justify bomber defense, futility of bomber defense.

Lt. Gen. Glasser, Air Force:  Justification for F-15 and A-Y, discussion of FB-111.

John Foster, Defense Department:  Justification for Triad, U.S. position on antiballistic missile and risk in delaying deployment.

Carl Kaysen, Princeton University:  History of Triad, sufficiency of submarine-launched ballistic missiles to meet deterrent needs.

Herbert York, University of California:  History of force composition, futility of damage-limiting strategies.

Charles Herzfield, American Telephone & Telegraph Inc.: Need for Triad but necessity to change emphasis to reflect technological changes.

John Craven, University of Hawaii: Need for weapons system design to meet controlability criteria.

Marvin Goldberger, Princeton University: Ending development of B-1 and proposed modification of existing bomber force.

Joseph Clark, World Federalists: Elimination of strategic bombers.

Dep. Sec. Packard, Defense Department: Soviet strategic momentum, rationale for antiballistic missile and multiple independently targeted re-entry vehicle programs.

Paul Warnke: Questions necessity of antiballistic missile and multiple independently targeted re-entry vehicle, effect of arms control negotiations.

Sen. Humphrey: Halt to multiple independently targeted re-entry vehicle program while Strategic Arms Limitation Talks continue.

Marshall Shulman, Columbia University: Soviet approach to Strategic Arms Limitation Talks.

Herbert Scoville: Lack of Soviet multiple independently targeted re-entry vehicle threat, its limitation highest priority in arms control, SS-9 performance.


*Prospects for Comprehensive Nuclear Test Ban Treaty, Subcommittee on Arms Control, International Law and Organization* (July 1971)
Y4.F76/2:N88/5

Philip Farley, Arms Control and Disarmament Agency: Potential advantages of comprehensive treaty, summary of previous negotiations.

Franklin Long, Cornell University: Improvements of monitoring systems, discussion of need for further nuclear testing.

Bernard Feld, M.I.T.: Influences of secondary

nuclear powers on arms testing.

Carl Walske, Defense Department:  Effects of tests cessation on reliability of nuclear weapons, need for Spartan missile in Safeguard system.


GOVERNMENT OPERATIONS COMMITTEE


*International Negotiation, Subcommittee on National Security and International Operations, Part 4* (March 1971)
Y4.G74/6:N31

Bernard Lewis, University of London:  Effect of U.S.-U.S.S.R. involvement in Middle East.


*--Part 5* (April 1971)

Robert Byrnes, Indiana University:  Implications of trends in Eastern Europe, China, and Southeast Asia for U.S. security policy.


*--Part 6* (April 1971)

Robert Conquest:  Soviet leadership, political implications of Soviet build-up.

# Research Note:

## Bibliographic Citations of Congressional Hearings

The only uniform numbering system for government documents is that provided by the Government Printing Office, which assigned a standard call number to congressional documents beginning in 1969.  Before that date there was no standard numbering system.  Although congressional committees and executive agencies number their documents and reports, these numbers are chaotic and intended for internal use.  Thus, most libraries file government documents and the like under the Government Printing Office number.  Using a number designation like the one below, one can find both executive and congressional documents without the help of a government documents librarian.

Y4.Ar5/2a:971-72/nos.

This sample call number can be broken down as follows:

Y4 - Refers to any congressional committee hearing.

Ar5 - Stands for the Armed Services Committee.

2 - This number indicates which House of Congress is involved.  (1) stands for the House of Representatives; (2) stands for the Senate.  Taken together the numbers Ar5/2 indicate the Senate Armed Services Committee.

a - Means that it is a Committee Print.

971-72 - Means the date of the congressional
session.

nos - Stands for Numbers:  some committees, including Armed Services, number their hearings,
prints, and reports consecutively through the
session; other committees such as Foreign Relations use instead an initial such as "M," which
might refer to the hearing on My Lai.

For purposes of correctly citing hearings contained
in this bibliography, the researcher should take note
of the correct procedure for listing a congressional
hearing source.  A correct bibliographic notation
should contain the committee name, the title of the
hearing, the number of the Congress and the date.  If
no date is available for the hearing, the Government
Printing Office date of release should be used.  There
are several acceptable bibliographic forms; two are
shown below:

House Appropriations Committee, Hearings on
Department of Defense Appropriations for FY
1959, 85th Congress, 2nd Session, April 29,
1958.

U.S. Congress, Senate Preparedness Investigating
Subcommittee.  90th Congress, 1st Session. *Air
War Against North Vietnam.  Hearings*.... 5 pts.
Washington, D.C.:  Government Printing Office,
1967.

Of course, when quoting from congressional hearings, it is necessary to add the page number of the
hearing at the end of the bibliographic notation.  It
should also be noted that if the hearings are held
before an identified congressional subcommittee, the
name of the subcommittee is used in the notation and
the full committee is not included.  (In the case of
the second illustration above, it was not necessary

376

to include the Senate Government Operations Committee in the citation.)

This bibliography contains all necessary information for correct citations. First list the House where the hearing occurred (House of Representatives or Senate). The number and session of the Congress is given in the section heading of each year's hearings. Names of committees and subcommittees are found either in the subheadings in each section or in hearing titles. Exact hearing titles appear in italics in this bibliography. Publication dates follow each title; if no date appears use the year in which the hearing appears. And, of course, the place and publisher of all hearings are "Washington: Government Printing Office."